Faith & Madness

Faith & Madness

A Spiritual and Psychological Journey

Sarah Slagle Arnold

FOREWORD BY
Eugene H. Peterson

CASCADE *Books* • Eugene, Oregon

FAITH AND MADNESS
A Spiritual and Psychological Journey

Cascade Books
An Imprint of Wipf and Stock Publishers
199 W. 8th Ave., Suite 3
Eugene, OR 97401
www.wipfandstock.com

ISBN 13: 978-1-62032-149-2

Cataloging-in-Publication data:

Arnold, Sarah Slagle.

  Faith and madness : a spiritual and psychological journey / Sarah Slagle Arnold.

  xvi + 196 p. ; 23 cm.

  ISBN 13: 978-1-62032-149-2

  1. Depressed persons—United States—Biography. 2. Psychology, Religious. I. Title.

RC537 .A74 2012

Manufactured in the U.S.A.

Grateful acknowledgment is made for permission to reproduce the following material:

GREAT IS THY FAITHFULNESS
Words: Thomas O. Chisholm
©1923, Ren. 1951 Hope Publishing Company, Carol Stream, IL 60188
All rights reserved. Used by permission.

The Way You Look Tonight
Words by Dorothy Fields
Music by Jerome Kern
Copyright © 1936 UNIVERSAL – POLYGRAM INTERNATIONAL PUBLISHING, INC. and
ALDI MUSIC
Copyright Renewed
Print Rights for ALSI MUSIC in the U.S. Controlled and Administered by HAPPY ASPEN
MUSIC LLC c/o SHAPIRO, BERNSTEIN & CO., INC.
All Rights Reserved Used by Permission
Reprinted by Permission of Hal Leonard Corporation

"Carol of the Bells"
By Peter J. Wilhousky
Copyright © 1936 by Carl Fischer, Inc. Copyright renewed.
All rights assigned to Carl Fischer, LLC
International copyright secured. All rights reserved.
Used with permission.

For my husband, Charles,
my sons, Christopher and Jonathan,
their wives, Melina and Erin,
my grandchildren, Niko, Maxwell, Liam, Zoe, and Matthew Finn

All of whom might have been lost to me.

And we know that all things work together
for good to them that love God . . .

ROMANS 8:28

Foreword

WE LIVE IN A culture impoverished in story. The widespread preference for a language of gossip and slander, polemics and advertising, and escapist distraction gives meager encouragement to nurturing a good life, living a generous life, an abundant life. But having observed that, it is also true that we are, in fact, blessed with magnificent storytellers.

The most satisfactory way to get acquainted with another person is by means of story. Story is our primary verbal means of getting acquainted, getting, as we say, *inside* another. For that we can be grateful for story is our most accessible form of speech. Young and old love stories. Literate and illiterate alike tell stories. Neither stupidity nor sophistication puts us outside the magnetic field of story. A good storyteller gathers us into the story. We feel the emotions, get caught up in the drama, identify with the characters, see into nooks and crannies of life that we had overlooked, realize there is more to this business of being human than we had yet explored. If the storyteller is good, and the writer of this story, *Faith and Madness*, is very good, doors and windows open. The only serious rival to story in terms of accessibility is song, and there is plenty of that in this book too. It is also evidence that nearly anything can be borne if only we can make a story out of it.

The art of the storyteller is to look long and lovingly at what at first sight looks or feels like chaos, fragments of broken expectations, disappointing circumstances or baffling dead ends, and discern a form that holds life together, a feeling for a comprehensive plot in process: a story in which all the parts are somehow being worked into something that holds together. A personal story, like this memoir, discovers in the telling perspective and energy and connectedness. It becomes a compelling witness that counters the frequently used depersonalizing abstractions that erode a sense of integrity and identity of *soul*.

A common consequence to losing this sense of connectedness and worth, this sense of inhabiting a story, is depression. For far too many, the final solution to depression is suicide. At the age of nineteen the story-teller in this memoir, Sarah, made elaborate preparations to end her life. She anticipated it as a kind of descent into hell.

Dr. Kay Redfield Jamison, in her book *Night Falls Fast*, reports that suicide in the young has more than tripled in the last fifty years. It is now the second highest cause of death among young people 16 to 24. Jamison also says that most suicides could be prevented with adequate help.

The "adequate help" that is reported in *Faith and Madness* is a conjunction of faith and psychology. The faith developed throughout a childhood expressed richly in hymn-singing in her home with her piano-playing mother and occasionally the voice of her agnostic father. The hymns supplied a wealth of vocabulary for articulating a life of faith in a musical context of melody and harmony. The hymns were supplemented by the sermons of two pastors, Presbyterian and Lutheran, through most of her adolescence and later through the teaching of an Anglican priest. Psychology came into the picture in the person of Dr. Frank Sellers with whom she met every Monday, Wednesday, and Friday for over a year after the onset of her depression. His patient, kind, and skilled presence eventually brought her through her suicidal depression.

She writes her story on a loom made of faith and psychology, weaving the threads of her depression into a story of healing, of wholeness, of praise. There is no lack of drama in this story but the writer does not exploit our emotions. The voice is reticent, quiet and modest, communicating whispers of hope to a generation impoverished by story. She lets us enter the story at our own pace.

Psychology and faith do not always make for an easy companionship. But Dr. Sarah Arnold's story is evidence that they can get along very well together. Neither has anything to fear from the other.

Eugene H Peterson
Professor Emeritus of Spiritual Theology
Regent College, Vancouver, British Columbia

Acknowledgments

THIS BOOK BEGAN IN a writing group in New York City convened by an excellent teacher and psychoanalyst, Susan Kaveler Adler, PhD. Four group members came together in Susan's office hoping to write professional papers. Before many meetings had elapsed all of us, Maria Luisa Bastos, PhD, Olga Marlin, PhD, Susan McConnaughy, MSW, and I were writing about our own lives, and I was beginning to write this story with encouragement and suggestions from each of them. I thank them all.

With a full-time practice of psychotherapy and psychoanalysis, and two school-age children, progress on the memoir was slow; but courses at the Writer's Voice in New York City kept me writing and were a lot of fun. There I found excellent instruction and superb mentors, including the always encouraging Charles Salzberg. His was the first writing course I ever took—on how to publish a non-fiction book. Little did I know then how much I would first need to learn about writing.

Patty Dann at Sarah Lawrence College made a huge contribution not only with her winsome teaching style, but in her encouragement and continued interest in the project. Patty read and made suggestions on the first complete draft.

After moving to Maine, at the suggestion of Rick Wile, for which I thank him, I entered the Stonecoast MFA program in Creative Writing at the University of Southern Maine. Rick has made major contributions to the manuscript in an ongoing writing group where we are members. The Stonecoast program proved tremendously helpful in pushing the project forward. Richard Hoffman, an instructor, was a strong influence as a memoirist himself, as was Baron Wormser, poet, teacher, and memoirist, and my chief mentor during the final drafting.

Others who gave generously of their time to thoughtfully read the manuscript and provide clarifying insights include my friends Marcie Jan

Acknowledgments

Bronstein, Susan Moran, Emma Stephenson-Smith, Katie Belmont, Madeline Dreher, Jo Belknap, Tracy Hotchner, and Jane DiMillo.

I am especially grateful to Eugene Peterson, prolific writer of Christian literature and author of the modern translation of the Bible known as *The Message*. After reading the manuscript, he phoned me and generously offered to write a foreword. I consider his thoughtfully written foreword on the importance of story a priceless contribution to the book.

Dr. Dale Irvin, president of New York Theological Seminary, of which I'm an alumnus, gave strong support for the book and valued encouragement in its final stages, for which I'm most appreciative.

I wish to thank especially Rodney Clapp, my editor at Cascade Books for his careful attention to the manuscript and his words of encouragement. Christian Amondson, Heather Carraher, and other staff at Wipf and Stock Publishers were most gracious in shepherding me through this process.

My deepest gratitude goes to my husband, Charles, and my sons, Christopher and Jonathan, writers in their own right, who thoughtfully read the manuscript in its various stages and gave generous feedback. Chris's periodic "Yuck"s in the margin told me when I was off track. I also thank them for their patience during the many hours I was closeted in an upstairs room, writing.

Introduction

DURING MY YEAR OF madness I did not consider myself "mad." I thought, as my father did during his manias, that I was seeing the world as it truly is. My illness was not anything like my father's. Thankfully, I had not inherited his manic-depressive illness as some onlookers feared; but I was severely disturbed and my faith as a comfort to me had vanished, replaced by an ever-present dread. Madness is chaotic, faith is ordered; madness is rudderless, directionless, faith is grounded, purposeful; madness is isolated, a silent void, faith has a shared community. I had suddenly lost all of the sustaining aspects of faith. I was in chaos.

My father's manic-depressive psychosis surfaced when I was five and my brother three. Before the arrival of medications, this was a fierce and terrible illness. The Great Depression was on as well; and yet my mother's faith that God would take care of us shielded my brother and me from what might have been truly traumatic. Between episodes of mania with their lengthy hospitalizations my father, who had been a pharmacist before the onset of this illness, cooked our meals and carried on good conversations with my brother and me. My mother worked as a salesperson in a large department store to provide our livelihood.

I had always felt a special love for my father and still do, but I did not want to be like him. At age seven as I watched his mania escalate for the third time, I vowed under my breath, "I will never let that happen to me. I will *never* let that happen to me." In spite of my vow, days before I began my sophomore year at Wayne University in Detroit, I too entered the realm of madness with the onset of a major depression. As sudden as darkening skies of a summer storm, strange thoughts plunged me deeper and deeper into a dark space. Soon I developed the twin dangers of anorexia and incessant urges to take my life. Despite my determination, despite my faith, patterned after my mother's, I had not escaped madness.

When a year later I recovered, my big question was what had caused this? Something happened to me that could have cost me my life. What was it? In a matter of days I had changed from a normal fun-loving college student, fully engaged in life, to someone totally different—a person who seemed strange, and had weird thoughts, who in time was bone-thin, and whose eyes looked dead.

Many years later, even though I had graduated from a theological seminary, obtained a PhD in Psychology from the University of Michigan, and had become a practicing psychologist and psychoanalyst in New York City, I still had no satisfying explanation for why I became so deeply depressed and anorexic, and wanted to kill myself. My psychoanalytic training required that I undergo my own psychoanalysis. Several times I brought up this terrible black year with my analyst and told him I wanted to know why this had occurred. Each time his dismissive, brief reply came back from behind the couch, "You were an adolescent. Weren't you?" His answer did not satisfy me. There had to be more pieces to the puzzle.

This memoir grew out of my need to examine the sources of this troubled period—my daily obsession with hell and my certainty that I was destined to go there. At times I thought my year of madness simply reflected a profound spiritual upheaval—an upheaval that began my first year at Wayne University when I discovered that most of my professors and instructors were either agnostics or atheists. My faith had been a bulwark for me growing up. As I saw it, only my mother's quiet faith in God enabled her to survive the wrenching sad periods of my father's illness, and keep our home a surprisingly cheerful and normal place. But learning and intelligence were also very important to me; so it came as a huge jolt to find that the "intelligentsia" considered my faith to be based on a myth, or a legend. Couldn't my religious questioning and confusion that first year in college account for this experience of dread—a "dark night of the soul" I needed to go through before I could comprehend God's grace? I wasn't sure.

Eventually, I came to have nagging doubts that my religious confusion explained everything that lay behind my illness. Perhaps there were other factors—such as psychological conflict that I wasn't aware of because it was deeply buried. In time I realized that in order to understand what had brought me to this year of madness, I needed to go back to the beginning—my earliest memories—and trace the experience of growing up in my family. I decided that the only way to unravel the various threads that fed into this experience when I was nineteen would be to examine carefully my life up to that point. I would need to go deeper into my memories.

Tennessee Williams wrote in the introduction to his play, *The Glass Menagerie*, "In memory everything seems to happen to music." I found this to be especially true of my memories—they were best triggered by music, whether the hymns I sang with my mother from an early age, the World War II songs we sang in elementary school or the the Swing and Boogie music the band belted out at our high school dances. I began to organize my recollections around the music that was important to me at different stages—until the advent of the depression when the music stopped abruptly. This too seemed significant—there was no music during this year of deep depression.

The memoir that resulted, *Faith and Madness*, is my effort to solve the mystery of what caused me to have a major depression at nineteen. As such it is a story of psychological discovery. It is equally the story of a spiritual quest—of growing my childhood faith into a full relationship with God and with Jesus Christ. These two elements, faith and madness, were not easy to untangle—they were as intertwined as two vines around a single tree. Unraveling them would take a lot of work. Ultimately, though, this is a hopeful story—the music does resume. It is a story set in an earlier time, the nineteen thirties, forties, and early fifties, a gentler time when, given my family's modest circumstances, I received more help than would be likely today.

The relationship between psychology and religion presents difficult choices for people of faith, and it did for me. I was sure no help would come from the psychiatrist I saw. I felt certain this was a spiritual problem, pure and simple, and the problem as I saw it was that I was irredeemably bad. I hear of devout people who fear that a psychologist or psychiatrist would tamper with their faith in God, but I never experienced any aspersions cast on my faith by my therapist. Other Christians feel that if their faith were strong enough they would be able to overcome their emotional problem by themselves. They see it as a weakness, or a lack of trust in God, to seek professional help. I now know I could not have recovered on my own. On the other hand are people who look to psychology to solve the whole problem of finding meaning in life, thinking it can substitute for a religious faith, when it cannot. This intricate relationship between psychological disturbance and religious faith was part and parcel of my confusion, the chaos of my "madness," and, as such, it is woven throughout my story.

one

"Jesus Loves Me"

"WHAT SHALL WE SING?" my mother would ask, the lilt in her voice brimming with pleasure. She loved to sing with me. "Jesus Loves Me" was almost always my first choice. Every day in our small apartment in Detroit in the early thirties, the years before I began kindergarten, I sang hymns with my mother. She sat on the piano stool with its round wine-colored velvet cushion. I stood next to her at the upright piano and rubbed my hand along its mahogany carvings of fruits and flowers which gleamed with a dark reddish brown from the furniture polish my mother used. After she struck the first chord we sang together,

> Jesus loves me, this I know,
> For the Bible tells me so.
> Little ones to Him belong.
> They are weak, but He is strong.

Then in a lusty voice I sang the chorus which several times repeats the words, "Yes, Jesus loves me. Yes, Jesus loves me. Yes, Jesus loves me. The Bible tells me so." I watched my mother's slender fingers move quickly over the keys and asked her how she had learned to play music like this. She said she took lessons on the pump organ in her parents' farmhouse. I decided that when I was older I would take lessons like she had.

By then I had a clear picture of Jesus in my mind. My mother read to my brother and me from *Hurlbut's Story of the Bible*, a large book of Bible stories written in language children can understand. This early edition had full page colored prints that in the New Testament section pictured Jesus as a young man in soft flowing robes with a short brown beard, slightly longer hair, and kind dark eyes. In one picture he's surrounded by children. A little girl holding a yellow flower is nestled in his lap. He looks as if he's telling them a story. I had some understanding that Jesus was God's son, and that God was in heaven because I knew the Lord's Prayer, "Our Father, who art in heaven." While I liked knowing I had a father in heaven, Jesus seemed closer—more like a friend. I can't say that at the age of three and four I talked to Jesus every day, but sometimes I did, and I knew that if I needed to I could. We often sang another hymn, "What a Friend We Have in Jesus," that said that we could take all our worries to Jesus in prayer. I knew that prayer meant talking to God or to Jesus. Even though Jesus didn't answer me in words, I never doubted that he was listening and that he heard me.

Before I was five I had learned a considerable number of hymns. The tunes and words of hymns such as, "Fairest Lord Jesus" and "Count Your Blessings" floated in and out of my mind daily. I found myself humming these hymn tunes when I was drawing or painting at my little table, or walking to the park with my mother, my younger brother in the green wicker baby buggy.

I sometimes attached peculiar meanings to words I didn't understand. There were words in one hymn that spoke about heaven:

> Tell mother I'll be there, in answer to her prayer.
> This message, blessed Savior, to her bear.

The last phrase led me to believe there must be a bear in heaven. One day when I took a sip of my painting water and my mother looked aghast and admonished me never to do this again, I started to fear I might die from the painting water and go immediately to heaven. I could picture myself with Jesus, my grandmother Janet whom I'd never seen because she died before I was born, and the bear. It was a friendly bear, a large man-sized bear standing on his hind legs. I expected heaven would be a pleasant place; but I didn't want to go there just yet and have to leave my mother. I wasn't sure why the bear was in heaven, but I liked that he was.

My mother was tall with dark wavy hair, smooth, ivory skin, and eyes as blue as sapphires. Every morning I watched her scurry around doing her housework—she had to have a neat house. This must have been the way she grew up because her sisters' houses in Canada were equally neat. She didn't have to do major cleaning because my father felt she should have a cleaning lady once a week. By nine o'clock she had finished with the breakfast dishes, making the beds, and whatever other straightening she had to do and was ready to read to my brother Danny and me, and teach us hymns and songs and poems. We sat in the living room amid sumptuous furnishings my father had purchased just before the Great Depression: a thick red and blue Persian rug, a long mahogany library table, an upright piano, and a sofa and two easy chairs upholstered in pale brown mohair. Any time I put my feet on the furniture my mother reminded me, "Sarah, mohair is very expensive." I didn't like the mohair very much because it was quite scratchy to sit on.

First the books would come out: big books such as *Grimm's Fairy Tales*, *Hurlbut's Story of the Bible*, and little books such as *Jack and the Bean Stalk*, and *Paul Bunyan and His Big Blue Ox*. My brother loved the Paul Bunyan story so much he wanted my mother to read it over and over and over. She would change her voice for each character in the stories. If she read what a princess said her voice became high and sweet, but if she were reading about what the big bad wolf said her voice became low and scary, yet not too scary. When one or the other of us became fidgety or started poking the other my mother would go to the piano and we would sing.

We sang songs other than hymns as well: "Old MacDonald Had a Farm," "Home on the Range," and the many Scottish songs my mother loved—"Annie Laurie," "Loch Lomond," and "The Road to the Isles," a fast, difficult song. She could play anything and had sheet music for some of the current songs such as "Indian Love Call" and "Deep Purple," which she played for her own enjoyment. Her face took on a wistful dreamy look as she sang these songs as though she was remembering something from a long time ago.

My mother told me that she had wanted to be a teacher like three of her four older sisters who went to Normal School and taught in one-room school houses until they were married. Every day as a little girl she played school with her dolls in the log playhouse her father built for her near their farmhouse. When it came time for her to go to Normal School, however, she was the last one at home and her parents told her they needed her to help on the farm. She never became a teacher, but I'm convinced she played school with my brother and me much as she had with her dolls. In the dining room there was a little table and chairs of varnished wood that looked just like grown-up furniture where we could draw or paint. We each had a small wicker rocking chair where we could look at books by ourselves. And there was the piano, all the books, my dolls and my brother's cars. It was a nursery school for two.

When my brother took his morning nap my mother taught me poems, and read to me from her thick book of poetry. She loved to read Gray's "Elegy Written in a Country Churchyard." Much of this poem I understood with her help and the opening lines still come back to me:

> The curfew tolls the knell of parting day,
> The lowing herd wind slowly o're the lea.
> The plowman homeward plods his weary way,
> And leaves the world to darkness and to me.

She told me that on her father's farm the cows came home following each other in a line at the end of the day just as in the poem. I could feel the sadness in this poem. Perhaps I felt my mother's sadness for the home her brother forced her to leave. After their father died her brother said he couldn't afford to keep her on one of the two farms he inherited, where she was caring for their mother, even though in her father's will he had said she could stay as long as she wanted. It was a harsh decision, but she was already in her early thirties, so if he hadn't done this, my brother and I might never have been born.

I loved when my mother told me stories of her earlier life—even sad ones like this one. I often asked her to tell me about the time she raced the hired man into town with her horse Billy hitched to a buggy. She said she had become sick and tired of hearing him brag about his fast horse, so when she met him on the road one day, they raced. She won, of course; but she had to take Billy to a stable in town and dry him down. I tried to picture living in a town that had stables for horses. I thought it must have been wonderful.

As much as I loved these mornings with my mother, her stories, the singing, and our trips to the park after our naps, the best time of day was at six o'clock when my father came bursting through the door in his white pharmacy coat full of energy and ready to play with my brother and me. With my mother we had orderly play and had to wear our slippers so as not to disturb our neighbors in the apartment below, but with my father we had raucous good times. After he hung up his pharmacy coat and went to the kitchen to give my mother a kiss, he would pick my brother up from his play pen and hold him high over his head until my normally shy brother squealed with delight. Then he'd get down on the floor and let us both ride horsey on his back. Sometimes our play became so spirited we did damage—like the night we played monkey in the middle with a large red and blue rubber ball and my father threw it over my head, too high to catch it, right at the lamp on the library table making a big crack through the beautiful red parrot on the black lampshade. I could tell my mother was upset, but all she said was, "I have some tape. After dinner I'll mend it." After that, even with the tape, when the lamp was lit you could see where it was mended. I sometimes saw my mother looking at the lamp shade, broken by my father's exuberance, and wondered what she might be thinking. Still, I loved these times with my father so much that often I could hardly wait another second to hear the sound of his key in the door.

My father stood two or three inches taller than my mother, fair-haired, his face open and trusting. His eyes were a much lighter blue than my mother's and they readily showed his feelings. He was almost always in high spirits, but once in a while I saw a hint of sadness in his eyes, and they often welled with tears if someone told a sad story or if he heard that something bad had happened to someone. He was sturdily built, neither heavy nor slender. To me he was completely charming.

The Great Depression was in full force during these years. When automobile production dropped from over five million vehicles in 1929 to a little over one million in 1931, the U.S. Census declared Detroit to be the hardest hit of 19 troubled cities. The idled Fisher plant served as a shelter for 2500 homeless men. The mayor came up with the inventive idea of Apple Vending. He bought apples from Canada that men were licensed to sell on the street for 5 cents a piece. At the peak there were 700 some vendors in Detroit. My father had a good job as a pharmacist at the Henry Ford Hospital, so I, who had a warm comfortable home, knew nothing of this—at least for a time.

Because our apartment was close to Ford Hospital my father came home for lunch every day. Being the outgoing person he was, he often brought a colleague along unannounced. My mother kept our dining room table set with white linen and her good silver just in case. On a day I remember especially well my father brought both a doctor and a nurse home. Hearing his hearty laughter accompanied by strange voices in the hallway, my mother whisked off her apron before the door opened.

"Mae, meet Louise Larkin, head nurse in peds. Dr. Matthews, their chief resident—my wife, Mae," he said ushering them into the front hall.

Miss Larkin had billowy red hair and wore dangling gold earrings with her white uniform. I thought she seemed uncomfortable to be coming for lunch with no notice.

"Dan insisted we come over and meet the children," she said.

My mother laughed her happy laugh. "He's always showing them off. Come right into the dining room. I know you don't have long for lunch." I loved it when my father brought people home like this. I think my mother did too. "Please help yourself to the tuna casserole and the salad," she said, putting on two extra plates and more silverware. "The hot biscuits will be out in a minute."

The three of them sat down, my father with Danny on his lap. I stood nearby so I could hear the grown-up conversation. In a few minutes my father put Danny in his play pen and took me on his lap.

"What did you do this morning, sweetheart?" he asked.

"Played with Mama."

"How old are you Sarah?" Dr. Matthews asked me. Dr. Matthews was a small man with a mustache and lively dark eyes.

"I'm three-and-a-half. And Danny is two," I volunteered. "Oh, and Mama taught me a new poem today," I remembered, turning to my father.

"Would you like to recite the poem for our guests?" he whispered in my ear, so I could say no if I wasn't ready or didn't want to do it. I climbed down from his lap and stood in the archway to the living room. I knew you couldn't recite a poem sitting down. My father's eyes met mine. In a sing-song voice I began,

The Little Brown Bug

A little brown bug climbed up to the sky,
And perched a way up on a daisy's bright eye.
The daisy did nod and dance in the sun.
"Oh," said the little bug, "What jolly fun.
No other bug in the universe wide
Is having like me so lovely a ride."
But just as he spoke a smart little bird
Out hunting for food nearby overheard.
He gobbled him up and flew away smug,
And that was the end of the proud little bug.

I ended with a curtsy I had learned in dancing class.

"That was very good!" exclaimed Miss Larkin, raising her water glass as if making a toast. "Do you know any more poems?"

By now I was back with my arms draped over my father's knee. "I know one about a turkey," I told her.

"Let's hear it for the turkey!" shouted Dr. Matthews, clapping his hands. I returned to the archway and recited a poem about a young turkey who wandered off alone when the grown-ups warned her not to go. It ends,

> "And so she made a supper for a sly young lynx
> Because she was so headstrong that she didn't think."

I went back to my father's lap.

"P-r-e-t-t-y s-c a-r-y poems!" said Dr. Matthews. "I feel sorry for the little bug, *and* the turkey."

"She should have listened to her Mama," I told him.

"That's right," my mother said laughing. She was coming in with lemon pie for dessert. Looking at Danny and me she said, "Time for naps." I started to go.

My father knew I hated to leave when we had company. "First give me a hug," he said. He knelt down beside me and gave me a warm crunchy hug, his face velvety smooth against my cheek. "When I come home tonight we'll play," he told me.

Although my mother and I sang hymns every day, the atmosphere in our home was not overly pious. My parents loved to have their friends over for parties where they got dressed up and my father served highballs on a silver tray. This was during Prohibition, so they likely obtained the alcohol for the highballs from Canada just across the Ambassador Bridge from Detroit. My mother made a beautiful flapper in her low-waisted sequined dresses she had saved from the twenties—a pink one and a black one—and her black satin shoes that had rhinestone buckles. The lights were turned down low and little candles were lit around the room. Soon the doorbell started ringing and the apartment filled with chatting dressed-up people. I wandered around and talked to the adults and ate the party food I'd helped my mother prepare—dishes of salted nuts and little canapés of cream cheese on crackers with a slice of olive in the center. I liked these parties so much that my mother despaired of trying to get me to go to bed before the last guest had left. My little brother by contrast was asleep long before the guests arrived.

Even more than parties, my parents' favorite activity was picnics. On my father's day off my mother packed our picnic basket with a jar of hot tea wrapped in newspapers to keep it warm, tuna fish sandwiches in waxed paper, some fruit and cookies, and we took off for one of Detroit's many parks in my father's green Willis Knight coup. I sat in the rumble seat for these trips with a big blanket wrapped around me. I never stood up while the car was moving. At the park we'd find a picnic table in the shade. While my mother set out the lunch on either her green or her red checkered table cloth, my brother and I played tag with my father or tossed a ball with him. He was great at thinking up new games for the three of us to play, such as the day he pulled a white linen handkerchief from his pocket and introduced us to blind man's bluff. He seemed never to run out of energy.

The spiritual part of our life was simple. We said our prayers with my mother at bedtime and before each meal either my brother or I would pray:

> Come, Lord Jesus. Be our guest,
> and let these gifts to us be blessed.

This blessing at mealtime reminded me that Jesus was there with us, which probably made me a little kinder towards my brother when he snatched my hair ribbon off my head or took off with one of my dolls to tease me. Every Sunday we went to Westminster Presbyterian Church, and we sang hymns daily.

My mother's home when she was growing up in the rolling farmland of Ontario, Canada had been much more pious; yet her life there was also laced with lively good times. She danced at the house parties of her friends, and nearly every night in winter, after she had milked seven or eight cows and put the milk through the separator, she told me, she went with her friends to a covered rink that had a band where they skated to music. She won most of the couples' races. She said, "All the boys wanted to skate with me in the couples' races. With my long legs, I could get around that rink faster than anyone."

Every morning after breakfast her family read a chapter of the Bible. "And if a hired man was there, he read too," my mother said, seeming proud of the fact. Her father, a soft-spoken man, as she described him, asked a blessing at the beginning of each meal and gave thanks at the end. On Sunday one couldn't read any book except the Bible or do any work, even sewing. While it was not considered a sin to miss church, no one ever did. For most people it was the major social event of the week.

The service was long and solemn. So long for a child that when my mother was small my grandmother took a large oatmeal-raisin cookie tied in a white handkerchief with a black thread for her youngest to eat midway through the service. "Sometimes I thought I couldn't wait another minute for my mother to begin unwinding that black thread," she told me.

After church all the young people came over to her family's home for a light lunch or, in good weather, a picnic on the grass. I've seen pictures of them on the front lawn of her farmhouse, the young women in long white frilly dresses and big white hats in summer, and the men, who had worn overalls all week, in three-piece suits with gold watch chains dangling from their vests. When I looked at these pictures I wished I could have lived then. It seemed such a lovely life with the women wearing long white dresses and the people getting together after church to have fun compared to the ordinary way women dressed in Detroit—and no one coming over after church for lunch.

On Sunday my mother took my brother and me to church. We walked three blocks from our apartment at Collingwood and Byron along Detroit's clean busy streets, less busy on a Sunday morning, past many neat little stores, all closed on Sunday, and crossed over the streetcar tracks on Hamilton Avenue to reach the church at Hamilton and Glynn Court. Westminster Presbyterian Church, a stately stone building with stained glass windows and red velvet cushions on varnished wooden pews, had been built in 1918. The sanctuary had a vaulted ceiling with windows rising up forever. Because I was small it probably seemed larger to me than it actually was. I found it huge and infinitely beautiful. The sun shining through the stained glass windows shed a rainbow glow on everything inside. I felt in a different world here than the world of every day—a world of mystery and warmth.

An even greater fascination for me was the music. The organist would play a soft, gentle piece called a prelude while people were coming into church. Then at the first strains of the opening hymn the congregation stood up and the choir began processing down the center aisle in their wine-colored robes with white satin collars. I watched them move two by two in time with the hymn. The voices of the choir and of the people soaring over the deep tones of the organ, and the light shining through the stained glass windows, created for me a sense that this was a holy place. This church was exactly the kind of house God would have, I decided, and I was excited to be there. Dr. Bush, the minister, was a tall, solidly built man. He followed the choir down the aisle wearing a black robe with black velvet bands on his sleeves. Older than my father, yet not very old, his graying hair circled a bald spot on the back of his head. He wore rimless glasses and spoke in a deep, strong voice that made me think he had to be speaking for God.

After an opening prayer and the reading of Old and New Testament Scriptures by different members of the congregation, Dr. Bush gave a five-minute children's sermon with the children gathered in front of him on steps in front of the chancel. On the next hymn the children were supposed to file out to their Sunday school classes, but I refused to go. My brother went, while I went back to sit with my mother in the pew. Fortunately she seemed to understand my wish to stay. To leave the splendor of this church to go and color Bible story pictures in a noisy classroom made no sense to me at all. Besides, I had heard these Bible stories at home with my mother, who did a much better job of telling them. I never went to Sunday school after the first couple of times. Here in the sanctuary I knew the choir would sing again soon—this time by themselves—and the organ would again fill the church with glory. On some of the lower tones the vibrations from the organ gave me shivers—good shivers.

Soon Dr. Bush would climb the steps to the pulpit in his black robe and speak in his rich, low voice. By the time I was five I understood many of the things Dr. Bush said about God and His care for us. I always listened intently and don't recall ever being bored. I wanted to hear him explain more about how God and Jesus managed to care for all the people on earth—how they kept the world going. I figured they must be very busy. To be part of this large group of people all speaking to God at the same time when they prayed the Lord's Prayer gave me a warm feeling. The pews were always filled.

The first Sunday of the month there would be Communion, or the Lord's Supper, with ushers passing silver plates that held little cubes of white bread down each pew. Everyone ate the cube of bread at the same time. Then heavier silver plates were passed that had tiny glasses of red wine set in little holes in the silver plates. When every one had a glass, we drank the wine together. It was really grape juice because the Presbyterian Church did not permit real wine. We put the glass in a little holder on the back of the pew in front of us. In time I became such a lover of sermons that I preferred the Sundays we did not have Communion because the sermon could be longer then. I wanted a full long sermon that usually had three points. But this was a few years later.

It's hard to separate out what I understood at ages three, four, and five from what came after. As a small child I never believed that Santa Claus was real. The first time my mother took me to see Santa Claus, before we got to the department store Santa I saw a Salvation Army Santa on the street. I knew then that Santa was just a man like my daddy. Yet, it made perfect sense to me that even though I couldn't see him, there was a God who made us and loves us—who made everything in the world that I could see, birds, flowers, the trees, the sky, clouds, the sun. I never felt afraid of God, or thought he would punish me if I did something wrong. It was a loving, enfolding God I came to know through my mother and in this church—someone you could depend upon to take care of you. I heard a fair amount about heaven at Westminster Church, but nothing whatsoever about hell.

At night we said our prayers with my mother's help. We never learned the one with "if I should die before I wake" in it. Ours were "thank you prayers" and asking God to bless Mama, and Daddy, and everyone else we could think of. We were sitting up in our beds, not kneeling beside them, and then scurried under the covers and received a good night kiss on the forehead from our mother. There was no reason to think that our happy mornings with my mother and exciting play every evening with my father wouldn't just go on and on in the same way. And while apart from the hymns we sang we did not talk about God very much at home, I always knew that God was in and around and underlying our warm convivial life.

Early on I came to know that my father did not think about God the same way my mother did. One time when friends were visiting I heard him explain that he had grown up on a farm near Canton, Ohio, the twelfth of thirteen children, where his whole family went to the Methodist Church.

He said that when he went to the University of Buffalo to study pharmacy, he began to question what he'd learned in the Methodist Church and decided he was really an agnostic. After the company left I asked him,

"Daddy, what is an agnostic?" I was about four.

He told me, "An agnostic doesn't say there is no God, honey. An agnostic says he just doesn't know for sure."

This answer puzzled me for a time. On everything else I trusted my father's opinion. I knew my mother thought my father was very smart because he had gone to college and became a pharmacist, which to her was almost the same as a doctor. Still, when it came to God I thought my mother's judgment was better. She knew what she believed, whereas my father wasn't sure. From time to time he came to church with us. He seemed to delight in trying to stump Dr. Bush with a difficult question on the way out after the service. This embarrassed my mother so much, I think she was glad when he stayed home.

After a while it didn't trouble me that my father wasn't sure about God. My parents seemed remarkably happy with each other. They had an easy way of doing things together and were openly affectionate. I took my cue from my mother that it must be all right for my father to have a different opinion about God.

Being an agnostic didn't prevent my father from having a favorite hymn. When my mother and I, and in time Danny, sang hymns at the piano, my father would frequently ask us to sing, "Lead Kindly Light," a hymn written by Cardinal John Newman that has beautiful sad words. Sometimes my father would come over to the piano and sing with us. In a clear tenor voice he sang out:

> Lead kindly light, amid the encircling gloom, Lead Thou me on;
> The night is dark, and I am far from home; Lead Thou me on;
> Keep Thou my feet; I do not ask to see
> The distant scene—one step enough for me.

There were three of these lovely mournful verses and I loved to sing all of them. I wondered if the "Kindly Light" my father liked to sing about was really another name for God.

two

"The Lord Is My Shepherd"

AROUND THE TIME I turned five, my mother helped me memorize the 23rd Psalm. During my brother's morning nap she would sit on the couch with her black leather-bound Bible in her lap and I would snuggle up next to her, glad to have my mother to myself for a whole hour or more. Each day she added a new line of the psalm. The first few lines were difficult because there is no necessary order to them. "He maketh me to lie down in green pastures" could just as easily come after "He restoreth my soul." The rest came quite easily. Eventually I could say the psalm all the way through. The 23rd Psalm is attributed to King David, and in the King James translation, the only version we had at the time, it reads like this:

The Lord is my shepherd; I shall not want.

He maketh me to lie down in green pastures: he
      leadeth me beside the still waters.

He restoreth my soul: he leadeth me in the paths of
      rightousness for his name's sake.

Yea, though I walk through the valley of the shadow
      of death, I will fear no evil: for thou art with me;
Thy rod and thy staff they comfort me.

Thou preparest a table before me in the presence
      of mine enemies: thou annointest my head with oil;
      my cup runneth over.

> Surely goodness and mercy shall follow me all the days
> of my life: and I will dwell in the house of the
> Lord forever.

In *Hurlbut's Story of the Bible* there was a picture of Jesus carrying a lamb, so from the beginning I thought Jesus was the shepherd. I could picture Jesus leading people through the valley of the shadow of death to keep them safe. We also sang a hymn, "Jesus, Like a Shepherd Lead Us." I didn't know that when David wrote this psalm Jesus had not yet come to earth. I found the psalm comforting, even though there wasn't as yet much need to be comforted. "Thou preparest a table before me," was the line that interested me most—I tried to imagine how Jesus would do that. I pictured a little table in the desert, something like a box with a white table cloth on it. I didn't know who my enemies were but I figured they were the bad people, like the witch in Hansel and Gretel.

I was not quite five when my father lost his job at the Henry Ford Hospital, a major hospital in Detroit. From listening to my parents' conversations I learned that my mother thought he lost his job because he had said something about a doctor at the hospital who was going out with a woman who wasn't his wife. My mother had urged him not to say anything. My father had a different explanation. He said that while we were away on vacation that summer, a few patients at the hospital died mysteriously. When he returned he discovered that someone had hooked up the apparatus for making glucose to tap water instead of to the distilled water. He thought impurities in the water might have caused the deaths. As it turned out, he was right; but this placed the blame on his department. Whichever it was, mentioning the affair or his disclosure about the deaths, perhaps both, he was fired.

He found another job almost immediately in the Fisher Building, a prestigious new twenty-eight story office building on West Grand Boulevard. It had a stunning pyramid-shaped gold dome you could see for miles when it was lit up at night. Shettler's Drug Store had a large space on the ground floor and hired my father as their pharmacist. Since he was the only pharmacist, it was a much more demanding job than the one at Ford Hospital had been. The Fisher Building was a long way from our apartment, so he could no longer come home for lunch. I missed that very much.

I began to notice little changes in my father after he took this new job. He grew a mustache that made him look different. I didn't like the feel of his mustache. When he kissed my cheek it was scratchy. His face had always felt so smooth. He seemed much more restless and wasn't nearly as much fun when he played with us before dinner.

One night I heard my mother ask him about a fur farm in Florida in which he'd invested some money. He tried to talk about something else—finally he told her that he had just learned that the fur farm did not exist. My mother sounded worried. She worried too that he was buying too many things we couldn't afford, such as the table and mirror he bought from a woman at work who needed money. My mother said we didn't need the table or the mirror. I thought they went very well in our dining room, the mirror with the table that fit under it up against the wall. But my mother was probably right about the money.

While he still came home and played with Danny and me for half-an-hour or so before dinner, he wasn't the same. He wasn't the joyful father we had known. I'd see him looking at his mustache in the new mirror, curling it this way and that. His expression was unfamiliar to me—strange. Some of the time I felt I didn't really know this new person who was my father.

One afternoon he took me with him to visit Aunt Daisy, one of his older sisters who lived a short car ride away. This memory is so vivid I still remember what I wore that day—a new blue and brown plaid dress my mother had bought me for starting kindergarten in a few weeks, and a brown cardigan sweater with two white Scottie dogs appliquéd on the front. I sat and listened patiently while my father and Aunt Daisy talked for about half an hour, but when we went to leave he stood on the front porch and continued talking to her for a long, long time. They were arguing about something. I grew tired of waiting and crossed the street to our car. I was not allowed to cross streets, I was not yet five, but it wasn't a busy street, and I was careful to look both ways. When he still didn't come I came back across the street and went up on the porch. "Daddy, let's go. It's getting dark." I tugged at his sleeve. But he kept talking, talking, talking to Aunt Daisy through the screen door. His face was getting red and his voice much louder now. I could have been a fly buzzing around him for all the attention he paid to me.

I gave up and started back toward the car. This time in the middle of the street I saw two headlights bearing down on me . . . a woman driver . . . a light green car. I didn't think I could make it to the other side in time. In my fright I fell down on the pavement and lay very still, as if I were hiding so the car wouldn't see me. Before the woman came to a complete stop her front wheels slid on either side of me. I think cars were higher off the ground back then. Something told me to keep my head down, and then the woman slowly backed up until she could see me. No part of her car had touched me. Something very bad had almost happened, but I wasn't hurt. I saw a slender blonde woman get out of the car. She looked terrified.

The screech of the brakes had alerted my father, who rushed into the street and gathered me in his arms. "Sarah, Sarah, do you hurt anywhere?" His voice sounded shaky but not angry. I shook my head to indicate I didn't hurt. Aunt Daisy rushed out too, her gray wispy hair flying around her face. "I believe she's all right," I heard him tell the blonde woman. The woman's face was a ghostly white. He kept asking me, "Are you sure you're all right? Can you move your arms—your legs?" When he saw I could move everything he seemed so relieved that I knew he wasn't going to scold me for crossing the street. He hugged me to him as he waved good bye to Aunt Daisy and carried me to the car. The blonde woman got back in her car and drove away very slowly.

On the way home my father said, "I think it would be better if you didn't tell your mother about this." I promised I wouldn't tell her, and I meant to keep that promise. But when I saw my mother, I burst into tears and ran to her saying, "Mama, I was run over by a car." Until that moment I hadn't felt nearly as frightened as I felt now.

She looked at my father with an expression that said, "How is that possible?"

"I crossed the street in front of Aunt Daisy's," I confessed. She put both of her arms around me. My father tried to explain what had happened. She didn't say anything. She just hugged me for a long time.

My father had never asked me to keep a secret from my mother before. Why hadn't he noticed that I was crossing the street? Was this the shadow of death, I wondered. I knew I was wrong to cross the street, but God had kept me safe. Goodness and mercy were following me.

A few weeks later I began kindergarten at the Doty School, three blocks from our apartment. My mother walked me there every morning with Danny in the baby carriage so we could go faster than a three-year-old can walk. Perhaps strollers were yet to be invented. At three o'clock when school ended she picked me up. My teacher, Miss Hill, a serenely pleasant woman with wavy silver hair, played the piano just the way my mother did at home. We sang songs and sat on a large round rug while she read stories to us. We played freeze tag on the playground and ran relays in the gym, more active games than we could play in our apartment where my mother was always afraid we'd disturb the neighbors and be asked to move. Apartments were not welcoming of children in these Depression years, so she had reason to worry.

A couple of months into the school year my mother picked me up after school as usual with Danny in the green wicker baby carriage. I was glad my mother was tall so I could see her a long way off. Still, I waited until I could see her thick dark hair marcelled in little waves around her face before I ran to meet her. Her eyes told me how glad she was to see me. Those eyes were bluer than anyone's. "What did you do with Miss Hill today?" She always asked that, and I always told her.

It was one of those crisp clear autumn days with the sun lighting up red, yellow, and orange leaves against a sky of intense blue. We went to the park where my mother pushed Danny in a swing with a bar across to keep him from falling out and I slid down the slide again and again, landing each time in a pile of dry brown leaves. I finally tired of that and went to the swing near Danny, a swing with no bar across, and let my mother push me too. When the wind blew colder we started for home.

Back in our apartment where it felt warm and cozy, my mother started getting dinner. Danny got out his cars and lined them up using the patterns in the Persian rug in the living room for roads. He always turned his cars upside down to see if he could find the engine inside. I sat on the davenport with my big doll I called Goll Goll and changed her dress so she'd look nice when my father came home. I sang Rock-a-bye Baby to her and rocked her in my little rocking chair.

It was nearly six o'clock, time for my father to come through the door in his white pharmacy coat. This day six o'clock came and my father wasn't home. It got to be ten after six, twenty after six. I had just learned to tell time and every few minutes I ran to the kitchen, checked the clock, and asked,

"Where is Daddy?"

"I don't know," my mother answered each time, and the last time she added, "Dinner's ready. I'm sure he'll be here any minute."

I was sorry to hear dinner was ready. This meant I would miss the most exciting time of the day—playing with my father was still very important to me even though he wasn't as exuberant as he used to be. "Now there'll be no time to play at all," I complained to her.

Soon she said, "Dinner's getting cold. We should go ahead and eat." We sat down at the dining room table. But it was impossible to eat when the question, "What could be keeping Daddy?" was hanging in the air like an enormous black balloon. He had never been late like this before without phoning. I ate a few of the peas on my plate and Danny ate some of his mashed potatoes, but I noticed my mother didn't eat a bite. She cleared away the dinner dishes and saved a plate of food for my father that she covered with waxed paper.

Danny played with his cars again, sitting as he always did, both legs bent back at the knees and his chubby calves flat on the floor. I was listening so hard for my father's key in the door that I couldn't follow the story my mother tried to read to us.

Finally the phone rang. I knew it would be my father and that he would tell us where he was and that he'd soon be home with us. But as I listened I could tell my mother wasn't talking to my father. She just held the receiver and kept saying softly,

"I see . . . yes . . . I see. Receiving Hospital? Yes, of course you can come over. Thank you." When she put the phone down she was crying.

"So where is Daddy?" I asked her as soon as she hung up the phone.

She was crying so much that for a moment she couldn't speak—then in between sobs she said in a shaky voice I'd never heard come from my mother before,

"That was the manager of the drugstore. He said Daddy wasn't himself today . . . late this afternoon he began preaching from the balcony of the pharmacy . . . they had to call an ambulance to take him to Receiving Hospital . . . that's where he is now."

I climbed onto the mohair sofa beside her. No one needed to tell me that preaching from the balcony was not a normal thing to do. I could see why this would make my mother cry. I wanted to cry too, but I didn't. Instead I sat trying to picture what "preaching from the balcony" was like. I could see my father standing at the railing that surrounded the pharmacy shouting to the people below.

We had visited my father at the drugstore once or twice since he took this new job. I remembered going up the spiral stairway to where the pharmacy was on an island elevated above the crowded main floor. I saw the four black telephones my mother said rang all day long—and the nurses coming in with prescriptions from the doctors' offices on the floors above. He was too busy to talk to us. My mother said afterwards that he was working way too hard. As I tried to imagine my father at that balcony preaching to the people below, I imagined the customers looking up at him. Were they frightened? I knew I'd be scared if I were in a drugstore and someone started preaching from up in a balcony. Maybe he spoke in a gentle voice the way Dr. Bush preached from the pulpit at Westminster Church. But would they take him away to a hospital if he were just speaking quietly? He was probably angry and raising his voice the way I'd seen him do with Aunt Daisy. Maybe he was waving his arms wildly. I hoped not, but in my mind's eye he was. He probably fought the people who came to take him to the hospital. I hated to think of him there all alone with no one to take his side.

My mother put her arm around me. I could feel she was still crying but without making any sound. Then, as if she couldn't sit still any longer, she stood up and started walking up and down the living room. She lit two more lamps and made a phone call, then came and sat down with me again. It frightened me that my mother didn't seem to know what to do. Until now I thought my mother would know what to do about anything. Danny came and put his head in her lap. I patted his blond hair that lay in a perfect swirl. He knew something was wrong, but he was too young to understand what my mother had said about the phone call. I wished I were too young too. Instead, I felt I understood perfectly. It was the séances. Aunt Daisy's séances were what made my father act so strangely. She held them in her house and I went to one once for a little while. I thought the séance was weird, frighteningly weird, so I left. My father no longer went to them, but he did a long time ago. It had to be the séances. Aunt Daisy felt she was a person the spirits could speak through to other people. My mother thought the séances were nonsense, but I wasn't so sure. To me they were scary and strange—the way my father now seemed strange.

In a little while two men came from Shettler's Drug Store to talk to my mother. I listened as she asked them the same questions I wanted to ask: "What is happening to him now? When do you think he can come home?" But they didn't have answers to these questions. They could only tell us what had happened, the same things the manager had said over the phone, and that was all. But how could that be all? We needed to know when my father would be coming back to us. They just said, "We feel so sorry." A big tall shadow followed the two men out of our apartment. Was this the shadow of death? Was my father going to die? Surely God would protect my father the way he had protected me when I was under the car. But then again maybe my father would become a spirit like the spirits that came to Aunt Daisy's séances.

It was past our bedtime. My mother had us get into our pajamas. She made a call to Mony, a friend who came to all my parents' parties. Her real name was Mildred but we called her Mony. Mony always sat and talked to me for a few minutes at the parties, something few of the other grown-ups did. I wanted to ask her what would make my father do such an unusual thing as preach from the balcony, but my mother said there wasn't time because Mr. Hinkle, a friend of my father's, was coming to take her to the hospital. Mr. Hinkle was a pharmacist like my father. He must be the person she called when she was walking up and down the living room. When he came she went down the hall and got Jack, the man who always stayed with us when our parents went to the movies.

My mother put on her coat and hat then stooped down, and hugged us both at once. "Go to bed nicely for Jack," she said. "Everything's going to be all right." How could everything be all right? It was all wrong for my father to be in a hospital and not home with us. Would I ever see him again? Nevertheless, I found my mother's words comforting. She seemed stronger now. I didn't know where Receiving Hospital was, but I knew hospitals made sick people get better.

Our apartment felt strangely quiet the morning after my father went to Receiving Hospital. I got ready for school. My mother helped Danny get dressed and made hot cereal for our breakfast. "Did you see Daddy last night?" I asked her.

She waited, as though trying to figure out how to tell me, "No, I couldn't see him." Then she added, "The doctors are taking good care of him, though."

"Do you think he'll come home soon?"

"I'm not sure, Sarah." I thought I saw tears in her eyes as she went to get the toast out of the toaster. I didn't like breakfast without my father there. It was too quiet without him giving Danny rides on his shoulder or teasing my mother about the bump in her nose looking like an Indian squaw's. I knew this meant he liked her nose.

We left for school. My mother pushed Danny's baby carriage faster than usual, as though she were in a hurry to get back home. At school I was relieved to find that kindergarten and Miss Hill were the same as they had been the day before. So many things had changed I feared this might have changed too. I didn't have much time to think about my father at school, but every once in a while when I remembered that he was in a hospital, a wave of sadness came over me. Then Miss Hill would call us to another activity and I'd have to leave my worries—which I was happy to do.

After school my mother took us to the park. She forgot to ask me what we did in school, but I told her anyway that Miss Hill pinned different colored leaves cut from construction paper on each kid's back and we had to try to keep the other kids from seeing what color our leaf was. "That sounds like a lot of fun," she said, but her voice sounded far away—I knew she was not really listening. She pushed both of us on the swings. I didn't feel like going down the slide by myself. I needed to be close to her and Danny. I needed to know that our family was almost the same as always. When we got home we had one of our favorite suppers, creamed chip beef on toast.

After supper my mother asked, "Which shall we do, sing or read a story?"

"Sing," I said. I almost always spoke first ahead of Danny. We sang some fun songs first, "Old MacDonald Had a Farm," "The Bear Went Over the Mountain," and then she played a hymn, "Count Your Blessings." I knew the first verse by heart:

When upon life's billows you are tempest tossed,
When you are discouraged thinking all is lost,
Count your many blessings, name them one by one,
And it will surprise you what the Lord has done.

We did have many blessings. We had our warm home. We had each other; and my mother seemed like her cheery self, at least while she was playing the piano and singing with us like this, one of us on each side of her. What I didn't know until much later was that after Danny and I had gone to sleep the night before, and for several nights after that, she walked the floor between our two beds, my bed in the sunroom and Danny's crib in her and my father's room, wondering how on earth she was going to take care of us. I never suspected she was feeling at such a loss.

In a week or so we received a letter saying that my father had been transferred from Detroit's Receiving Hospital to Ypsilanti State Hospital. Ypsilanti was a long way away—near Ann Arbor, my mother said. My Aunt Kathryn lived in Ann Arbor and I'd been there many times. It was a long way. My mother was still not allowed to see him.

It was clear that my father was not coming home for a long time. My mother knew she'd have to go to work, and that she could never make as much money as my father made. My father had earned $35 a week as a pharmacist, and our rent was $35 a month. Some changes would have to be made.

My mother's first move was to negotiate with the super for a cheaper apartment. She took me with her when she went to see him. The super, a short portly man with a bushy mustache, told her, "The only apartment I have, Mrs. Slagle, is in the basement next to the laundry room. I don't think you'd want that."

"I'd like to look at it," my mother told him in a determined voice. The apartment he showed us had once been an office.

"This was the entrance hall for the office," the super was saying as he unlocked the door and we walked inside. I saw that the walls separating the rooms had frosted glass from half-way up the wall almost to the ceiling. "And this room to the left might be large enough for a living room." My mother and I walked around. The kitchen was small—no room for a table. We looked at the bathroom and the two other small rooms that could be bedrooms. "The outer walls are mostly underground," the super pointed out. "That's why the windows are so high up and don't let in much light." It was already dark, so we hadn't noticed the windows.

"We couldn't see out of them very well either, I suppose," my mother said. I was relieved that she could see this would not be a good place for us. But then she said, "We could make this entrance hall the dining room, Sarah." She told the super, "I'll take it."

On the way back upstairs I said, "We can't move down there. It's too dark, and it's ugly."

"You'll be surprised at how pretty we can make that apartment," she reassured me. "It's only half the rent we're paying now."

When the basement apartment was freshly painted a light ivory and our furniture was in place, it did look surprisingly bright and cheerful. Our round oak dining room table and six chairs filled the entrance hall almost to overflowing. My mother stored some of the living room furniture, but she kept the piano so we could still sing our hymns and songs. Danny and I shared one of the little rooms and the other one was my mother's, but I thought of it as my father's too. He was in the hospital. He hadn't died. I knew that God must be watching over him too, just as the psalm said—"I will fear no evil for Thou art with me."

Not long after we moved into the new apartment I went into our much smaller living room and found my mother sitting on the couch crying. Since the night my father didn't come home until that moment, I had not seen her cry. Going over to her I said, "Don't cry, Mama. God never let us go hungry yet." She put her arm around me and pulled me down beside her. We always had plenty of food. I just couldn't think of anything else to say. How could I know that on a recent day my mother had made lunch for my brother and me and had nothing left for herself? That afternoon a friend had come and bought the green wicker baby carriage for five dollars, so we had food. When my mother told me this story some years later, she added, "Back then you could fill the trunk of your car with groceries for five dollars."

I grew to like the little bedroom Danny and I shared. Danny still slept in the crib which folded down into a trundle bed he could get in and out of easily. I had a little nightstand by my bed now with a lamp that gave the room a cozy glow. One night, I remember, my mother had heard my prayers, and Danny was already asleep. She lay down across the foot of my bed. She looked very tired. I was about to get under the covers and lie down too when she said, "Sarah, would you say the 23rd Psalm for me?" I felt so happy that I could do this because I knew it would make her feel better. Softly, so as not to wake Danny, I began,

> The Lord is my shepherd. I shall not want.
> He maketh me to lie down in green pastures: he
> > leadeth me beside still water . . .

The psalm made me feel better too. "Thou preparest a table before me . . ." Of course God would never let us go hungry. In 1935 people were going hungry, but I didn't know that then.

three

"Just the Way You Look Tonight"

CHRISTMAS MORNING I WOKE early. The bedroom Danny and I shared opened into the entrance hall that was now our dining room. I slipped quietly through the door in my nightgown and bare feet and was astonished to find our round dining room table completely covered with brightly-wrapped packages piled one on the other, two, and in some places three, layers deep. In the past, I remembered, our Christmas presents were always placed under the Christmas tree. Then I saw it—in the middle of the table, a scrawny little artificial Christmas tree about two feet high with red plastic berries at the end of the branches. With a sinking feeling I realized the gifts *were* under our Christmas tree, or at least around this pitiful little tree. There'd be no beautifully decorated real tree like the ones we had always had before which reached to the ceiling and glowed with colored lights and splendid ornaments my father had collected. I remembered watching him carefully place strands of tinsel, one at a time, along a branch, and then move on to the next branch until the whole tree shimmered with silver. My father would never have allowed us to have such a silly little tree. But he wasn't here. He was far away in Ypsilanti State Hospital, a place I could only imagine as dark and lonely with no one to be with him for Christmas.

My mother once told me that growing up in Canada she had never had a Christmas tree. She and her brother and four sisters hung their stockings up by the fireplace on Christmas Eve. In the morning they'd find a few small presents inside their stocking along with the best gift of all, an orange—"the only orange we would see all winter," she said. It didn't sound like much of a Christmas to me.

I was fighting back tears when Danny stumbled out in his blue flannel pajamas with feet in them. He looked very sweet with his Buster

Brown haircut. At not quite four he was too young to care what kind of Christmas tree we had. I would have cared at his age though and would probably have complained. He was a much nicer child than I was—an easier child, at least.

My mother came out of her bedroom. Seeing the tears I was struggling to hide she picked up one of two toy banjos, gifts too odd-shaped to wrap, and started to sing a little song to cheer me up. I started to smile. I could see she was trying to make this as happy a Christmas as she could with all these beautifully wrapped presents. I didn't say anything about the tree.

Although we usually waited until after breakfast to open Christmas presents, my mother decided we should open some now. There were so many. I had the feeling our friends tried to make up for my father not being here by giving us more gifts than ever.

After reading the tag on it my mother handed me a large box and said this was a present for me from Mrs. Carter, a woman in the building whom I knew a little but not very well. I opened the box. After sifting through the first few layers of tissue paper, I stood back in awe of what I saw. "Look Mama!" I said, "It's a beautiful doll. And Mrs. Carter has made a box full of clothes for her."

My mother came over to my side of the table where amid the layers of tissue paper I was finding outfit after outfit and carefully lifting them out of the box. "It's a wardrobe for a princess," she said. The doll was about a foot-and-a-half tall. Mrs. Carter had made her a long party dress and a fur cape, several beautiful shorter dresses, and a black and white tweed coat with a collar of real fur and a matching hat with a little red and green feather tucked in the hat band. The tweed coat and hat were already my favorites. They were exactly like what a grown-up would wear.

My mother was fingering the beautifully tailored little coat. "We must stop by her apartment a little later and thank her," she said. And we did.

My brother was already playing with some additions to his car collection, lining them up on the little bit of space remaining on the table and making car noises as he pushed them along imaginary streets. We took a long time opening the presents. I felt sorry that my father wasn't there opening gifts too. He loved Christmas trees so much.

That afternoon we were invited to our friends the Fellowes' apartment in the building. Nancy Fellowes was my age and my friend, so our mothers became friends as well. After lunch the three of us went up there, but as soon as we arrived my mother realized she'd forgotten the box of Whitman's chocolates she had bought for the Fellowes. She asked me to go downstairs to get it.

I ran down the three flights of stairs to our basement apartment. The door was unlocked, and as I opened the door I could hear that the radio in the living room had been left on. It was one of those radios with a curved top that sits on a little table. Just then a song came on the radio and something about the mood of the music made me want to listen. It must have been Bing Crosby who was singing:

> Someday,
> When I'm awfully low
> And the world is cold
> I will feel a glow just thinking of you
> And the way you look tonight.

I sat down next to the little radio and listened to every word. I could not possibly have left before the song was finished. The song continued:

> Oh, but you're lovely
> With your smile so warm
> And your cheek so soft,
> There is nothing for me but to love you
> Just the way you look tonight.
>
> With each word your tenderness grows,
> Tearing my fear apart.
> And that laugh that wrinkles your nose,
> Touches my foolish heart.

The refrain was the best part:

> Lovely!
> Never, never change.
> Keep that breathless charm
> Won't you please arrange it, for I love you
> Just the way you look tonight—
> Just the way you look tonight.

With all my heart I wished I could hear the song again from the beginning. The words were exactly what I wanted to say to my father, "Never, never change." I missed him so much the way he used to be. Why had he changed? The lights in the apartment had been left on and even though my father had never lived in this apartment, the room felt aglow with my memories of him—the excitement I felt waiting for him to come home from work—the way he used to bring people home for lunch—how happy he was at the parties in our upstairs apartment. He had looked so handsome serving highballs to our guests on a silver tray. "Breathless charm," that's what my father had for me. Even at five-and-a-half I knew what that meant. When the song finished, I sat there for several minutes thinking about him. I hated to break the spell the song had cast. But I had to take the box of chocolates back upstairs, so I did.

Not long after my father had been transferred to the state hospital at Ypsilanti, my mother received a letter asking her to come to talk with a social worker, Miss Anderson, about my father. My father's sisters, Aunt Daisy and Aunt Kathryn, learned that she had this appointment at the hospital, and insisted on going too. When my mother came through the door after her long ride home on two buses, her eyes were still red from crying. I asked her what had happened. She said, "It's too long a story, Sarah." She paid Jack for babysitting with Danny and me. No sooner had he left than the doorbell rang and it was Mrs. Fellowes who came to see how my mother's trip to the hospital had gone. I was glad she came. Maybe now I'd find out why my mother had been crying so hard. She made tea for the two of them, then took the tea into the living room and began to tell Mrs. Fellowes what had happened. I sat at my little table in the corner and drew a picture of my mother and Mrs. Fellowes talking while I listened.

"I still couldn't see Dan," my mother was saying. Over several cups of tea she poured out the whole story. Her telling was so vivid I felt I had been there myself. I could picture Aunt Kathryn in her green silk suit with a fox fur around her neck, her brown wavy hair and lipstick just so, and Aunt Daisy in a housedress, her gray hair popping out of the topknot at the back of her head, all of them crowding into Miss Anderson's small office. Miss Anderson had to bring in an extra chair, my mother said. From my mother's telling, this scene still exists in my mind:

Searching Miss Anderson's face for clues, my mother asked, "What is happening with my husband, Miss Anderson? Have you seen him?"

Miss Anderson hesitated. "I have to be honest with you. He's higher than a kite." A slender blonde woman a little younger than my mother, she folded her hands firmly on her heavy oak desk and wearily let out a little sigh, "Yesterday he pulled all the stuffing out of his mattress. But he can't hurt himself. He's perfectly safe."

"What is wrong with him?" my mother asked in a plaintive voice and then looked down at the floor as if talking to herself. "He was always so smart. I never expected anything like this could happen to Dan." When she looked up again tears glistened in her amazing blue eyes. Then, as if answering her own question, she said, "He worked too hard at Shettler's Drug Store. The job put too much pressure on him."

Just then Aunt Kathryn broke in, her voice high-pitched and angry, her lips with the perfectly applied lipstick spitting out the words, "I'll tell you what happened to him. He was bored out of his mind. Everything was the children. The two of you never went anywhere without them." Then she looked right at my mother and said, "You should have been dressed up and ready to go places when Dan came home, Mazie. No man likes a scrubwoman!"

My mother had often seemed a little afraid of Aunt Kathryn, but this day she stood up to her. "Are you saying it was my fault Dan took sick, Kathryn? He loves his children. He always wanted to be with them."

Knowing she was landing a hard blow, Aunt Kathryn said, "Well, that's not the way it was with Grace. Dan was used to more bright lights." My mother wiped her tears with the linen handkerchief she always carried. Miss Anderson remained a calm observer of this sudden squall.

My mother, composed again, said calmly, "I think you're wrong, Kathryn. Dan loved our life together the way it was."

Aunt Kathryn picked up her purse, gloves, and briefcase. As secretary to the director of the McGregor Foundation she had important things to do. "I can't stay. I've a meeting back in Ann Arbor, but the other thing I need to tell you is that Tracy McGregor said the Foundation will make funds available for Dan to have a thorough evaluation at a clinic he knows in Philadelphia. It was good to meet you, Miss Anderson."

Before she could exit, my mother had the last word, "Thank Mr. McGregor for me, Kathryn. Tell him we'll go to that clinic as soon as Dan's able to travel."

"I will," Kathryn said as she and Aunt Daisy left together. Aunt Daisy, awed by her younger sister, hadn't said a word.

Once the sisters were gone, my mother gave in to her urge to cry, but only for a few moments. Miss Anderson came out from behind her desk and sat next to my mother. "You must understand one thing. No one causes this kind of illness. It runs in families. We don't know what causes it, but you didn't do it." She took a yellow pad off her desk and began taking notes on my father's history. "Did your husband ever have this kind of problem before?"

My mother thought for a minute. "I—I'm not sure. When I met Dan he had his own drugstore in Buffalo. People couldn't always pay their bills to him—still he wouldn't refuse medicine to anyone. In the end he couldn't pay his creditors and felt he had to sell his store."

Miss Anderson wrote that down. "That had to be a blow."

My mother leaned forward. "It was. He's told me several times, 'When I didn't have those keys to the drugstore in my pocket, I didn't feel like myself.'"

"Were you married then?"

"No, not even engaged. Dan was at loose ends after he sold his store. Daisy and Kathryn had moved to Detroit—his mother too—so he moved there. He was feeling pretty low. Kathryn wrote to me inviting me to come for a visit thinking it would cheer him up. If they hadn't sent for me, Dan and I might never have gotten together."

Miss Anderson leaned back in her chair and chewed on the end of her eraser thinking. "You know, he was showing signs of this illness before you married him."

My mother looked surprised. "Really?"

"That was the depressive phase. What you're seeing now is the manic phase. I bet he had other depressions before he sold his store."

My mother hesitated a long time. She wasn't sure she should tell this next part, but then she did. "You heard Kathryn speak of Grace. I don't think they were ever married. They lived together a while and she helped in the store. Grace ran off with a pharmaceutical salesman. Dan told me he was depressed after Grace left. He felt betrayed. He discovered she'd been taking money from the store for some time. That may have been the real reason he lost his store."

"How terrible!" Miss Anderson said. Then checking her watch she said, "We have to stop, but I'm coming to Detroit next week and I'm going with you to Hudson's Department Store." She stood up and so did my mother.

"Since you worked there before, they just might give you a job." At the door she said, "Don't pay any attention to Dan's sisters. He had this illness long before and they knew it. We're going to focus on getting him better and in the meantime on getting you a paycheck."

My mother would have left then to start her long trek home on two buses, one into downtown Detroit, and another out to where we lived. From what I heard her tell Mrs. Fellowes the main thing she took away from that meeting was that Aunt Kathryn thought of her as a scrubwoman. If at that moment I could have slapped Aunt Kathryn's face, I would have done it—as hard as I could. No one called my mother "Mazie" except my father's family. Her name was Mae, or Mary. And no one would *ever* call her a scrubwoman. She cried and her eyes became red again when she told this part of the story to Mrs. Fellowes.

From that time on I hated Aunt Kathryn for what she had said to my mother, even though Aunt Kathryn was always good to me, giving me lovely gifts she brought from her trips to Europe. In my five-year-old way I understood how painful my father's illness was for my mother. To have his family turn against her and blame her seemed terribly unfair. They should be helping her, not criticizing her.

Her own sisters were completely different from Aunt Daisy and Aunt Kathryn. They wrote urging her to come back to Canada where they would help her raise her children. But it was an offer she had to refuse. I heard her tell Aunt Sadie on the phone, "I have to stay here and keep a place for Dan to come home to when he's well." If she hadn't, she said, my father might have spent the rest of his life in a state hospital. I've often wondered what I'd have done in her place. I've since learned that more than 90 percent of people with manic-depressive illness become divorced. Her decision was based on more than duty, though. She deeply loved my father and whether he was sick or well, that never changed.

In allowing me to overhear her conversation with Mrs. Fellowes, my mother let me hear about Grace. I'd seen pictures of a blonde woman among the family snapshots and when I'd ask, "Who's that?" my parents just said, "Oh, that's Grace." It didn't trouble me that my father might have had an earlier girl friend, or even a wife. As with his being an agnostic, whatever he thought or did was honorable, I was sure, and was done for a good reason. From here on there wasn't much my mother kept from me. At age five I was becoming as much her friend as her daughter.

What did trouble me were the bizarre sad stories about my father—that he pulled all the stuffing out of his mattress. I pictured him in a cell of some kind—like a prison cell. I imagined metal bars keeping him enclosed in a small space while he did this wild thing of pulling the stuffing from his mattress. Later I learned that he was on a ward with about 200 men. In my adult life when I worked on a hospital's psychiatric unit we had a "seclusion room" padded and safe for out-of-control patients; so he may have been secluded during times he was out of control. I figured my father tore the stuffing out to get back at the people who had locked him up, and sort of cheered his fighting back. Still, it was an ugly image—and hard to reconcile with the gentle, loving father who would get down on the floor every night and play with Danny and me.

In pictures my parents took the day I began kindergarten, standing next to my father who is kneeling down beside me wearing a dark suit, I look like a happy child; and I could be a feisty little girl. My parents had said, "Sarah's so persistent" so many times, Danny began saying, "Sarah's so persint." In this way "Persint" became my nickname for several years. It is true that I insisted on staying up for all my parents' parties—and when my grandmother, a tough one to go up against, tried to have a new head put on my battered doll, Goll Goll, I protested vehemently, "Then she wouldn't be Goll Goll," and hugged Goll Goll to me so tightly that there was no way my grandmother could take her away. But by the end of the school year, in the kindergarten class picture I'm in the back row, almost hiding behind the child next to me and looking very forlorn and beaten down. Like most five-year-old girls I totally adored my father. I found it hard to understand why he was behaving like a strange, wild man. Worse, I felt my father's behavior reflected on me and worried that whatever this wild thing was that was in him, was also in me. Everyone said I looked like him, and that my brother looked like my mother. I used to like that I looked like my father. Now I wasn't sure. By the end of kindergarten my feistiness was crumbling.

With the Great Depression still cresting, it was not going to be easy for my mother to find a job. She had worked at Hudson's Department Store until just before I was born, but if Miss Anderson, the social worker from

Ypsilanti State Hospital, had not gone with her, Hudson's probably would not have hired her. Hudson's was a generous, large store that contributed significant amounts of money to help the unemployed, but the depression-size salary they could offer my mother was only $13.50 a week plus 1 percent commission. She quickly said, "I'll take it." With the lowered rent of our basement apartment, she could now manage all the necessities and pay Edith, our baby-sitter, five dollars a week. She had to have been a wizard with money because all during this time I never *ever* felt that we were poor.

Friends helped too. Our good friend Mildred White, whom we called Mony, sent us $5 a month anonymously as soon as she learned my father was ill and couldn't work. We knew it was Mony because it was the kind of thing Mony would do. When I grew out of the new clothes with which I began kindergarten, Mrs. Carter, who had made the elegant doll clothes for me at Christmas, said she would sew new clothes for me if my mother bought the material. Mrs. Carter made me a bright red corduroy jumper and five frilly long-sleeved white blouses, one for each school day. The blouses were each so different that I didn't mind wearing the same red jumper every day. In fact, I thought the jumper was beautiful. To save my school clothes, Mrs. Carter also made me a play dress with matching bloomers that I changed into after school, carefully hanging up the jumper for the next day. Girls never wore long pants then, only skirts and dresses.

Until the government passed the forty-hour work week law in October, 1938, my mother worked six days a week. This meant that she cleaned and did laundry after church on Sunday. She began losing weight. Dr. Chase at the Employees' Health Service at Hudson's thought she looked too pale. He wrote her a prescription for a bright green tonic and then gave her his charge plate so she could buy it at once at Hudson's pharmacy. I tasted this tonic once or twice and liked the taste. It may have had a little alcohol in it. Dr. Chase also arranged for Hudson's to pay for a cleaning woman to come once a week to clean and even do the washing and ironing, which took a huge load off my mother. Personal interest of this kind in an employee's well-being would seem unusual today, but at that time it wasn't. The *Detroit News* reported that with these years of rising joblessness came an increase in kindness. The hymn was right. We could "count our blessings" and "name them one by one" in the kind deeds of our friends and even my mother's employer.

But for my father we could only wait. In 1935 there were no medications for this illness, not even the heavy tranquilizers like Thorazine, which would not arrive until the early fifties, eighteen years later, and Lithium later yet. My mother was told it would take several months for his mania to run its course, and that severe depression with a high risk of suicide usually follows mania. After the depression diminished and he was only moderately depressed he could come home.

In time Danny and I got used to having a baby sitter instead of our mother at home with us. I missed the songs and stories with my mother, but most of all I missed my father. On Friday nights, to add a little liveliness to our week, my mother had our baby sitter take Danny and me to meet her at the bus stop, and the three of us went to a neighborhood restaurant for supper. We were excited waiting to see "Is she on this bus?" and if not, "Surely she's on the next one." Then we'd see her coming down the steps of the bus in her black crepe dress or her navy blue one with the cape—she only had two—all smiles and happy to see us. She never seemed tired on Friday nights. The baby sitter would leave and we'd walk the two blocks to the restaurant, one on each side of her trying to tell her our stories of the day, or waving a drawing we'd made in front of her face.

The restaurant had booths of shiny dark oak wood in which my brother always sat next to my mother and I sat across from them. The menu consisted almost completely of different kinds of hot sandwiches, chicken, roast beef, roast pork, made with white bread and covered with thick pale-brown gravy. Each time Danny said, "I'll have what Mama's having," while I made it a point to choose a different hot sandwich than the one they ordered. I saw my mother as Danny's partner, and I knew that the seat next to me was vacant. My partner was missing.

After we got home from the restaurant we read stories or sang a few songs at the piano before getting ready for bed. One of these Friday nights my mother played a song I hadn't heard before. The melody was plaintive and the words went something like this:

> Tell me the tales that to me were so dear,
> Long, long ago. Long, long ago.
> Sing me the songs I delighted to hear
> Long, long ago, Long ago . . .
> Then to all others my smile you preferred.

Love when you spoke gave a charm to each word.

Let me believe that you love as you loved

Long, long ago, long ago.

The song made me think about my father, of course, far away in a state hospital. Did he still remember me? I felt sure he did. I pictured him being as lonely for us as we were for him. In fact, this troubled me the most—that he was all alone there while we had each other. It did seem a long time ago, that night when he didn't come home. "Love when you spoke gave a charm to each word." There was that word "charm" again— like "breathless charm." I don't know how I knew the meaning of the word charm at age five, but I did, and I knew it was what my father had for me—long, long ago.

four

"O Little Town of Bethlehem"

AFTER EIGHT MONTHS, AN eternity to my now six-year-old self, my mother received a letter from Ypsilanti State Hospital telling her that my father was ready to be discharged. It was late August and I was marking off the days on the calendar before I would begin first grade; but on this day something far more important was happening—my father was coming home. Uncle Charlie, one of my father's brothers, drove my mother to Ypsilanti State Hospital. I persuaded Edith, our baby sitter, to go home from the park early because I had to be there when my father arrived. It had been very hot at the park, but now our basement apartment felt beautifully cool. I watched as the minute hand got closer and closer to five o'clock, the time my mother said she and Uncle Charlie would be back with my father.

Barely able to contain our excitement Danny and I began to chant in unison, "Daddy's coming home. Daddy's coming home," jumping up and down in the entry hall turned dining room. "Don't be disappointed if they're late," Edith cautioned us, "There's traffic this time of day." Edith was our cousin by marriage, married to Aunt Daisy's adopted son, Johnny. Tall and pretty with pale skin and thick dark hair, she was a younger version of our mother and we liked her very much. They weren't late. A little before five o'clock the door opened and my mother came in wearing the navy blue dress she wore to work. My father came right behind her, carrying his suitcase. Uncle Charlie must have dropped them off and wasn't coming inside.

Our exuberance quickly hushed, as we waited for my father to say something. He put his suitcase against the wall, squatted down and held out both arms to us. With that much invitation we jumped all over him, arms around his neck, shouting, "Daddy, you're home, you're home, Daddy," almost knocking him over. Looking up I saw my mother had tears in her eyes but these were not happy tears because her eyes looked troubled and she was biting her lower lip. It was then I noticed my father's appearance. He was very thin. His navy blue suit was too big on him. His face had no color and he looked much older than I remembered.

After a moment he stood up and looked around at the basement apartment he had never seen. My mother had everything sparkling and just so for my father's return, but even her best efforts couldn't make this apartment as lovely as the one upstairs had been. My father said nothing about the basement apartment. Bending down again he took both of us in his arms and hugged us to him, saying, "Sarah, Danny, I've missed you so much."

Danny took his hand. "Come and see our new house, Daddy. I'll show you where I sleep." Relieved that Danny was taking charge, I followed behind while he took our father into each of the small rooms showing him finally where he would sleep with my mother. Bewildered at how changed he appeared, I wondered if he would ever again pick Danny up and hold him over his head the way he once did when he came home from work. Of course Danny was bigger now. I wondered if he'd ever laugh and have fun with us again. He looked so serious.

Soon after my father's return home my parents went to the clinic in Philadelphia for the evaluation that the McGregor Foundation arranged. Danny and I stayed with Aunt Daisy that week. In the past I had never enjoyed our visits to Aunt Daisy's large, dark, cluttered house. The house was filled with stuff she would never use. If I opened the door to any of the bedrooms upstairs, I saw old furniture stored there with books piled on top and even a few stuffed birds peering down at me from a shelf. Her own oil paintings, all dark scenes of barren fields and trees, leaned against the wall in every room. To me it was a scary house filled with spirits from her séances. The one time I went to one of her séances the spirits spoke by making the table legs rise and fall. One tap was for "yes" and two taps for "no." At least that's what Aunt Daisy said caused the taps. My mother said Aunt Daisy made the table legs make those sounds. I didn't like the idea of staying in her house at night, perhaps with spirits flying around. But I knew the trip to Philadelphia was so important, I didn't protest. I would have agreed to do anything that might make my father well again.

From the time I first heard about Aunt Kathryn arranging for my father to go to a city called Philadelphia for his illness, I had hoped that doctors in that other city would be able to explain what made this happen to him—and not only explain it to us, but fix it. Until now my mother's explanation was that, "Daddy had a nervous breakdown." But what was a nervous breakdown? And why did it make him do things like preach from the balcony of the pharmacy or, even worse, pull all the stuffing out of his mattress? I wanted to hear what these new doctors would say.

Upon their return our parents picked us up at Aunt Daisy's late in the day in my father's Willis-Knight coup. As usual, I rode in the rumble seat. Our orderly apartment looked so good to me when we walked in the door after a week at Aunt Daisy's. That night while my father listened to the baseball game in the living room, my mother put Danny and me to bed. I waited until we had finished our prayers and I had crawled under the covers. The little blue lamp on my nightstand with its white shade gave off a warm light. The time seemed right, so I said, "Mama, tell us what the doctors said." She sat down on my bed and looked at both of us for a few seconds. Again she bit her lower lip on one side which told me that, as at other times lately, she was figuring out how to explain something complicated in words that we could understand.

"The doctors told us Daddy is manic-depressive, Sarah. They don't know what causes it, and right now there's no medicine for it." She was still wearing the black dress with the white lace collar she had worn on the trip.

"That was all?" I was greatly disappointed. I had expected more than just a name for this illness. "But what does it mean, manic something-or-other?" I said impatiently. My mother took a deep breath and chewed on her thumbnail a moment. Then speaking slowly she explained.

"Manic means a person becomes very excited, the way Daddy did in the drugstore when he preached from the balcony, and depressive is when someone becomes very, very sad the way Daddy became in the hospital. He's still a little sad." I agreed he was still sad. He had hardly played with us at all since he came home. He just listened to the radio or read *The Detroit News*.

"So manic is when you get too excited? The other part, de-something, de-pressive means you're too sad?" It was so important to me to understand this. Was I right that it came from the séances at Aunt Daisy's?

Both the séances and my father's behavior struck me as strange and out-of-the-ordinary, almost frightening, so I still connected them.

"That's right. We all have times we're happy and times when we're sad. Daddy's happy and sad times just go too far. He becomes too excited and a few months later he becomes too sad. But it's not his fault. It's an illness." My mother looked very pretty just then, her dark hair framing her face in the lamp light. Although it was a worried, tired face, her blue eyes had a sparkle. Now that my father's eyes never shone the way they used to, I was glad to see my mother's still did. She had lots of energy and enjoyed small everyday things in a way that made me sure our life would go on almost as normal.

Until now Danny was just listening. Leaning on his elbow in his bed, his blond hair golden in the dim light, he asked, "Is he all better now, Mama? Will he ever have to go to the hospital again?"

Once more she hesitated before she spoke. "The doctors said this could happen again, Danny. He could become over excited. But I'm hoping he won't. We'll just have to pray that God will show us how to keep Daddy well." She got up from my bed. "Go to sleep now, my dears. It's been a long day." She gave us each a goodnight kiss and left the lamp lit. I turned the word "manic-depressive" over in my mind for a long time. What could we do to keep Daddy from getting too excited, I wondered? Already Danny and I didn't ask him to play horsey or hide and seek with us anymore. We could see he wasn't in the mood for that. Sometimes we played hide and seek in the apartment just ourselves. Maybe we shouldn't even do that.

My father took another job as a pharmacist at Herman Kiefer Hospital, a small hospital that paid him less money than he had earned at the Henry Ford Hospital or Shettler's Drug Store. My mother kept her job at Hudson's Department Store. There was no mention of her staying home with us again. I could tell that this was never going to happen. With my father earning less money we needed my mother's paycheck too. And besides, what if my father had to go back to the hospital? It was hard to think about that, but the doctors had said that it could happen.

Before we knew it, it was Christmas time again. On Saturday, my father's day off, he decided to go downtown to do some Christmas shopping and asked if I would like to go with him. My mother worked on Saturdays and Danny was content to stay with Edith, our baby sitter. I was eager to go downtown with my father. He no longer seemed as quiet and sad as he had the first few months he was home—sometimes he did play with us now, and he was always happy to answer my many questions. I put on my dark blue winter coat, my tam, my snow boots, and was all ready to go. Before we left, though, my father took me into their bedroom and took a silk scarf of shocking pink from my mother's bureau drawer. He tied it around my neck, as if to dress me up more. The scarf was so long it came to the bottom of my coat, and the color was much too showy for a little girl. I knew it didn't look right, but I was afraid I'd hurt his feelings if I refused to wear it. We took the streetcar downtown. Despite how uncomfortable I felt in the pink scarf, I was happy to be riding the streetcar alone with my father for the first time ever. I took his hand.

We got off the streetcar and headed for Hudson's Department Store. Downtown Detroit was aglow with Christmas trees lit up and holiday wreaths with bright red ribbons everywhere. A light snow was falling. Merry tunes of Christmas carols mixed with sleigh bells filtered down from a loudspeaker through the snow and the bustle of shoppers as we hurried along the street. We passed a Salvation Army Santa ringing his bell outside Hudson's. My father put a dollar in his big pot. I knew that was a lot of money.

The elevator door opened on Hudson's twelfth floor and we entered a child's paradise. Here we wandered among brightly lit glass showcases filled with the most wonderful dolls and toys I had ever seen.

"Sarah, look at all these dolls! Which one would you like for Christmas?" My father's voice sounded too loud in a worrisome way. I looked at the dolls in the cases and on top of the cases, baby dolls, large and small, older-looking dolls in long silky dresses. "These are wonderful. Look at that doll, and what about this one?"

"I don't know, Daddy." All of a sudden I didn't feel much like choosing a doll. I felt embarrassed that his voice was so loud. Other customers seemed to be noticing.

"Which one would you like, honey? I know how much you love dolls." I could hear the excitement in his voice. He was moving too quickly from case to case for me to have time to look at the dolls. There was a large baby doll in a pink bunting in a case and when I pointed to her my father called a saleslady over to take her out of the case. I held her in my arms and saw that she had shiny blue eyes that opened and closed, and long brown eyelashes.

"I'd like this one, Daddy, the baby doll," I told him.

"That's a great choice, sweetheart." He asked the saleslady to wrap the doll as a present; then he took out his wallet and paid for it.

We looked at toys for Danny next. He bought him several different models of little cars, knowing that Danny could play with cars all day long. He bought him a large red fire engine as well, and a pick-up truck. Then he wanted me to pick out another doll.

I told him, "One is enough, Daddy. I like the doll in the pink bunting best of all of them." He looked so hurt that I did find another doll I liked, a Deanna Durban doll with long black hair and a royal blue satin dress. Normally I would be thrilled to have these dolls, but I could see he was spending too much money. I was afraid he would spend his whole week's pay, which I knew was $28. I watched the dollars come out of his wallet until there were no more left.

We took the escalator down to the sixth floor to see my mother and get money for the streetcar home. When we reached her department and found my mother she looked at the scarf around my neck and then looked at me. Her eyes told me that she knew what I knew, that my father was becoming manic. My mother went to her locker to get us some money for the streetcar and my father and I went home carrying all the presents. Riding home on the streetcar with all these bundles I did not feel as happy as I had on the way downtown. My father was very cheerful and continued to talk loudly. It didn't seem to bother him that he had spent his whole paycheck on toys, but it troubled me. I knew we needed that money to pay for food and pay the rent. There had never been a sharp division of adults and children in our household, so I heard all the discussions of finances between my parents. They never disagreed—just planned. Only now my father did not seem to be concerned about paying our bills—only about buying loads of presents.

That night and over the next few days it was impossible for my father to stop talking. He slept only two or three hours a night. He talked until he pretty much lost his voice. He was angry that Dr. Chase had sent my mother a cleaning woman. He thought there must be a romance between my mother and Dr. Chase. She tried to explain that Hudson's, not Dr. Chase, paid for the cleaning woman. Eventually he was up all night for several nights and would certainly have lost his job at Herman Kiefer Hospital if he had tried to go to it.

Late at night after Danny and I were in bed, I could hear my father's loud talking in the dining room. I went to the door of my room and opened it in time to hear my mother say, "Perhaps we should go back to the hospital, Dan, and see if they can give you something to help you sleep?" She said this quietly, knowing my father would most likely refuse to do that.

"There's nothing wrong with me. You're the sick one," he shot back, pointing his finger at her. "You're a nervous woman!" He was shouting and I had never heard my father shout at my mother before or even be angry with her. By now Danny had joined me in the doorway. My father's face looked red. He loosened his tie and opened his shirt collar as he walked up and down the little area beside the table in the dining room.

My mother stood in the doorway to the kitchen. Ignoring his angry accusations she said calmly, "Dan, you're not eating. You can't sleep. Maybe the doctor could help you." It was now almost midnight. Neither of them paid any attention to Danny and me standing there watching. To my surprise my father said my mother could phone Uncle Charlie to drive him to Receiving Hospital. The doctors there admitted him. I could see now why the people at Shettler's Drug Store had to call an ambulance when he was preaching from the balcony. He was such a force, like a steam engine that keeps on going. No one could reason with him. After Uncle Charlie left with my father Danny and I went back to bed. I asked God to help my father calm down and to bring him home to us in a few days, but I wasn't sure even God could do this.

The next morning before she went to work my mother put all the presents my father had bought for us on the dining room table. "Choose one present you'd like to keep for your Christmas present from Daddy," she said, explaining that she had to return the rest to have money to pay our bills. Neither Danny nor I objected. In fact, I wasn't sure I wanted either of the two dolls. I kept the baby doll, but I never played with her. Playing with her would make me remember how my father had spent all his paycheck on toys because he was too sick to know better. At the same time I could never part with this doll—never give her away. She is still in the cedar chest I inherited from my mother looking as beautiful as the day my father bought her as a present for me. Once in a while I take her out and look at her. It was the last time my father had any money of his own to buy me a present. After this second time he went to the hospital the doctors advised him not to go back to pharmacy again, and that was the only kind of work he knew.

In the days that followed, the songs we sang at the piano were mostly Christmas carols. It was hard to sing joyful Christmas carols, such as "God Rest You Merry Gentlemen," after seeing my father leave in such a worked up state and knowing he was still at Receiving Hospital. Even though I prayed that he would be able to come home, I knew in my heart that we were going to have another Christmas without my father. In one carol we sang, "O Little Town of Bethlehem," the words and the music seemed to match my melancholy feeling.

> O little town of Bethlehem, how still we see thee lie.
> Above thy deep and dreamless sleep, the silent stars go by.
> Yet in thy dark streets shineth the everlasting light.
> The hopes and fears of all the years are met in thee tonight.

I could picture the dark streets—and the words, "hopes and fears of all the years," spoke to me. I was learning about hopes and fears—hopes that my father would come home and stay well, and fears that he would not. And the "everlasting light"—was that the same as the "kindly light" my father liked to sing about? Somehow there was hope here to counter my sadness, without denying the sorrow. "O Little Town of Bethlehem" became my favorite Christmas carol from then on.

My expectation that my father would not be home for Christmas was borne out. Instead he was again transferred to Ypsilanti State Hospital for a second lengthy stay. My mother explained to Danny and me that our prayers are not always answered in the way we hope, but that God is still watching over us. I believed her and this made it much easier to accept what was happening, that God was with us. I also felt certain God was with my father too whether he believed in him or not. God wouldn't let anything bad happen to him.

After six months my mother received another letter from Ypsilanti State Hospital telling her my father was again able to come home. This time he would come home to an entirely different neighborhood. I had finished first grade at the Doty School in June and my mother decided it was time to move from our basement apartment. She had discovered a good residential area of Detroit called the Northwest Section and rented the ground floor of a two-family house on a street named Ilene. The house had a nicer living room and a real dining room, a kitchen you could have breakfast in, and two nice-sized bedrooms. Danny and I were getting too old to share a bedroom, my mother thought, so she gave me the bedroom and a studio couch in the dining room became Danny's bed. From this time on Danny slept in the dining room of the several similar flats we rented. I never once heard him complain. Even as a teenager he just had a little cedar chest on the table under a mirror in the dining room where he kept his wallet and all his valuables, the same table and mirror my father had bought from the woman who needed money. Every morning the bedding was put away, so it never looked like anyone's bedroom. Looking back I think he was such a remarkably sweet kid to accept this lack of privacy without a word of protest.

My mother told me that the buyer for her department at Hudson's, Miss Hughes, who had taken a special interest in my mother, chided her for paying so much rent in this nicer area, given her salary. Normally my mother would not contradict Miss Hughes, but this time she told her, "It makes sense to pay a little more rent in a better area because then you have good schools, and the neighborhood is safer for Sarah and Danny while I'm at work." I could see that my mother was a wise person. Now Danny and I had a backyard with grass and trees. We could go outside by ourselves here and play with other kids. It was a longer bus ride to downtown for my mother but it was clearly a better place for children. As we prepared for my father's second home-coming, my mother said she hoped he would like our new house. In the past she had asked my father about everything, such as what medicines to give us when we were sick; but now she had to decide many things on her own. I felt confident that she would be able to manage whatever came up.

I could hardly wait to see my father. Maybe by now the doctors would have done a better job and he would be completely better. I wanted him to be the way he used to be when he came home for lunch and brought people from work home with him. I still liked to think about those times when my father went to work in his white pharmacy coat, and we had a car with a rumble seat and went on picnics. By now we had sold our car to save money and, with his illness, my father was not supposed to drive, in any case. We no longer had a telephone either because it was considered an unnecessary expense.

On a Sunday Uncle Charlie drove my mother to Ypsilanti State Hospital for the second time to bring my father home. Aunt Lottie, Uncle

Charlie's new wife from Germany, stayed with Danny and me. My mother left dinner all ready for Aunt Lottie to heat up at the right time. This time when the door opened and my father came in Uncle Charlie carried his suitcase. The first thing I noticed was that he looked thinner than ever. I looked at his eyes. They still did not shine the way they once had. That had been too much to expect, I decided. My father hugged Danny and me, but when he said "Hello" to Aunt Lottie his eyes looked down at the floor. He must be embarrassed, I figured, to have her know he'd come from a mental hospital. I watched him carefully but I couldn't tell if he liked our new house or not. He didn't look around to see the different rooms or the backyard. He just sat in the living room with Uncle Charlie, so I climbed up and sat next to him on the couch.

My mother put on an apron and began to help Aunt Lottie with the dinner. Soon we were all seated at the table in what was now a real dining room, set up like our usual Sunday dinner with a white linen tablecloth and our good dishes. Danny said our usual blessing, "Come Lord Jesus, be our guest, and let these gifts to us be blest," and we all said, "Amen."

People were passing a platter with baked chicken, a bowl of mashed potatoes, and a dish of green beans. There was the usual fruit and Jello salad and a green salad that were always part of Sunday dinners. But once the food was passed there was silence. We began eating, and no one said a word. I couldn't remember a dinner this quiet. When I couldn't stand it any longer I said,,"The chicken's very good, Mama."

"Not as good as your father makes," my mother said, and smiled at my father. They had begun cooking together after my father's first hospitalization. There was more silence. No one wanted to say, "How was it in the hospital?" and yet I imagine that is what everyone was thinking—it was what I was thinking.

Uncle Charlie was very brave, I thought, when finally he asked, "How often did you see a doctor in that hospital, Dan?"

My father smiled a funny little smile. "Not often, Charlie. Every doctor has about two hundred patients. They do the best they can."

My mother got up to get dessert—apple pie with ice cream. Except to say her pie was delicious, everyone was quiet again. This was so different from the lively times my parents used to have with company—when everyone talked about President Roosevelt or the movies they had seen that week.

Aunt Lottie helped my mother with the dishes. In the living room Uncle Charlie tried turning on the radio, saying, "Maybe we'll get some news." But my father didn't seem to be paying attention to the news, so he turned it off. My father got up, went to his suitcase that was still sitting inside the door, and took out two little packages neatly wrapped in white tissue paper. He gave one to Danny and one to me. Sitting on the floor in front of my father we opened them expectantly and found each package contained a pair of beautiful wooden bookends with a metal plate on the bottom, the wood carved and varnished to a high gloss. Danny's bookends were in the shape of an owl with finely carved ridges indicating the owl's feathers and his two big eyes. Mine were much simpler, a smooth surface of gleaming wood with a little groove that made a border around the edge.

"I made them in the craft shop at the hospital," my father said.

"Thank you, Daddy. I like the owls. Oooooooh" Danny waved one of his bookends in a flying motion and hooted like an owl.

"I like mine too, Daddy. They feel so smooth," I said rubbing my hand over the silk-like varnish. To be honest, I liked Danny's owls a little better than my plainer bookends, but I liked mine too. "Danny and I have a lot of books," I told him, and got up and gave him a kiss.

As soon as the dishes were done, Aunt Lottie and Uncle Charlie left. My father looked tired. My mother must have noticed that too because she said,

"Maybe you'd like to go in and take a rest, Dan."

"I would," he said. They both went to their bedroom. Danny went outside to play with his friends and I found Goll Goll, the large baby doll that had remained my favorite doll from before I was two. I rocked her in my mother's rocking chair that was now in my bedroom. I told her how bad I felt that my father was so quiet and tired. I couldn't imagine him ever laughing and playing with us again. I talked to Goll Goll a long time before I made my decision. This felt like such an important decision I thought I should tell my parents about it right away. I tiptoed into their bedroom in case they were asleep, but they were still awake talking. Holding onto the dark metal foot board I pulled myself up onto their bed and wiggled into a space between their feet on top of the covers. Then I told them, "When I grow up I'm going to have babies, but no daddy."

They looked at each other and smiled an amused smile.

five

"In the Gloaming"

YPSILANTI STATE HOSPITAL, A few miles south of Ypsilanti, Michigan, opened in 1931 with six mental patients. Within a year it housed 900, and at its peak in the 1950s over 4000. My father was first admitted here in 1935. Albert Kahn, who designed the famous Angel Hall and Hill Auditorium at the nearby University of Michigan, designed the red brick buildings that made up the complex. Each one had tall white pillars at the entrance. Although surrounded by generous areas of lawn, all kinds of shrubs, and oak and maple trees, the buildings still looked institutional. They were only three stories high but endless in length—like shipping containers. Plans for this large mental hospital were made just before the unexpected Great Depression. In 1932 Dr. O. R. Yoder, the long-time director, had only 80 cents a day to spend on each of the 900 patients. My father would be hospitalized here thirteen times.

In time Danny and I were able to go with my mother on her trips to see my father at this hospital. We were not allowed inside, so we had to be old enough to be left alone on the grounds—beginning at about ages five and seven. My mother left us sitting on one of the many green benches placed on the grass near the cement walkways, but as soon as she left we ran and stood beneath the window where we thought our father would soon call down to us. Despite the well-kept grounds, I only needed to see one of the forlorn-looking patients who wandered by on a pass to know that this was not a happy place. I looked in the windows and I couldn't see any lamps shining inside, no sign of a cozy atmosphere within. With the windows covered as they were by heavy screens, I saw only darkness.

When my mother reached the visiting room where she visited with my father, she opened the window and he would call down to us. The window always seemed to be high up on the third floor and the screen looked very thick. We couldn't see my father's face, but we recognized his voice as he called, "Sarah, Danny, up here, it's Daddy," his face pushed up against the screen. We called back up to him, "Hi, Daddy," "Come home soon, Daddy," and, "We miss you, Daddy." We couldn't carry on a conversation with him as much as we tried. One time I told him, "I got all my spelling words right on the test this week, Daddy," but I didn't think he heard me, or if he did I couldn't understand his answer. "Watch this, Daddy," Danny said, and turned a somersault on the grass. Again, we couldn't hear his response. After a few unsuccessful attempts like this we gave up and took to playing tag or just running around on the grass. Still, we never refused a chance to go on the long bus ride so we could see him, even at this unsatisfying distance.

When my father was nearly well enough to come home, he was able to get a pass to come outside and have a picnic with us. On this particular day Danny and I waited and finally he came out of his building walking with my mother and wearing a white short-sleeved shirt and striped seersucker pants. As he got closer I thought he looked very well-dressed compared to other patients I saw on the grounds, except that his black shoes weren't shined as well as he shined them at home. After many hugs and kisses, we each took one of his hands and walked to find a green bench for our picnic. There were no picnic tables. We tried to sit one on each side of him as close as we could get, but then there wasn't room for my mother, so Danny and I sat on the grass in front of him. My father was very quiet during this lunch. Once in a while he smiled at us, but he hardly talked at all. He acted like an uncomfortable guest.

A bedraggled man dressed in brown tattered clothes with a red bandana tied over his long hair walked up behind my father and asked, "Could you spare a cigarette, sir?" My father reached in his shirt pocket for his pack of Camels and gave the man two or three. "Thank you, sir." The man smiled as he sauntered away. I thought my father looked embarrassed at our seeing him as one of these pitiful-looking people. He needn't have felt embarrassed though because I never associated him with the people I saw on the grounds. Many of these patients, I've since learned, remained at this hospital for years, abandoned by their families. My mother was right when she told Aunt Sadie, explaining why she couldn't go back to Canada and let her sisters help her raise us, "I have to keep a home for

Dan to come home to." Otherwise he might have been one of those who remained there for years and years.

My mother took out the tuna fish sandwiches and the hot tea and china cups and some cookies from the little picnic basket she'd brought. She used the lid of the basket on the space on the seat between them for a table. The lunch was exactly like the picnic lunches we used to have in the parks around Detroit, only then my father would have played ball with us, or thought up some great game for us to play. Now he just sat quietly, and wasn't even that interested in his tuna fish sandwich. Danny and I finished our sandwiches and drank our tea. We ran to a nearby knoll where we ate cookies and then played tag while our parents talked.

All too soon it was time to leave on the bus that pulled up in front of my father's building. I looked at this building and thought, "If I were inside there and couldn't leave, I would feel that I was in a prison." I hated to say goodbye and leave him in this dreary place. He hugged my mother.

"Thanks for coming, Mae," he said.

"As soon as the doctors say you can come home, I'll be here," she said quietly and smiled her most encouraging smile at him. He kissed my mother and kissed Danny and the two of them boarded the bus. Then, as he often did at home, my father stooped down on one knee to give me a hug. "Don't worry, Sarah," he said. "I'll be home before long," and he kissed my cheek. His face felt as smooth as it always had. I didn't want him to see my tears, so I hugged him quickly one more time and got on the bus. I slid into a window seat behind my mother and Danny where I could wave to him again as the bus was pulling out. He waved back, and then turned toward the door of his building. With his pass he could have stayed out longer, but he went inside.

I moved to the empty seat across the aisle from Danny and my mother so I could talk to them. My mother handed me some paper on a clipboard and a package of crayons she'd brought along and I started drawing a picture for my father, a picture of my new Edgar Guest School that he hadn't seen yet.

"Don't you think Daddy looked good?" she asked.

"I thought he looked good," Danny said without looking up. His voice sounded as if he was just agreeing with my mother. He was drawing too.

"I thought he looked good, but he's very quiet," I said. "Do you think he'll ever want to go on picnics and invite friends over the way he did before?" My mother leaned over and put her hand on my arm.

"I don't know if he'll ever be exactly the way he was before, Sarah. But as long as he's well enough to be out of a hospital and home with us— I'll settle for that." She looked at me with those royal blue eyes, a serious look, and I couldn't help but agree with her.

"I'll settle for that too," I told her and went back to my drawing, but I wasn't sure I meant what I had said. This wasn't my father as I used to know him and I wanted that father back. And yet it was true that I'd rather have him at home than at Ypsilanti State Hospital. Not long after this visit to the hospital, my father was home again.

During these years, our school-age years and beyond, it felt as if my mother and Danny and I had made an unspoken pact in which we agreed to do whatever it took to keep my father well. Whether we were right or not, we believed that if we kept everything at home as calm and peaceful as possible, my father would be less likely to become excited and eventually manic. There probably was *some* truth to this. When we noticed that on a vacation to Canada my father became a little agitated, we no longer went on vacations. If we had company it would just be one person, usually our friend Mony, the one who had sent us five dollars a month anonymously when my father first became ill.

Often I found the calm we tried to maintain excruciatingly dull. I felt bored, restless, in need of more activity. The drone of the Tiger baseball game my father listened to on the radio on Sunday afternoons was the worst. I can still hear the announcer's voice slowly calling, "Ball three. Three and two." I didn't understand the game, never having been to one, and couldn't see why every word that announcer said seemed of such importance to my father. I could never pull him away from a baseball game to go on a walk. Baseball and the newspapers, or news on the radio, were the only things that interested him now—aside from our dinners, which he prepared with great care.

At times, however, my father surprised me. I was home from school one day, almost recovered from the measles, when I took him a recipe I'd found in a magazine and asked him, "Would you make cream puffs with me, Daddy?" I wanted to see how the hole formed in the middle of the cream puff. I was ten.

He studied the recipe. "We can make cream puffs, honey," he said. In the kitchen he began assembling all the ingredients listed in the recipe and placing them on the counter. "Did I ever tell you that I cook the same way I used to fill prescriptions?"

"What do you mean?" I was putting on one of my mother's aprons.

"I take out all the ingredients, and then put each one back as soon as I've used it. That way you will never use the same one twice by mistake."

"No wonder the kitchen looks so neat when you're cooking," I said. I stirred the hot liquid once it had boiled while he added the flour mixture quickly as the recipe said to do. When the flour was absorbed my father broke three eggs into the mixture while I continued to stir rapidly. Soon it seemed just the right consistency and he scooped round lumps of batter onto a greased cookie sheet. "Let me do some," I said after I watched him do a few. We had a dozen in all and put them in the pre-heated oven. By now the light in our sunny kitchen was hurting my eyes after spending days in a darkened room with the measles. I had to face away from the windows.

While the puffs were rising in the oven we made the creamy custard filling. The timer went off and my father took the puffs out of the oven. They looked just like the picture in my recipe, perfectly round and a light golden brown.

"We'll have to wait until the puffs cool down a bit," he said. "And we'll need to find something to inject the custard into the puffs." We rummaged through all the drawers and came up with a cake decorating utensil I didn't know we owned. I had a hard time waiting then for the custard to cool, but finally he said it was cool enough. We took turns injecting the puffs with the custard.

"This cake decorator works perfectly," I said as I pushed the plunger and watched the thick yellow custard flow neatly into the puff.

"Shall we sprinkle them with a little confectioner's sugar?" he asked.

"Oh, yes! Then they'll look like they're just out of a bakery." My father made coffee for himself. I made some weak tea for me and we sat down at the kitchen table to try one.

"They're delicious. Did you ever make cream puffs before?" I asked.

"No," he said. This is the first time."

Despite working full-time, my mother made every effort to compensate for the lack of excitement my father required. She wanted so much to create a normal life for Danny and me, and tried to make sure we had what other kids had. Every birthday was celebrated with a special dinner, a cake, and presents. No matter what else was happening, a Sunday dinner followed church on Sunday and now we could invite a friend. There were new clothes at Easter, and except for that first Christmas, a well-decorated tree at Christmas with presents. It fell to Danny and me to buy the tree. Each year we trudged from tree lot to tree lot in the snow in search of the perfect tree.

When the Ringling Brothers-Barnum and Bailey Circus came to Detroit each year, my mother took us. Truthfully I never enjoyed the circus very much. People looked as though they were having a good time, but to me it looked like fake joy—the clowns especially; and the trapeze acts, some without a net, I found downright frightening. I didn't like Clyde Beatty, the man who went into the lions' den with a whip and a chair and ordered the lions around. I thought he was cruel to the lions, and was afraid that one of them would attack him. I didn't want that to happen even though I didn't like him. It could be that I sensed the same underlying sadness in the circus that I knew permeated our family—not all the time, but at times when we worried about my father. Clowns and circuses, I've since learned, are thought to cloak a hidden melancholy. I just know that I always walked into that dark circus tent with a feeling of reluctance, and yet said nothing because I didn't want to spoil my mother's treat.

I did enjoy the trips the three of us took in the summer on the Bob-lo boat, a large boat with music and dancing that made several daily trips to Bob-lo Island in the middle of the Detroit River. Even when my father was home, he preferred not to come. We were too young to dance, but we liked watching other people dance. During the trip Danny and I explored the several decks, and the bow and the stern of the vessel. Bob-lo Island had an amusement park, and though I've never liked amusement parks any more than I liked circuses, this one was especially clean and had a few rides that didn't throw me around too much. There were areas on Bob-lo Island with flower beds and large shade trees with picnic tables under them where we ate the ample lunch my mother packed. She encouraged each of us to bring a friend on this trip, but until seventh grade when I had a best friend, I often didn't have a friend I knew well enough to invite, nor did Danny. This was because we moved so frequently.

I went to five different grade schools in eight years. Although I knew my father as this gentle man who would bake cream puffs with me and who never hurt anyone, once the neighbors heard the police sirens that often accompanied my father's hospitalizations, they were afraid of living near a mentally ill person. I could see why they might be frightened if they heard one of his angry tirades that sometimes spilled over into the street outside our house. One time when Aunt Daisy visited I saw my father usher her out to her car, shouting at her. As he opened the car door he broke the steel handle on her dark blue Buick right off. Manic people are incredibly strong. Two women out in their yard appeared petrified. I saw them talking to each other. The neighbors would talk to our landlord and when our lease came due my mother would be handed a notice to move.

My mother always found another place in the Northwest Section, but every time we had to change schools. Each new two-family house was exactly like the one before: a living room, dining room, bathroom, two bedrooms, and a kitchen at the back of the house. It could be upstairs or downstairs. With the help of tall, slender Uncle Charlie to drive her, my mother would have all the dishes in the cupboards, our clothes in the closets, and the rugs down before moving day, so all the movers had to do was put the furniture in place. By nightfall there was nothing left in boxes and the house looked as though we'd always lived there. Our mother was extremely well organized. The hard part was leaving our friends, and the prospect of starting over to make new ones. In each new school I felt like an outsider for a long time.

After a while I developed a desperate desire to be included in the in-group of my class. At the beginning of fifth grade I switched schools again. The first few days of the new term I made friends with Doris Jean Finley, another newcomer. Doris Jean lived halfway along the mile-long route I walked to school, and by now Danny walked with other boys, so she and I began walking home together. Mrs. Finley usually invited me in to play for a while. The family had moved to Detroit from somewhere in the south and with her thick southern accent and hair still in pigtails, Doris Jean seemed younger than the rest of us. She had something called childhood diabetes and had to take medicine in school. Kids teased her about all these things that made her stand out. I liked Doris Jean a lot, but I was keenly aware that as her friend, I too would be rejected by most of the other kids.

On the way home from school one day, six or seven girls from our class came up behind us and started calling Doris Jean names and imitating her southern accent with taunts like, "How y'all doin?" They even began to hit her teasingly with small branches they found lying on the ground. The last block before we reached Doris Jean's corner house, I found myself joining them in mocking her and even picked up a little branch myself. Doris Jean's mother was in the backyard and saw all too clearly that I was one of her daughter's tormentors. Filled with shame, I put my head down and didn't look up until I reached my house.

All that evening the memory of how I had betrayed my friend plagued me. The next day in school I couldn't summon the courage to speak to Doris Jean, let alone tell her how sorry I felt. On the way home that day I considered going a different way, but instead walked my usual route past her house alone. To my amazement Mrs. Finley stood at the fence smiling and calling to me, "Sarah, please come in." As I pushed open the gate to their yard I made some limp reference to the previous day in an attempt at an apology, but before I could get the words out Mrs. Finley brushed them aside with, "Oh these things happen. I know you and Doris Jean are still good friends." Doris Jean was smiling. She too had forgiven my dreadful moment of disloyalty. I saw lemonade and home-made oatmeal cookies on the picnic table. "Wouldn't you girls like to go under the sprinkler when you finish your snack?" Mrs. Finley asked with her soft southern voice. In late September Detroit was still stifling hot. Doris Jean went and got one of her bathing suits for me and one for herself and in a few minutes the two of us were running squealing through the cold spray of the rotating sprinkler, laughing as if nothing at all had happened. When I think of this incident, though, I'm struck by the power of this wish to belong that could push me to go so against all my usual concerns about right and wrong. Like Peter denying Jesus, everything I'd ever learned in my much-loved sermons at church went out the window in the face of this need to be included, at least for that moment. No matter how skilled my mother became at moving, she couldn't shield us from the pain of leaving our friends and feeling like outsiders in a new school. But the forgiveness Doris Jean and her mother extended to me taught me something about grace and forgiveness I never forgot.

During these school-age years, any time my father was in the hospital my mother always left two nickels for Danny and me on the lace table cloth in the dining room so we could buy a treat at the local candy store after school. Unless I went to a friend's house, like Doris Jean's, I went straight home, picked up my nickel and my roller skates and skated to the local candy store, a mom and pop store that welcomed kids. I almost always chose chocolate covered ice cream on a stick. Skating back, eating ice cream, I tried to decide what I would do for the rest of the afternoon. The choices were to play Red Rover and Freeze Tag outside with other kids, or go in and listen to the fifteen minute serials I followed on the radio: Jack Armstrong, Captain Midnight, and Superman. In third grade Aunt Daisy had given me a child's size violin she had bought for her son John, now grown, and Detroit schools gave free music lessons, so I usually spent some time practicing the violin. Occasionally I peeled the potatoes and set the table for supper to surprise my mother, but not often.

Many days when my father was in the hospital, I sat for an hour or more at the upright piano where I'd sung hymns and songs with my mother as a little girl, and sang songs—mostly melancholy, mournful songs if I could find them. On this particular day with my father away and Danny out playing Red Rover with his friends, the house was wonderfully quiet. The afternoon sun filled our flat with a fading light. I loved this time of day, and felt drawn almost as by a beckoning force to the piano. Since I had learned to read music in my violin classes, I was able to pick out melodies on the piano. I opened the large green songbook my mother had recently bought, *Robbins Mammoth Collection of World Famous Songs.* The price listed on the cover was, "One Dollar." Starting at the beginning I began flipping through the pages, stopping at a song I wanted to sing. It seemed that all the songs that caught my attention were about loss, brokenhearted songs.

I stopped first at the song, "I'll Take You Home Again, Kathleen," and sang all three verses. I loved the part, "The roses all have left your cheeks. I've watched them fade away and die. Your voice is sad when-e'er you speak. And tears bedim your loving eyes." I pictured a beautiful young wife longing for her home in Ireland. I figured it must be Ireland and Ireland was very far away. Then I sang, "When You and I Were Young, Maggie." I loved the line, "They say we are aged and gray, Maggie, as spray by the white breakers flung, but to me you're as fair as you were, Maggie, when you and I were young." Even though things changed, his love for Maggie remained the same. I liked that. Then I came to, "The Band Played On." I read the words, "Casey would waltz with a strawberry blonde, and the band played on." I knew this song, but it didn't appeal to me. So I turned the page and began to sing, "Gone are the days when my heart was young and gay. Gone are my friends from the cotton fields away." I could picture old black Joe. I could picture Casey too, but I preferred old black Joe. I was enjoying this so much and hoped that Danny wouldn't come in just yet and disturb my singing.

Next I came to the song I loved better than any song in the book, "In the Gloaming." I played and sang it a couple of times, both verses:

> In the gloaming, oh, my darling, when the lights are soft and low,
> And the quiet shadows falling softly come and softly go,
> When the winds are sobbing faintly, with a gentle unknown woe,
> Will you think of me and love me, as you did once long ago.

I could hear those winds sobbing faintly, and loved the mournful tone in the second stanza, "For my heart was filled with longing. What had been could never be. It was best to leave you thus, dear, best for you and best for me." I knew my love for this song had to do with my father being away in Ypsilanti State Hospital, or even more with the way he had changed, and that he never came back as the father he had been before. As to the other melancholy songs, I wasn't sure of the connection to them. I just knew I loved them. I played several more, "The Lost Chord," "None but the Lonely Heart." These last two were not songs I had sung with my mother. I discovered them on my own. "The Lost Chord" speaks of someone seated at an organ— searching for a chord he'd once played that was so wonderful, but which he could never find again—a little similar to what I was doing at the piano—searching for something I had lost. And "None but the Lonely Heart" is Goethe's poem set to music by Tchaikovsky. The words, "None but the lonely heart can know my sadness, alone and parted far from joy and gladness," I found very beautiful. I sang one more song, "Silver Threads among the Gold," and then I'd had enough. I got up from the piano. My mother would be home soon. Singing these sad songs lifted my spirits.

My mother, too, had ways of lifting her spirits. Someone sent her a little booklet called *Daily Word* that came in the mail every month. It had a reading for each day that began with a quotation, such as this one for July 7, 1936, "The presence of God within me assures me of abiding peace." Then there was an explanation of the quotation, and after that a verse from the Bible. I knew my mother read *Daily Word* every morning, usually on the bus on her way to work. Many days, though, if we had time, she would read the page for that day to us—just standing beside the dining room table before the three of us left the house for school and work. We didn't always understand all of it, but the words were encouraging with thoughts such as, "God is in every person you meet," or "God's peace will be with you throughout this day." I would have preferred that my mother read a chapter from the Bible the way she said they did in her family when she was growing up. I liked the stories she used to read us from *Hurlbut's Story of the Bible.* But there was not enough time for that in our hurried departures in the morning. There wasn't always time even for *Daily Word,* but when there was I was glad to listen.

I remember one morning before we left for school my mother said, "Let me read to you from Daily Word this morning. We have time." She read the passage. The day's message reminded us that God is always with us. "That means God is with Daddy in the hospital too," she told us. I could tell *Daily Word* meant a lot to my mother because after she read the message for the day she seemed cheerful and full of energy as she put on her hat and gathered up her things, her purse and gloves. She closed the door behind us and we headed down the street, Danny and I to school, and she to work. I felt cheerful too.

six

"A Mighty Fortress Is Our God"

THE SUMMER BEFORE I began sixth grade we were forced to move again but there was no Presbyterian Church in our new neighborhood. Danny and I scouted the area and saw that there was a Lutheran church a few blocks away. We told my mother that we thought we should go there; she agreed to try it. Pastor Wacker, the senior minister, welcomed us warmly the first morning we showed up for the service. The sanctuary had a particularly warm glow formed by soft lighting on the brown wooden pews and the large ivory candles that were lit on the altar. It was not Gothic and awe-inspiring the way Westminster Presbyterian Church had been, but enveloping and comforting. I felt at home immediately.

Covenant Lutheran Church differed in other ways from the Presbyterian Churches I'd known. As a Missouri Synod Church, it was highly traditional and conservative. We could square dance in the basement of the Presbyterian Church, for example, but never in this church. Lutheran churches are liturgical, which means the Eucharist, what Presbyterians call Communion, is celebrated every Sunday, and a set liturgy is sung by the congregation with words such as:

> O Christ, Thou Lamb of God, who takest away the sins of the world,
> Have mercy upon us. (Repeated three times, and the third time
> ending with, "Grant us Thy peace.")

The pastor reads or sings passages from the New Testament and the Prayer Book that tell how Jesus instituted this sacrament with his disciples at their last supper the night before his death. Real wine is used instead of grape juice, and the congregation goes by rows up to the altar and kneels to receive first the bread, in the form of a thin wafer, and then the wine served from a silver chalice. It's a lengthy process toward the end of the Sunday morning service. But happily celebrating the Eucharist did not cause Pastor Wacker to shorten his sermon to a homily. His sermons were full bodied and meant to be taken seriously.

I had always paid attention to sermons. Just as I had at Westminster Presbyterian Church when I was five or six, now I loved to listen to the minister talk about God and about how he wants us to live our lives. My mother never spoke much about her faith. I think I looked to the sermons to spell out what I saw my mother lived by, but that she couldn't explain to me. The faith she had grown up with was so natural to her she didn't have to put it into words. I wanted what she had.

Still, I wasn't particularly pious. Many times when I sat in the choir loft at Covenant Lutheran Church one of the youth choir members would say something funny and I could not suppress the giggles that bubbled up in me the whole rest of the service. This was particularly true if my witty new best friend Pat, who had long brown hair and freckles and lived down the street from me, had made the remark. Our always warm and encouraging youth choir director, Mrs. Septke, had to have seen our snickering, but never once chastised us.

I had sung Martin Luther's stirring hymn, "A Might Fortress is our God," before coming to Covenant Church, but here we sang it often and lustily. I loved the strength of the words:

> A mighty Fortress is our God, a Bulwark never failing.
> Our Helper He amid the flood of mortal ills prevailing:
> For still our ancient Foe doeth seek to work us woe;
> His craft and power are great, And, armed with cruel hate,
> On earth is not His equal.

This hymn, written in 1529, speaks unashamedly of the Devil as a powerful force for evil, something I'd not come across in the liberal Presbyterian churches I'd attended until then. In fact the Presbyterian hymnal has two versions of Luther's hymn, the original and a sanitized version with no reference at all to devils. In the third verse Luther puts it even more graphically,

> Although this world with devils filled should threaten to undo us;
> We will not fear for God has willed His truth to triumph through us.

I didn't find these words disturbing—perhaps because everyone else was singing them too and did not find them frightening. Besides, the hymn made it clear that God would triumph over all devils. These words did make me think, however, of Aunt Daisy's séances and my theory that the séances had contributed to my father's illness. Were the spirits floating around Aunt Daisy's house evil spirits, devils even, I wondered—or some of them at least?

By now I had even more evidence for my theory about the séances. In his repeated periods of mania, my father several times thought he was another spirit. One time he thought he was Sitting Bull, whose spirit he claimed to have met at one of Aunt Daisy's séances. Someone had given my father a long ornate pipe with a beautiful lacquered orange bowl at the end which, as Sitting Bull, he tried to smoke as a peace pipe. Another time he thought he was Jesus Christ. I don't remember what my father did as Jesus Christ, but the most frightening time of all I do remember. My father went striding up and down our living room shouting menacingly, "I *am* the Devil." The fierce look that shone from his eyes was altogether someone else—and I thought at the time it *could* be the Devil, or a devil. I was perhaps seven or eight. When my father was this out of his mind he would be taken to the hospital fairly quickly, so my memories of these times are like little snippets and not whole scenes.

At Covenant Lutheran Church these dark powers were labeled as evil and as something to be avoided. In Aunt Daisy's séance, the one I went to when I was five, I couldn't be sure what kind of spirits she was calling upon when the table rose and fell tapping out answers to the questions the people gathered around her card table asked about their dead relatives. I only knew I felt very uncomfortable about those spirits, and so I had slowly removed my hands from under the hands of the people sitting next to me and snuck out of the darkened room. Singing Martin Luther's hymn now I felt confident that whatever evil spirits there were, Christ "will win the battle," as the second verse of the hymn proclaims quite clearly.

That there was a battle going on in our life that required a Mighty Fortress I had no doubt. The battle was to keep my father well and out of a hospital for as long as possible, with God's help. God would provide all the protection we needed. After all, He was the Mighty Fortress, a bulwark never failing.

September came and with it my first day at the Noble School. Mrs. White, my sixth grade teacher, stood at the front of the class. I was happy to see that she was young, but not too young. She looked confident and experienced—and she was elegantly dressed in a white blouse with long flowing sleeves, a slim black skirt and black patent heels—her dark hair cut in a long page boy. I liked her instantly. She wrote a long list of school supplies on the blackboard which I copied neatly on the paper she had given us. At the end of the day she reviewed long-division and gave us five problems for homework. I'd never had homework until now, so I was excited at the prospect, which felt very grown-up. I determined I would get all of the problems right.

At home I raced up the steps to the second floor and opened the door to our flat. Our door was never locked in the daytime even when my father was in the hospital. But now my father had been home several months.

"Daddy, I'm home," I called out. Then in the dining room I stopped short—and drew in by breath. On the dining room table were two blueberry pies and a peach pie my father must have baked that day. Was it starting again—so soon? I could hear a lot of commotion in the kitchen which meant he was busy making something else.

"What are you baking?" I asked, trying to sound nonchalant.

"A chocolate cake, honey. Did you see the pies?" He was stirring a thick brown batter in an ivory mixing bowl.

"They're beautiful, Daddy." His eyes had that watery glassy look they always had when he was becoming agitated, and his face was flushed, but maybe it was just from the heat in the kitchen. I hoped it was the heat.

"Next I'm going to bake an angel food cake—your favorite."

"You don't need to make it today, Daddy. It will take us a while to eat the chocolate cake and the three pies." His long white apron was splattered with flour and a few drops of chocolate batter. Mixing bowls and baking pans covered the kitchen counters. Normally the kitchen was the picture of neatness when he cooked our dinner. I knew he would make the angel food cake no matter what I said. There was an engine running inside him and he couldn't shut it off.

"I have homework now, Daddy. I want to get it done before supper." I went to my room. A sick feeling in the pit of my stomach was slowly getting worse. The familiar mix of fear, anger, and sorrow for my father were all tangled up together. The long-division problems that had seemed so easy a short time ago in school seemed impossibly difficult now, but I kept working on them.

About 6:30 I heard my mother's footsteps on the stairs and went out to the dining room. I wanted to be there when she saw the three pies, and now two cakes. We looked at each other, our eyes telegraphing the silent message: Daddy's becoming much too excited again and there's not much we can do about it.

My mother went to the kitchen and gave my father a hug the same as she always did when she came home. He was getting supper now and stopped just long enough to give her a quick kiss.

"The pies and cakes look lovely, Dan," was all she said, and went to change her clothes. Danny came in from playing with his friends. He knew right away what was happening, but he didn't say anything. Danny rarely talked about our father's illness the way my mother and I did. His face just lost color—as if he felt too devastated to put into words what he was thinking.

I followed my mother into the bedroom and whispered, "I'm so sorry." She had taken off her work dress and was putting on a cotton house dress. When she finished she sat on the edge of the bed and motioned for me to sit next to her.

"I know, Sarah. It's very discouraging. But we'll get through this. We always have. Just say your prayers that we'll know what to do for Daddy. She gave me a warm hug and then we both went to the kitchen to help my father get dinner.

At supper my father did all the talking, telling us stories we'd heard dozens of times before.

"You see my mother had eight boys, and there were five us in a row— Albert, Charles, Harold, Arthur and myself—so she had to teach some of us to cook. It's a good thing. That's how I worked my way through the School of Pharmacy at the University of Buffalo. I made candy in the window of a drug store, all kinds of candy."

My mother gently reminded him that his dinner was getting cold, but he continued on in a loud voice.

"Those were the days! The professor of pharmacy used to embarrass me every week. 'Here's Slagle with another 100,' he'd say. 'What's the matter with the rest of you?'" The only time my father ever bragged about how well he did in college was when he was becoming high. Danny looked down at his plate. He picked at his food, eating hardly any of it.

My mother had said she would take us to buy our school supplies after supper, but none of us wanted to leave my father when he was this excited. Out of earshot of my father I asked her if she still thought we should go for school supplies. She hesitated—then she said, "All the other kids will have theirs. Let's go quickly." Telling my father where we were going, the three of us walked up to Cunningham's Drug Store on Grand River Avenue. Cunningham's, part of a large chain, was a beautiful corner store that carried a huge selection of school supplies this time of year: rows of colorful notebooks of all sizes, different kinds of pen holders, pen points, even green ink, pencils, erasers, and pencil sharpeners. I usually picked out a couple of things that weren't on the list, and had planned to find a little notebook for my homework assignments, but this time we quickly picked up the essentials and left. Hurrying along the two residential blocks from Grand River, our only conversation amid long silences was to wonder what we would find my father doing when we got home.

For three days my father baked furiously. He made three or four kinds of cookies, a pineapple upside-down-cake—anything in the cookbook that caught his eye. He made the candy he always made at Christmas—maple, chocolate and vanilla fondant patties about the size of a silver dollar with a perfect half-walnut pressed into each. The results were beautiful. He even made some dipped chocolates, the kind he made in the window of the drug store as a student. He still had the little notebook full of recipes he had written out on that job. Some of these goodies he gave to Miss Petty, a very thin woman who lived downstairs from us, and who welcomed the rich desserts. Since we'd just moved to this house, Miss Petty had never seen my father in his manic state. She probably thought he was just an out-going man who never stopped talking.

My mother had to use all her will power to go to work and leave my father during the next few days. She had the highest sales record in her department year after year, so I don't think she would have been fired if she had stayed home a day or two, but she would never risk it. In school my mind wandered constantly to what might be going on at home. In the morning I dressed quickly, not caring what I wore, so I'd be sure to be ready to leave when my mother left for work. Danny did this too. It was the only time the three of us could talk without my father thinking we were plotting against him. When we were far down the block, Danny said, "Daddy's going to have to go to the hospital again, isn't he?"

"We'll have to wait and see," was all Mother could say. "We'll pray that he'll calm down." In the past this had only happened once. That was the time on vacation when he started talking way too much, but we came home early and he was all right. But he had never calmed down once he reached the point that he was at now.

"This keeps happening over and over and over," I stomped my foot with each "over." I felt angry, and totally frustrated that this was happening so soon.

"I know. It's very hard. But Daddy doesn't do this on purpose, remember. It's not as if he were a drinker or a gambler." We didn't know back then that these were illnesses too.

"I know," I said. And I did know. I believed that he couldn't help it, and still a part of me thought he should be able to control himself and calm down. Inside I was still saying, *I would never let that happen to me, I would never let that happen to me.*

"He probably *will* have to go to the hospital again," my mother said, "but he'll get better again too." At the same time I could tell she was as upset as we were. When we reached the corner where we would go our separate ways she took a little card out of her purse that a woman at work had given her. She always had it with her, along with *Daily Word.*

"Saint Paul said this, 'And we know that all things work together for good to them that love God . . .' That is in Romans. We have to believe that." At the corner she kissed us good-bye. "I'll be home at 6:30. If you need me you know how to phone me from a neighbor's." She crossed the wide main thoroughfare of Grand River Avenue to get her bus to downtown. Danny and I walked together until we neared the school where he ran ahead of me. His legs with his knobby knees looked so skinny in short pants.

The nights were the worst part. From my bed I could see the gloomy cast of light from the bathroom shining out into the hallway all night long. I knew my father was up puttering at the medicine cabinet, putting on different kinds of salves and ointments as if trying to cure himself of the invasion of the strange feelings and thoughts taking hold of him. I lay there wondering what is he doing now, is it dangerous, and when will things really get bad? I knew from past experience that soon his behavior would go beyond what we could manage at home.

The fourth night after I first saw the pies I dropped off to sleep watching the ominous yellow light shining from the bathroom. Suddenly I was awakened by a loud thumping noise. I listened. The sound was coming from the dining room. I jumped up and ran out. There was my father, completely naked except for gobs and gobs of cold cream smeared all over his body, running around and around our round dining room table. My mother was watching from the archway to the living room, and Danny was sitting up in his studio couch bed in the dining room. He must have been the first to be awakened by the thumping. It was like being awake in a nightmare. I had never seen my father without clothes. Once when I was quite small he didn't shut the bathroom door tightly and I caught a glimpse of his penis, but that was the only time. Now what he was doing was so bizarre, it didn't seem to matter that he was naked.

As if trying to make some sense out of this scene for me, my mother said,

"Daddy says he's training to fight Joe Louis."

"I don't just *say* it." He was puffing a little. "I *am* training to fight Joe Louis, I tell you, the heavyweight champion of the world." On "world" his voice boomed out as if he were announcing a recent victory for Joe Louis.

"I know who he is, Daddy," I said.

I knew we couldn't stop him or reason with him, but we'd have to do something soon. Danny was still sitting up on his bed, his face a ghostly white. My mother went to the couch in the living room and motioned for me to follow her.

"We can't let him go on this way. He'll have a heart attack," she whispered. "I'm going downstairs to call the police. We have no choice." I noticed now that my mother was already dressed, or maybe she had never undressed that night. "I hate to wake up Miss Petty, but she's probably already awake. Tell Danny where I am if he asks."

"Hurry back," I whispered. My father didn't notice her leaving, or if he did he still kept circling the table. Danny came and sat next to me on the couch. I told him, "Mama went downstairs." I didn't need to tell him why. Soon the door opened and she was back.

"Miss Petty was already awake," she said softly. She went and stood in the archway again. "Dan, don't you think you should take a little rest?"

"Can't stop—not much time—before the fight." She came back and joined us on the couch. On the way she turned the porch light on for the police. It was still pitch black outside. In minutes we heard the police sirens. From past experience we knew there would be a police car and a patrol wagon with lights flashing and sirens blaring. I was tense wondering what my father would do when he heard the sirens, but he just kept on running.

My mother had left the doors unlocked. We heard footsteps. Two officers came up the stairs and into the flat. At first when they saw the scene they looked as though they were having a terrible time stifling a laugh. But they treated my father most respectfully. He saw the officers and spoke first.

"You'll have to wait, officer," he told them. "I'm—uh, I'm going to fight Joe Louis—for the championship—in a few weeks." He was beginning to sound winded now. "I have—to finish—my training." Around he went, more slowly, but still doggedly.

"I understand that, Mr. Slagle, but I think you've done enough training for tonight. Tomorrow's another day," the officer said. My father was not going to be easily dissuaded. I could have told them that. He kept on running around and around the table. The other officer tried to intercept him and got a big smear of cold cream on his uniform. My father nimbly crawled under the table to try to get to the other side. Soon there was an even more outrageous scene with two police officers diving under our heavy oak table in pursuit of a man clothed only in cold cream, their navy blue uniforms becoming more and more smeared with the greasy substance. Twice he eluded them with sheer slipperiness. I found myself rooting, for the moment, for my father to get away as if it were a chase scene in a movie and my father was the good guy.

Soon the officers had a firm hold on him, and he seemed to recognize they had the upper hand. They were very gentle with him as they persuaded him to let my mother wipe off the excess cold cream and help him into his pajamas, and then his bathrobe and slippers for the trip to the hospital in the patrol wagon. He gave us goodbye, smiling a sad wild-eyed sort of smile that did not look like my father, and yet I could still see him there somewhere— in the way he looked back at us, I knew he wanted to stay with us.

As I watched him go, escorted by two policemen, I felt terrible. We had each other but my father had no one. The sirens started again and each of us sank into one of the chairs in the living room or onto the couch. My mother was crying silently and blowing her nose in her handkerchief. I followed my father in my mind for as long as I could hear the sirens.

Why did they have to use those sirens? The neighbors would have heard them, and once they learned that my father had been taken to a mental hospital, we'd probably be asked to move again. But I'd worry about that later. The storm we'd been riding out for days had passed, for us at least, though not for my father. We talked about how relieved we felt that he would now be safe in a hospital. Not totally safe, of course—he once had four ribs broken by another patient—and yet we knew it was the only place for him to be when he was like this.

It was about four in the morning, but none of us could think of going back to bed.

"That was pretty smart of Daddy putting cold cream all over himself so he'd be hard to catch," Danny said. Danny still had an ashen color.

"Yes, with all that cold cream it was like trying to catch a greased pig," I said, and we couldn't help but laugh at that idea. My mother laughed too. She motioned to Danny to come and sit next to her in her chair. Putting her arm around him she asked,

"What would you like me to make for breakfast? It's almost daylight." Looking up at her Danny grinned, the color coming back into his face.

"Ralston with brown sugar on it?" he said.

Despite the night we'd had, after breakfast my mother got ready to go to work and Danny and I went to school.

At age eleven the worst part for me wasn't seeing my father with no clothes and cold cream all over him. The more devastating part was to see him become almost unrecognizable. The father I knew was an intelligent, loving person, and in these few days all vestiges of who he was had been destroyed. The person I loved was lost to me. He had disappeared into the world of his agitation and weird ideas.

This time my father's stay in the hospital was shorter than usual. After about two months he was home with us again. This was fortunate because another battle was brewing that year. I hadn't paid much attention to it until we came home from Covenant Lutheran Church on December 7 and found my father listening intently to reports coming over the radio from Pearl Harbor. I was glad to have him home as I sat with him beside this larger radio we had now, an ugly big square box on four long legs someone must have given us. We listened to report after report, the substance of which was voiced by President Roosevelt, "America is at war."

As frightening as this news was to us, the threat from outside forces felt less unsettling than the ever present threat that lurked inside our home.

World War II galvanized the entire country into one great larger purpose—the War Effort. We collected scrap metal and rubber, massaged an orange pellet into white margarine to make it look yellow like butter, and got used to meatless meals to meet the limitations of food rationing. As the war continued, all through eighth grade Monnier School excused me fifteen minutes early each day to care for two children whose mothers worked in war plants. Both had husbands in the Navy. At the house the mothers shared I took care of a seventeen-month-old boy, Denny, and an eight-year-old girl, Cindy, during the three-hour gap in the mothers' shifts when they were both at work. This was my contribution to the war effort, as I saw it.

At school a new music was becoming familiar to me, the tunes of war. In the music class we had twice a week we sang almost nothing now but the songs of the four major services: "From the halls of Montezuma," "Anchors Away" and "The Caissons Go Marching Along." Our voices soared, and in our imaginations we flew as we sang,

> Off we go into the wild blue yonder,
> Climbing high into the sun.

But like the World War I song, "Over There," which we also sang, that is where World War II was for us—over there; and we were safe in Fortress America. I don't think the war itself touched me very deeply except for the fervor and excitement we all felt in banding together to defeat the Japanese and the Germans. The movies we saw every Saturday at the local cinema depicted easy victories for the Allies and showed practically no casualties on our side—not an accurate picture by any means. I would have to wait until I was older to understand the real horrors of World War II—or even know about them, especially the Holocaust. My father's war was much more real to me, and for that I needed a Mighty Fortress. My mother's faith in God and the time I spent at Covenant Lutheran Church—these formed that fortress.

seven

"Whispering Hope"

OUR SUPPER OF SALMON loaf, scalloped potatoes, and peas was over. My father, who had taken over the cooking for some time now, had made dinner, so my mother and I did the dishes while he took the *Detroit News* to his favorite green leather chair in the living room. My brother was already outside with two friends riding the red Schwin bike he had just bought with his paper route money. After we hung up our dish towels my mother asked if I would like to play some violin and piano.

"Sure. I've nothing else on for tonight," I told her. So often I had choir practice or a Walther League meeting. Walther League is the youth group at the Lutheran Church. Or my friend Pat and I might be going to see Greer Garson and Gregory Peck in *The Valley of Decision* for the fourth time. We adored the love scenes, especially the one in the attic where Gregory Peck finally kisses her as the flood waters rise. At the piano in a corner of the living room I opened my violin case and put some rosin on my bow. My mother struck an A on the piano and I began tuning my violin. The scraping of the bow on the A and D strings played together, then the D and G, and finally the A and E until they sounded smooth and just right filled the room with sound.

"Will our playing disturb you, Dan?" my mother asked. Her voice sounded tender. She still took great care to provide a restful atmosphere for my father.

"Not at all. I enjoy it," he said, looking up from the classifieds. At least once a week he checked the advertisements for pharmacy positions. Sometimes he told us about the good salaries pharmacists were making these days, his voice sounding apologetic as if he still thought he should be out earning that kind of money and sparing my mother from having to work so hard for less than he could earn. She usually said something to reassure him that she actually liked her work. I believe she did like it. She treated her salesperson's job as a career and took pride in having had the "highest rating" in her department every year since she went back to work. The rating was based on sales, days absent, and days late. Despite this perfect record, she was extremely well-liked by the other saleswomen.

My mother began chording to "Turkey in the Straw" while I fiddled the melody. She used to play for dances in Canada when she was young and played the accompaniment for her cousin who wore a kilt and sang Harry Lauder songs at parties, so she knew lots of old tunes. It sounded like a real hoe-down when we played them. Sometimes we broke out in laughter at how corny we sounded. I struggled to keep up with her tempo. But hymns were what we enjoyed the most. Next we played and sang "Abide with Me," a lovely hymn for evening—

> Abide with me. Fast falls the eventide.
> The darkness deepens. Lord with me abide.
> When other helpers fail and comforts flee,
> Help of the helpless O abide with me.

I loved this hymn, especially "fast falls the eventide." The words had such an old-fashioned, homey feel to them. I could feel God's presence as we sang them.

I asked if we could play 'Whispering Hope." I was hoping to get a job the very next day. Tomorrow, July 7, 1944 would be my fourteenth birthday, and now that the government had lowered the age for working permits, I could apply at Hudson's Department Store. It sounded like unbelievable good fortune that someone my age could have a full-time job there for the summer, but it was true. My mother opened a different songbook and found the page for "Whispering Hope." We had sung this piece often—especially at times my father had gone back to the hospital. This time it was about my hoped for job. As we played the gentle melody we sang the words together:

> Soft as the voice of an angel, breathing a lesson unheard,
> Hope with a gentle persuasion whispers her comforting word.
> Wait, till the darkness is over. Wait, till the tempest is done,
> Hope for the sunshine tomorrow after the shower is gone.

And then the chorus:

Whispering Hope, Oh, how welcome thy voice,
Making my heart in its sorrow rejoice.

We played two more hymns—"Sweet Hour of Prayer" and "Fairest Lord Jesus." Then from his chair in the corner of the living room we heard my father say, "How about, 'Lead, Kindly Light?'" So we played and sang that hymn too, his favorite. Sometimes he came and sang it with us, but tonight he just listened. His face looked thoughtful and a little sad. I don't know why he liked this hymn so much, but I loved it too. The poetry in the words is beautiful. "Lead kindly light amid the encircling gloom. Lead Thou me on. The night is dark and I am far from home. Lead Thou me on." We sang all three verses, and then decided to stop for the night. I loosened the hairs in my bow, put my violin back in its case and followed my mother to the kitchen where she was beginning to fold laundry. I sat down at the table with its soft red and white checkered tablecloth to chat with her for a while. Her sleeveless blue flowered housedress picked up the last rays of the setting sun. She looked as fresh as she had at breakfast. No one would guess she had worked downtown all day. When my father was home and well she lost that worried expression her face often wore when he wasn't home.

"Won't it be great if I get that job tomorrow?" I said. "We'll be able to ride the bus together there and back—maybe even have lunch together." I had always wanted more time with my mother. During school vacations I made sure I was up in time to have breakfast with her before she left for work. I needed that taste of her cheerfulness and energy to get my day off to a good start. Just the way she hurried around the kitchen getting breakfast, wearing one of her few dark work dresses, her nails polished and her hair set at the beauty parlor, made me feel I should get going on some projects of my own—practice my violin or take my books back to the library. Now we'd have all this time, just the two of us, to talk. I needed to talk to her about what clothes I would buy for starting high school in September—her ideas about what I could get Pat for her birthday—and if I should take private violin lessons now that I would no longer have them free at school. "We can even stop for coffee at Greenfield's Cafeteria downtown—that's if I get the job."

"With the war on they are really short of people. I'd be surprised if they didn't hire you," she said as she folded a faded blue bath towel neatly in thirds. "Just go to the Personnel Office on the fourteenth floor. It's the other end of the floor from the Employees' Cafeteria, and you've been there with me many times." Her voice sounded as happy as I was at the prospect of my going to work with her.

"I'm so excited. I can't wait for it to be tomorrow—when I'll be fourteen."

"It's hard to believe you'll be fourteen, Sarah." She looked up from folding a green plaid dish towel and studied my face. "You probably should wear a little lipstick so they won't think you look too young." I had lipstick but I usually didn't wear any. My friend Pat was a year younger than me and didn't wear lipstick yet, so I usually didn't either.

"I will. I ironed a white blouse today to wear with my navy skirt and I should shine my black shoes. But I think I'll go down to Pat's house for a while and see what she's up to." Pat and I had been friends since I began seventh grade and we rarely went a day without seeing each other. I patted my father's shoulder as I passed him reading his newspaper. "Goodbye, Daddy. I'm going to Pat's for a while." He looked up from the paper with a worried look.

"I'm sure glad your brother's too young for this war," he said, motioning to an article on the front page about the number of troop ships the German U boats were sinking.

"I'm glad too." I had never thought about my brother going to war. "The war's bound to end before he's draft age. He's only twelve," I reassured him. My father was very fond of my brother, although they didn't talk to each other the way my father and I did. In one of his manic periods he wrote a poem about Danny in which he called him "Sunny Dan." Danny *was* a sunny kid except when my father was becoming ill again.

The next morning I didn't ride the bus with my mother. I wanted this to be my project. Once I had the working permit firmly in my hand I headed for Hudson's Department Store. I felt marvelously grown up. A job at Hudson's would be a real job—not like baby sitting. I pictured myself opening the same brown envelope my mother received each week with a stiff green paycheck inside. If I got this job I could buy my own clothes and then save the rest for college. I didn't know which college I would go to, but I always knew I would go to college like my father had.

On Hudson's fourteenth floor I found a door marked Personnel Office in black block letters on frosted glass. Slowly I opened the door and peered inside. Behind the counter an older gentleman wearing horn-rimmed glasses motioned for me to come in. "I'd like to apply for a job as a stock clerk," I told him handing him my newly minted work permit.

He smiled what seemed to me an amused smile. Did he think I looked too young? "Just fill out this form," he said in a kindly voice and handed me two copies stapled together and a pen. "You may sit at that desk over there." I sat down and hurriedly filled in the blanks—name, address, phone number. The questions were all simple except for one, "Reason for seeking employment?" "To make money" was the first reason that popped into my head, but that sounded too blunt. "To make money for college," I wrote. With that done, I took the form back to Mr. Horn-Rimmed Glasses. He appeared to be over sixty—all the younger men were in the service. He separated the two sheets I had filled out and barely glanced at what I had written before he said,

"This seems in good order. Are you prepared to start today?"

"I'd be glad to start today," I said in my most formal voice. I was trying desperately to hide my surprise and thrill at being hired so quickly without even a real interview. To be truthful, I was disappointed not to have an interview. They had no idea who I was or if I could do this job. I guess they really were short of help.

"I'm going to send you to Miss Clancy then. She's in charge of all the stock clerks and people who check merchandise in and out of fitting rooms." He took me to the door with the frosted glass window and pointed to a counter about a hundred feet away. "Take this paper to her and tell her you're permanent for the summer." Now I knew why I had to fill out two copies.

"Thank you, sir," I said. I took a deep breath and wondered if he'd made some huge mistake. Was I really ready to be a full-time employee at Hudson's like my mother?

Behind the counter I found a petite bespectacled woman standing straight as a pencil behind her desk, keeping an eye on whatever was happening. Her slightly graying dark hair, parted as with a ruler, formed tight curls around her sharp, pointy features. Miss Clancy, I would soon learn, was known as the Mother Superior of stock clerks and fitting-room checkers. She looked quizzically at the paper I handed her. Did she recognize the name and know my mother worked at Hudson's? I hoped not. I didn't want them to give me this job because of my mother, but because of me. In a terse voice, as if she had said this hundreds of times before, Miss

Clancy informed me, "The dress code requires you to wear dark skirts or dresses, white blouses only, silk stockings with the seams straight and dark, well-polished shoes."

"Yes ma'am," I said, my voice barely audible. Most people did not intimidate me. Being so long my mother's confidant I was usually at ease with adults, but Miss Clancy cowed me from the start. I knew the dress code and had dressed accordingly. Still, I began to run my hand down the back of my leg to make sure my seams were straight.

"They badly need a stock clerk in Misses' Inexpensive Dresses on the sixth floor, so I'd like you to start today. Find Miss Shinkman. She's the assistant buyer. Tell her this is a permanent assignment."

With another mumbled, "Yes ma'am," I took off for the sixth floor, glad to be out from under Miss Clancy's scrutinizing gaze. Misses' Inexpensive Dresses was on the opposite end of the floor from where my mother worked in Misses' Moderately Priced Dresses. I was glad to be near my mother's department but I hoped this was a true coincidence and not because Miss Clancy knew my mother worked on the sixth floor.

Hudson's store was a world of its own. Privately owned by the Webber family, it covered a city block, and vied with Macy's in New York and Marshall Field's in Chicago for the most floor space and the highest sales volume in the country. Moreover, Hudson's was beautiful. The first floor had the elegance of a Tiffany's with smooth wood paneling everywhere, and seemed to shimmer softly with dimly lit glass show cases filled with jewelry and expensive perfumes. The elevators too were wood-paneled and operated only by slender fair-skinned black women in gray fitted uniforms with white lace cuffs. Each department at Hudson's was decorated in perfect taste. Serenely quiet dining rooms on the eleventh floor served elegant food. My mother and I had lunch there once for the fun of it. We joked about our splurge that day like two kids skipping school. You could buy anything at Hudson's, from a shoe lace to a grand piano.

Despite Hudson's size, a warm family feeling prevailed among the salespeople and floor managers—extending even to the buyers, although everyone held the buyers in awe. One Thanksgiving my mother's buyer, Miss Hughes, had her husband deliver a sumptuous basket of food to our house. Standing outside I saw my father come to the door and take this basket from a man a foot taller than himself. I felt sorry for him. I was sure he felt embarrassed to be accepting a food package from another man, yet I knew Miss Hughes had only the best of intentions and only wanted to help my mother.

I reached Misses' Inexpensive Dresses, one of the larger departments, and found Miss Shinkman. "I'm Sarah, your new stock girl," I told her, "and I'm a permanent assignment." By now it was so close to lunch hour that we only talked a little. She decided I should take the eleven o'clock lunch hour, the one she took, and she'd show me around when I got back. I went to find my mother, still not quite believing I actually had this job. "You were right," I told her, "They hired me in two minutes." She signaled her floor manager and we headed excitedly for the Employees' Cafeteria.

During lunch I told my mother all about Miss Shinkman. "She's young, sort of medium pretty, with a very good figure," I told her. "And she wears her hair pulled back with a barrette that leaves soft brown curls showing at her neck." As soon as my hair grew longer I planned to wear it that way. I went on and on. "She's new too, she told me—just graduated from University of Michigan last month. I know I'm going to like her."

"You've barely touched your lunch, Sarah." I looked down at my tuna fish salad of which I'd taken one bite.

"I know. I'm too excited to eat."

"She's probably in the Executive Training Program if she's a college graduate." My mother looked thoughtful. "They'll be grooming her to be a buyer."

"Didn't Hudson's ask you to be a buyer one time?" I asked, although I knew the story. I wanted to hear it again.

"Yes. I had to turn it down because it meant I'd be away from you and Danny overnight. Before you were born I was an assistant buyer in suits at Eaton's in Toronto. I enjoyed that. I did some modeling then too." I pictured my mother, like Miss Hughes, standing tall and regal in that suit department. She was still a handsome woman. In my imagination she was wearing a pink suit.

I knew that Miss Hughes had a daughter, Dixie, six months older than me because I inherited some of her elegant clothes. Having a child didn't keep Miss Hughes from being a buyer. Surely on a buyer's salary my mother could have afforded a baby sitter to stay all night. Then again, perhaps my father's lengthy, frequent stays at Ypsilanti State Hospital would have made buying trips to New York very difficult if not impossible. I wanted to ask if she ever regretted her choice, but decided not to. Her not becoming a buyer reminded me of how she didn't get to go to Normal School to be a teacher because her parents needed her to work on the farm. Both times she was cheated, but it would not be her nature to feel sorry for herself. I think she really believed that verse in Romans that she quoted to us so often, that, "All things work together for good to them that love God, to those who are called according to his purpose." She told me one time that she felt her purpose in life was to keep a home for my father to come home to and to raise my brother and me. I hoped that my life would have a purpose too.

"I'd better get back and find out what Miss Shinkman wants me to do," I said when we were walking out of the cafeteria.

"I'm going into the Employees' Health Service to see what I weigh," she said. She always watched her weight. If she gained five pounds she ate only Jello or a half a grapefruit for lunch until she lost it. She told me that it was wonderful having me here and suggested I meet her at her locker to go home. Then she gave me a hug.

I found Miss Shinkman in the sewing room having a piece of chocolate with the two ladies who did alterations. She introduced me and offered me a chocolate. Then she talked about work. "I unpacked some dresses this morning. Come, I'll show you where we throw the boxes." We gathered boxes off the stockroom floor into a big cart and with both of us pushing wheeled them toward the center of the building. There a door you'd never notice led into a small square room with walls painted a gun-metal gray.

"You open this door on the wall and throw the boxes down the chute. It's an incinerator," she explained.

"That looks easy," I said, but when I leaned over to look down the chute, I had an uneasy feeling. I didn't see any flames as I expected in an incinerator—only darkness—and the chute looked large enough that a person could fall in, except the door was a little high for that. We threw in box after box and heard them clatter down six flights of metal walls. The sound gave me a slight chill—as when you look over the edge of a cliff.

"The chute runs the length of the building so you can use it on any floor," Miss Shinkman told me. I knew Hudson's was 23 stories high. I pictured a long metal funnel running through the heart of Hudson's store.

Miss Shinkman took me to a rack of dresses and said, "You can start going through these. Make sure the size is correct for that rack, do up any belts and buttons that are undone, and if anything needs fixing, take it to the ladies in the sewing room. If you have any questions, come and find me." I thought these dresses lacked style compared to those in my mother's department. Most were tailored cuts in dark purples, browns, and teal blue crepe—old ladies' dresses. I guess you have to pay more to have stylish clothes, I concluded. Still, I was determined to make my department look as beautiful as possible. I wanted to be as good at my job as my mother was at hers.

On the way home my mother said, "Let's stop at Awry's bakery and buy one of those seven-layered cakes for your birthday—and to celebrate your new job." My mother loved these seven-layered cakes. I liked them too, but not as much as she did. We got the cake. I knew that along with the cake would be some well-chosen presents my mother had hid away. And we talked all the way home, just as I had dreamed of doing. We talked about my new job and what I would buy with my first paycheck. I told her I'd like to buy a desk for my room since in high school I would have a lot more homework. She said we could look at desks the next day on our lunch hour, and we did. We found the perfect desk, a dark mahogany keyhole with a matching chair that had an upholstered seat of red and gold stripped satin material. It would take two paychecks to pay for it, but we ordered it anyway.

eight

"Follow I Will Follow Thee, My Lord"

WHEN THE SUMMER ENDED and it was time to go back to school, I began my freshman year at Cooley High School, glad that I could still work at Hudson's on Saturdays and again next summer. Cooley was one of the best high schools in Detroit, but I didn't know this at the time. It had opened in 1928, and its opulent design and well landscaped grounds bore witness to the pre-Depression prosperity Detroit had enjoyed. As soon as I laid eyes on the school I loved its pale orange brick and the brown marble pillars at the two matching front entrances. I thought it looked like a castle. Both entrances led into a marble hall with high ceilings, more Greek revival pillars and elegant bas-reliefs. Glass cases housed Cooley's many athletic trophies. Off this huge hall were doors to a magnificent, large auditorium. Soon I would play my violin here in shimmering Christmas Concerts and Spring Concerts wearing a formal, see theater productions by the drama club, and eventually play for graduations. The student body at Cooley was around 4,000.

Owen A. Emmons had been principal from the time the school opened, a soft-spoken man who always wore three-piece gray suits and stood noticeably straight at assemblies, his feet spread apart and his hands behind his back. The Assistant Principal, Miss Farnsworth, her black hair piled in a roll upon her head, dressed in high-necked long black dresses that made her look like a stolid figure out of the 1800s. Her whole de-meanor signaled, "You must behave with dignity here." Although we could have fun walking through the halls between classes as lively kids, Cooley was a place of serious order and I liked this. When our Latin teacher, Miss Wells, who also always dressed in black, gave the class an assignment and then left for half-an-hour to listen to President Truman's inaugural address after President Roosevelt's death in office, no one moved from his or her seat. She returned to a quiet classroom and told us she thought the new president was going to do just fine. We were so well-behaved. This appealed to me—no doubt because at home the quiet order my mother established could disappear in a day. We never knew why, but if my father took off his shoes and stockings in the living room, planting his pale white feet in the tufts of the carpet, this signaled another period of mania was about to begin. Danny and my mother and I would exchange helpless glances. Over the next several days our order would be totally disrupted, ending in a painful hospitalization for our father. Fortunately these disruptions were interspersed with long peaceful periods, but we never knew when a disruption would occur.

At Cooley High School I entered a happy interlude best represented perhaps by the music I found there. For the next four years my head was full of orchestral passages, popular wartime melodies, Swing, Boogie, and the beginning of Rock and Roll at the Cooley dances, and the hymns and choral music of Calvin Church where I went with my high school boyfriend. At the first Christmas concert I heard the music to "Hark how the bells, sweet silver bells, from everywhere, filling the air," sung by a large choral group, and the spiritual, "I wonder as I wander out under the sky, why Jesus my Savior did come for to die," sung by a senior, Chuck Hutchins, who had a wonderful tenor voice. I loved all this music. I took private violin lessons with Jack Bosen, a first violinist with the Detroit Symphony, and went to every outdoor summer concert I could so I could watch him play. With many other interests opening up—the school newspaper, the yearbook, the church choir, and my continuing Saturday job at Hudson's—I didn't practice enough to become a truly fine musician, but this didn't trouble me. I enjoyed singing in the choir at Calvin Church, playing my violin in the orchestra, hearing the big band music of Glen Miller and Tommy Dorsey on the radio, and engaging in a wide range of pursuits, including boys.

On a Saturday at the start of the second semester of ninth grade, I was riding the bus to work in downtown Detroit with my mother when I told her, "I wish you could have seen the boy who walked into my English Lit class. He's at least six feet tall with thick dark hair, and has these sparkling blue eyes with the longest black lashes I've ever seen. He had on a canary yellow shirt with a red plaid tie, and danced a little jig all the way to his seat in the back of the room."

"Sounds like a colorful fellow," my mother joked. We both laughed.

"Colorful! He was in Technicolor." Technicolor films had just become popular. "His name is Bob Alexander and he's so cute."

"Well, who knows, maybe you'll get to know him better."

"I've tried walking home on the streets he takes—he's in two of my other classes too, so who knows?"

"With that red plaid tie he sounds like a Scot," my mother said. As a former Scotch Canadian she liked all things Scottish.

I kept walking down the streets Bob took on the way home, even though he often walked with a girl named June, and in a few days we did start talking. In time he told me he had noticed me that first day of class too. He said, "You wore a light blue sweater with a matching band in your long brown hair."

We had a lot of snow that winter and on one of these walks toward his house and my bus, Bob asked me if I would like to go tobogganing with the Christian Endeavor group from his church that coming Friday night.

I told him, "I would like that, that would be great," knowing I had neither ski pants nor a ski jacket for the occasion. I had never been tobogganing. When my mother learned that I was going tobogganing she did not like the idea at all. She had skated the night away as a girl in outdoor covered rinks near her parents' farm in Canada, but she knew nothing about tobogganing and thought it sounded dangerous. This is the same woman who told me how she rode her horse Billy bareback, and with Billy hitched to a buggy raced the hired man for eight miles into town. She hadn't always been so cautious. I think my father's illness impressed upon her how quickly life can change. I had been telling her about Bob for weeks now and she liked the fact that his parents were from Canada like herself, so she didn't say I couldn't go exactly, only that she would worry. My friend Pat loaned me her navy blue ski pants and her mother loaned me her light blue ski jacket. Both were happy to support my first date with Bob—my first date ever. As I left the house that night my mother was still saying, "I sort of wish you weren't going." I felt guilty about making her worry—she had enough worries—but I was too excited about my date with this handsome boy with the sparkling blue eyes to let anything stop me.

It was a crisply beautiful night with a sky full of stars. Once on our way, joking with Bob and the other kids, thoughts about my mother's fears and my guilt quickly faded, then disappeared. The hill at Rouge Park had a deep layer of fresh snow. On the toboggan nestled in the shelter of Bob's arms, I felt very safe. Even when the toboggan overturned at the bottom rolling us out into the soft snow, I could see there was no danger here. Time after time we lugged the toboggans up the hill and sped down, our shouts and squeals piercing the chill night air. Back at Bob's Presbyterian Church I drank hot chocolate and talked with some of the kids in his Christian Endeavor group. They were such a warm friendly bunch. Most of them went to Cooley. I began to think that maybe I should try going to Bob's church. This was a much larger youth group than the Walther League I belonged to at Covenant Lutheran Church.

That night I wrote in my diary, "I've never had so much fun in my life." High school was becoming all I had hoped it would be. I turned out the light and pulled up the covers, too tired to offer more of a prayer than, "Thank you, God, for this beautiful night—and this handsome boy."

After a year of seeing each other several times a week, on the way home from school one Friday Bob asked me, "What would you think about going steady, you and me?" I didn't *need* to think about it. I was thrilled.

"Sure. That would be great," I told him.

"We can call it 'liberal going steady' if you like." I wasn't sure what that meant but I said that was fine too. Just as we reached my bus stop Bob took out his Order of the Arrow pin and gave it to me to wear. I had heard that it was a top honor in the Boy Scouts to belong to the Order of the Arrow.

"Oh, Bob. Are you sure you want to trust me with this. I might lose it."

"I trust you *not* to lose it," he said with his infectious grin. He was looking down at me with those amazing blue eyes—the same blue as my mother's, I noticed. He put his arms around me until my bus came. I felt completely happy.

As soon as I got home I told my mother, "Bob and I are going steady," shouting over the sound of the vacuum. It was her day off and she was vacuuming the living room. She turned off the vacuum and laughed when I repeated my announcement.

"You're much too young to be going steady, Sarah," she said, still laughing, as though she couldn't take this seriously. I felt more than a little hurt. By now she had to know how crazy I was about this boy. Her mild disapproval wasn't going to stop me.

"I'm Bob's steady girlfriend, Mom, and that's that. Besides, everyone at Cooley goes steady." That was true. I felt confident that I knew more about modern dating than my mother. She came from a different era entirely, I told myself. She probably never dated at all back on the farm, but just skated with the boys she met at the ice skating rink.

I've read that in wartime people dance—and dance we did. The Big Bands and the fledgling Rock and Roll music counteracted some of the heaviness of the war. When I was finally eligible—you had to be in tenth grade—I went to every single Friday night Rhythm Romp at Cooley. At first I went with my girlfriends and met Bob there. Then Bob asked me to go to the next Rhythm Romp with him. This was before we began going steady. I was in a joyful daze the whole week thinking about the dance. On Friday night I waited in a new coral dress and black patent pumps I'd bought with my money from Hudson's. The hour got later and later— eight o'clock, eight thirty. I began to shed a few tears. I couldn't bear that I was missing so much of the dance and couldn't imagine what had happened to Bob. At nine o'clock the doorbell rang. My brother answered the door. I heard Bob's voice ask, "Where's your sister?"

"Crying," Danny responded."

Younger brothers can be so embarrassing, even Danny, I thought as I repaired my smeared make-up and grabbed my coat. We still had two hours left of the dance. Bob had finally figured out that I had expected him to come to my house and had a friend drive him here.

The gym looked amazingly lovely for a gym—balloons in rich autumn colors, and branches of fall leaves surrounded the bandstand, and the lights were turned down low. The band—two clarinets, a saxophone, a bass, and drums—was playing the final measures of "In the Mood," a lively jitterbug number, when we arrived, then moved to the slow strains of "Tangerine." Bob and I drifted slowly across the dance floor. I was in paradise humming the music, and in my head hearing the words, "Tangerine—she is all they say." Bob lifted my chin up so he could see my face.

"How are you doing, Breezy?" he asked. Breezy was his nickname for me. It didn't quite fit me, but I liked it.

"Now that we're here I'm just fine," I said smiling. "It was an understandable misunderstanding."

"I just thought we'd meet here as always," he said. "I'm sorry I made you cry."

"I'm not sad any longer. I'm very happy," I told him, leaning my head against his shoulder.

We danced the rest of the night, mostly to such dreamy slow melodies as, "I'll Walk Alone," "I'll be Seeing You," and "As Time Goes By." World War II had introduced a whole new repertoire of nostalgic, melancholy songs I loved to sing and dance to. They replaced the mournful songs I used to pick out at the piano. I'd sing them walking along the street. "I'll walk alone, because to tell you the truth I am lonely," was a sentiment that felt familiar to me. By this time I didn't make the connection to my father, however—some of the most obvious connections go underground.

I did begin to go with Bob to Calvin Presbyterian Church, although I felt guilty about leaving the Lutheran church that had been so welcoming to us. For a while I went to both churches and managed to sing in both choirs. At Bob's church I learned yet another kind of religious music we called "Choruses." At the beginning of the Christian Endeavor meeting, every Sunday evening at six o'clock, we sang a host of them. There was no book for these that I ever saw—you just learned them. Like the hymns my mother taught me before kindergarten, these choruses stayed in my mind and were very reassuring. There must have been twenty or more of them that all of us knew. Two I liked in particular. This one is actually a refrain to a hymn, "Jesus Calls Me, I Will Follow":

> Follow, I will follow Thee my Lord.
> Follow every passing day.
> My tomorrows are all known to Thee.
> Thou wilt lead me all the way.

I especially liked the thought, "my tomorrows are all known to Thee," —as though God had a plan for my life. And it didn't matter that I didn't know what it was because He did.

And the other one I liked:

> Turn your eyes upon Jesus.
> Look full in His wonderful face.
> And the things of earth will grow strangely dim
> In the light of His glory and grace.

I wouldn't say that I understood the Christian faith in a very full way at all at this time, but these melodies became something I hummed without realizing I was doing it. At times when I didn't know what I'd find my father doing when I got home—he might be baking too many pies and cakes or arguing with Aunt Daisy—the words of these choruses made me feel that God was with me and that meant everything—"the things of earth will grow strangely dim in the light of His glory and grace." Events happening here were only temporary, whereas God's love is eternal. It put my concerns in perspective.

Many of us donned wine-red choir gowns and sang in the youth choir for the evening church service that followed the Christian Endeavor meeting. A stocky, exuberant man named Jack Phlieger led a spirited hymn-sing at the beginning of this service using a different hymnal that set a whole other tone than that of the one used for the morning worship service. Instead of solemn, lofty hymns such as "Holy, Holy, Holy," in the evening we sang, "Amazing Grace," "Shall We Gather at the River," and "Bringing in the Sheaves." I liked both the lofty hymns of the morning service and the lively, more down-to-earth hymns we sang at night. I would not have wanted to give up either sort. At the Lutheran Church we had only sung "lofty." In time, my mother and my brother began going to Bob's church with me and we left Covenant Lutheran behind.

At one of these Sunday evening services, John Frame, a missionary doctor home on furlough, told about his work in Teheran, Iran. Dr. Frame was a tall, angular man, who seemed fairly shy. He was not a gifted public speaker, but he made a lasting impression on me nonetheless. I felt great admiration for him as I heard about the way he took care of sick people in a hospital the Presbyterian Church ran in Teheran. There were no services for the poor in Iran back then, so without this hospital many people would be without medical care. In some individual cases he described, his being there made a huge difference. I knew that was exactly what I wanted to do with my life, something that would make an important difference. Until that night I had thought I wanted to go into retailing like Miss Shinkman;

but after I heard Dr. Frame I changed my mind. The thought of going to a far-away country and doing something useful had even more appeal than going on buying trips to New York. Again, I found myself thinking, "I want my life to have a purpose—like his—and like my mother's does." I mentioned this to Bob on our way home that night, the idea that one's life should have a purpose. He said something that sounded as though he felt the same way and I'm sure he did feel the same. Bob was always helping people. But it had snowed and he began to throw snowballs at me. The mood shifted away from any serious discussion. I was disappointed. I had wanted to talk about this more, but we went back to our usual playful bantering and played in the snow all the way to my house.

For the next two and a half years I couldn't get over my good fortune to have a handsome boyfriend like Bob who was also a good friend and a lot of fun. Our good times together usually ended with some passionate kissing we called "necking." We could sit in the back of Bob's father's car and kiss endlessly, our excitement mounting, with no thought of going beyond this great new pleasure. One time Bob thought his tongue touched my lips and he feared I would never speak to him again because I'd think he was, "trying a French kiss." I didn't know what a French kiss was until he explained it to me. Ours was a very innocent time I see in retrospect—a very good time.

I have to admit I enjoyed the envy of more than a few girls in our class at Cooley High School. From time to time one of them would ask me, "Are you still going steady with Bob? If you're not we'd like to invite him to a party." "Nothing has changed," I'd tell them, feeling wickedly smug. Not that I didn't have my own qualms and uncertainties common to this age, because I did. I deemed a group of leaders in the school to be the "big wheels," and did not count myself among them. Bob, who had this exuberant outgoing personality, was a "big wheel." I figured that I was included by virtue of being Bob's girlfriend. In Christian Endeavor, however, fostered by some truly unusual adult sponsors of the group, everyone was included on equal footing.

Then, in senior year a strange thing happened. My friend Don Stewart asked if I would help on the campaign for class president of a fellow named Eric Anderson. Our class was so large that I had never even heard of Eric Anderson; but Don persuaded me that because Eric was from our Study

Hall I should help him. At Eric's campaign meetings, I began painting signs and banners. Then one day he offered to drive me home from the meeting. We sat talking for a long time in his car in front of my house. He told me about his plan to go to medical school and then go as a medical missionary to some place in Africa that needed physicians. I'd never met anyone at this age with such definite ideas about what he wanted to do in life—he was extremely idealistic. Eric made me think of John Frame, the medical missionary I had heard speak at Calvin Church two years before. After a few more such talks with Eric I just wanted to talk to him more and more. I was mainly attracted by his plan to be a missionary doctor and help people less fortunate than we were.

Where Bob was tall and blue-eyed with dark wavy hair, Eric was of average height, brown-eyed, and wore his light-brown hair in a pompadour, as my father did. Bob and I rarely talked about anything very serious. The qualities I loved in Bob showed up in what he did—making sure my friend Pat got home safely after a dance, almost missing a Halloween party we were going to because he wouldn't cut short taking a neighbor child trick-or-treating. Eric was almost always serious. He ran track, wrestled, and wrote poetry—lyrical poetry about nature. He worked hard on weekends pumping gas in his father's gas station. It was the way he talked about his feelings and his faith that most intrigued me—I found this unusual for a boy. Bob was by nature a happy person who didn't seem to have a dark side. Eric was a brooder. He worried about all the suffering in the world and wanted to do something about it. I found his idealism inspiring, and our talks fostered an intimacy between us that was hard to resist. I began to fantasize about going off with him to do some kind of heroic work.

Eric, though truly a dark horse, won the election over a very popular student. The campaign meetings ended, but not my fascination with Erik. Bob and I had been going steady for over two years. If I were to see Eric, I would have to tell Bob I didn't want to go steady any longer. This was the toughest decision of my life until now.

I didn't want to hurt Bob. He had been a truly good friend to me, a wonderful boyfriend. We now shared so many friends at church, had been to Christian Endeavor weekend conferences together, and knew each other's families. How could I give all that up? How could I hurt him like that? But I didn't want to give up talking to Eric either. In January of senior year I suggested to Bob that it might be a good idea if we dated some other people for a while since we had only dated each other for such a long time. I felt very guilty doing this, although Bob had suggested the same thing the year before and then changed his mind. I knew that the only person I wanted to date was Eric. So what I was suggesting was very dishonest and I knew it. Bob agreed to try it.

Soon after, on the way to work at Hudson's one Saturday morning my mother and I stopped, as we often did, at Greenfield's Cafeteria for a cup of coffee. As we drank coffee and ate a French cruller my mother asked me, "Tell me why you're seeing this fellow Eric now instead of Bob Alexander? What do you see in him?"

"I don't know how to explain it. There's just something about him that makes me think he's wonderful," I told her.

"Your father and I were talking the other day. We both think you seemed much happier when you were seeing Bob." I was surprised, yet pleased, to hear that my father had an opinion about my boyfriends. And I didn't disagree with their observations.

Twisting uncomfortably on the stool where we sat at a counter, I said, "I know. I *was* happier with Bob—more carefree. Eric is very serious. He wants to be a doctor, so he can help people." I didn't tell her that he wanted to go to a far off country in Africa, and that we had talked about my going with him as a teacher. That would really give her cause for alarm.

"I guess we have to go," she said picking up her purse and gloves. "I'm just afraid you'll be sorry someday when you see Bob Alexander walk down the aisle of Calvin Church with somebody else." I was even more surprised to hear my mother talk about marriage. We were all so young, after all. She had a point though—in time nearly all the young people in Christian Endeavor married within the group. Since most of them went to Wayne University, their relationships just proceeded on through college and into marriage. Breaking up with Bob was definitely a road not taken.

I hurt Bob badly, as it turned out. Bob's older sister told me, "Girls don't think that boys go home and cry when they get hurt, but they do." Bob had done nothing to deserve my wanting to stop seeing him. If I could have split myself in two and continued to see both of them, that's what I would have wanted. I wrote in my diary that I loved them equally. Bob was like my energetic, fun-loving mother with her same blue eyes, and I loved him for that. Eric was like my sensitive, more soul-searching father in his out-and-out idealism. And when I had to choose, I chose the idealist—the one who was planning to be a missionary. In actual fact, I believe Bob was just as idealistic as Eric. Like my mother, he didn't talk about his beliefs as easily as Eric but I believe they were rock solid.

By spring Eric and I were "going steady." As guilty as I felt about leaving Bob, I felt extraordinarily happy any time I could be with Eric. We never ran out of things to talk about—our views about God, life, our future together—how many children we'd like to have. Our talks led to the same passionate kissing I had known with Bob. It was only the serious discussions with Eric that were were different. At times Eric gave the sermon for the evening service at his church, a denomination called the Church of Christ. I loved listening to his ideas that seemed much more complex than my own—and his knowledge of the Bible went far beyond mine. I felt a deep respect for him as well as love. I was sure I could happily be with him forever.

During this time my brother Danny had a job on weekends at a branch of Cunningham's Drug Store, the big chain store in Detroit. By now Danny was six feet tall, still on the thin side, but a good-looking fellow with deep-set blue eyes, and a great sense of humor. Any girl in the Christian Endeavor group would have happily been Danny's girlfriend, but he didn't have a steady girlfriend yet. He happened to mention to his boss at Cunningham's that his dad had been a pharmacist. The boss asked if his father might be interested in a job. "They need a pharmacist at a branch not far from where you live," he told Danny.

That night at dinner Danny told us about this conversation. My mother and I remained silent, waiting to see what my father would say. "Naturally, I'd like the job," he told Danny, "but I'm not sure I could still do pharmacy. It's been a lot of years since I last worked as a pharmacist." It had been about thirteen years. He'd been doing so well. Did he dare to rock the boat? He'd even gone on a short vacation to Canada with my mother and me earlier in the year and had not become overly excited. I thought about the way he read the classifieds and would mention what good money pharmacists were making now. All these things flashed through my mind as I waited to see what he would say next. "Find out the number tomorrow, Danny, and I'll give them a call." I was glad—yet frightened about where this might lead.

In the end he couldn't refuse so tempting an offer—a salary twice what my mother made at a location a short bus ride away. Nor could we bring ourselves to discourage him. It would mean so much to him if he could return to his profession. He had been so proud of putting himself through the University of Buffalo's School of Pharmacy where the studies had come easily to him. He had owned his own drug store at such a young age. He would regain much more than money if he could return to pharmacy.

The first day at his branch of Cunningham's Drug Store he was relieved to find he remembered virtually all his pharmacy. When we all arrived home that night he told us, "I think I'm doing pretty well. A couple of the newer drugs I had to look up, but almost everything else is the same. It's all coming back to me."

"That's wonderful, Dan," my mother said as we sat down to a dinner of meatloaf, mashed potatoes, and green beans they had worked on together. We were all nervously optimistic that night. My father seemed unusually happy. He told Danny to thank his boss for him for telling him about this opportunity.

I'm sure the three of us prayed that our father would make it. I know I did. He was on my mind all day at school. I'd look at the clock and think, "He only has four more hours to go," or "It's almost quitting time. I bet he's on his way home now." When my mother and I caught a few moments together walking to the bus, we talked about nothing else. "Wouldn't it be amazing if he could keep this job and not get sick again?" I said. "I believe it can happen. Other illnesses are curable—or go into remission—why not this one?"

"It would be wonderful, Sarah, but I keep thinking about those two doctors who advised him not to go back to pharmacy. Still, I'm not going to say anything to discourage him." We walked the rest of the way in silence both wondering, I'm sure, how we'd find my father when we got home that night after his second day on the job. It was a jittery time. But the second day had gone well. The third went well also. Then on the fourth day things began to unravel. We could see that his mood was too high in that driven unnatural way. He began setting the table for supper and putting the dishes on so fast he broke one. I felt a huge let-down—nothing had changed after all. By the next night he wasn't sleeping. Again I saw the yellow light shining from the bathroom late into the night—always before a sign that things had gone too far to turn around.

"I think it would be good if you took a break for a day or two," my mother said, knowing that the chances of his doing this were close to zero.

"Are you imagining that I'm sick again, Mae? I'm fine—I enjoy what I'm doing. I never felt better. What's more they need me there." His speech sounded combative, on the verge of anger, his cheeks flushed with the excitement he felt.

By the end of the day on Saturday my father agreed that he was in the throes of another manic period and needed to go back to Ypsilanti. On Sunday our next-door neighbor, Tom Mohan, drove him back to the hospital, one of the few times he went willingly. My mother went with him. This was one of the saddest hospitalizations for all of us—our hopes had been raised to such a height. It had to be doubly hard for my father. I could see how much he truly loved pharmacy.

A couple of weeks later the pharmacist at the branch where my father had worked for only one week phoned to say he had a paycheck for him and wondered if my mother could pick it up. When she returned from Cunningham's store she told us with a quiver in her voice, "You know, the head pharmacist had tears in his eyes when he gave me your father's paycheck. He said, 'I never had a pharmacist any better than Dan—he remembered everything.' He felt so bad for him." I put my arm around her. I was glad to hear he had done well. I especially liked knowing that my father was still such a smart man. But to me it underscored even more how much this illness had robbed him of his life. He never complained about his illness and how much he lost because of it—especially the self-respect that comes from being able to take care of his family. And yet he did take care of us with all of his fine cooking when he was home. And he did take pride in that.

Before I realized it, the time had come to decide about college. A very high percentage of the students at Cooley went on to college. I don't think I knew anyone who didn't. Among my friends most were deciding between the University of Michigan, forty miles away in Ann Arbor, and Wayne University in mid-town Detroit. At first Michigan seemed out of reach for me financially. Then Mildred White, the friend we called Mony, who had sent us five dollars a month when my father first became ill, encouraged me to apply to the Student Aid Foundation in Detroit where she was secretary to the board. In the end I received a Regents Scholarship from U of M for tuition, a small Phi Beta Kappa stipend, and the Student Aid Foundation agreed to cover all the rest, even my books. So I now had the choice of either school.

Bob and Eric and most of my close friends planned to go to Wayne University. Their families must have agreed with my mother who said, "It's silly to pay more to go away when there's a perfectly good university right in town." My mother's thinking that I should go to Wayne was in large part, I'm sure, because she wanted to keep me nearby. My father gave no opinion. In the absence of arguments to the contrary, I was happy to go where my friends were going, especially since Eric would be there.

Mony was upset when she learned that I was turning down the Student Aid Foundation's scholarship to Michigan. She secured an invitation for Sunday dinner from my mother so we could discuss the question further. When we were assembled in the living room, my parents and Mony and I—my brother was studying in my bedroom—Mony chose her words carefully.

"Mae, you and Sarah are wonderfully close," she began, "but you can be too close. This little distance from home, forty miles, would help Sarah gain some independence. It's very important at this stage of her life." Mony's strategy seemed to be to focus on my welfare, knowing that my mother would always want what was best for me. But in a tone my mother only used when she wanted to get rid of an unwanted phone call, she said dismissively,

"We can't afford to send Sarah to Michigan, Mony. It's just out of the question."

"But there's nothing to afford. Her scholarships will cover everything—even her books." Mony crossed her shapely legs and held out her hands in a beseeching gesture. My father sat mute while my mother said again, "You don't understand, Mony. The University of Michigan is expensive. She can go to Wayne for $75 a semester. And she can live at home." Had my mother suddenly become deaf, or brain dead? I was embarrassed by her inability to respond to what Mony was actually saying. My father still said nothing. Why doesn't he say which school *he* thinks is the better choice, I wondered? He's the one who's been to college. Had he begun leaving all the important decisions to my mother at some point? Or did he sense how much my mother depended on me?

Mony tried one more time. "Mae, it's such a different experience to live in a dorm and take part in late-night discussions with other students. I see this when I visit our scholarship students."

"But don't you think it's silly for her to go so far away when there's a good university right here in Detroit?" I could see this was not a dialogue.

It was two people talking past each other and neither hearing what the other had just said.

"I could come home on weekends," I interjected. Mony was at least persuading *me* that I shouldn't pass up such a significant opportunity so quickly.

"I appreciate all you've done, Mony, but you've got to understand. Given our situation, it's really not possible." Suddenly it became clear to me that "our situation" had nothing to do with money. In all my growing up years my mother never said that anything I wanted was too expensive. I heard my father chide her more than once with, "If Sarah wanted the moon you'd find a way to get it for her." But this was different. "The situation" was simply this—my mother wasn't able to part with me. She needed my companionship in case my father became ill again—or even when he wasn't ill. I had become her closest friend—she needed that. "You two talk for a few minutes while Dan and I get dinner on the table. I'm sure it's ready," she said. My father was already in the kitchen pulling things out of the oven. Mony moved over closer to me on the sofa, "If you do go to Wayne," Mony said, "the Foundation will take care of your tuition and books. It's just that, well—they were willing to give you so much more."

Over the next few days I found myself agreeing with Mony that I should take advantage of the opportunity to go to Michigan. I didn't know much about the relative merits of the two schools. Actually they were both excellent schools. Michigan may have had a little more prestige, but it was having the experience of living on a college campus that was drawing me toward Michigan. I told my mother I had decided I should use my scholarships and go to Michigan in September. She seemed to accept this, saying only, "I still think you'd be happier at Wayne with your friends."

A day or so later, though, my mother became ill with some unexplained illness. She was in bed for nearly a week—someone who never ever missed work. Every morning when I went in to see her before going to school she looked very pale, and had no energy at all. Each day I took her breakfast to her, a soft boiled egg or oatmeal, toast and coffee, but she only ate a corner off the toast and a sip of coffee—saying she had no appetite. It worried me that she was sick for this long. She was the one who kept things going—paid the bills, cleaned the house, and provided the high morale she generated in the family—not to mention that she was the sole bread-winner. I didn't think for an instant that she was faking illness.

I could see she really was not well. But I began to suspect that the thought of my being away—even forty miles—was more than she could bear and it was making her sick.

I remembered her telling me years before that she would never have left her own home had her brother not forced her to leave. My grandfather had owned two farms and left them both to his only son, which was the custom, but with the stipulation that my mother, the only unmarried daughter, should have a home there as long as she wished. She was doing all the chores and taking care of her mother on one farm while her brother's family lived on the other. One day her brother came across the road, she told me, and said he couldn't afford to support her there any longer. She'd been devastated. She went to Toronto and took a job at Eaton's Department Store. But she was dreadfully homesick for a long, long time. Her mother did not live very long after she left. I could see that it might be hard for her to understand why I would choose to live away from my family when she had found it so painful leaving hers.

One way to find out if the thought of my leaving was making her sick, I reasoned, was to tell her that I had changed my mind and had decided to go to Wayne after all. I took another uneaten breakfast tray away that morning and came back and sat on the side of her bed. Her face looked so pale against the white pillowcase and her eyes had a lifeless look I'd never seen there before. In as casual a way as I could manage I said,

"You know, I've been thinking it over, and I think Wayne would be a better school for me. I think I'll miss Eric too much if I'm off in Ann Arbor for four years." She lifted herself up against her pillow, almost to a sitting position.

"Are you sure, Sarah—that this is what you want to do?" she asked, but her eyes, so lifeless moments before were definitely brighter.

"I'm positive. Most of my friends will be at Wayne. I can still work at Hudson's on Saturdays if I go to Wayne. I think it will be better all the way around." It wasn't a long discussion. Much of what I said was actually true. I would miss Eric enormously if I went away, and I'd miss Calvin Church and singing in the choir and my friends there. I'd miss my mother too, *and* Danny *and* my father.

"Well, I thought that you'd miss your friends if you went that far away," was all she said. Forty miles to her must have seemed a long way— too great a distance between her and me. My hunch proved to be correct. By afternoon when I came home from Cooley, my mother was feeling much better. She got up for dinner that night and the next day she went to work. The decision was settled. I couldn't go away just yet. That was "the situation."

Graduation day dawned hot and muggy. When the concert mistress sounded her "A" in the orchestra pit that morning, I realized with a start that this was the last time I would play my violin with the orchestra at Cooley High School. A wave of sadness—I might better call it grief—swept over me that made it hard to keep back my tears. I wiped them away with the sleeve of my gray graduation gown so I could see the music, and lifted my bow to start the processional march. The best period so far of my whole life was coming to an end. This was supposed to be a joyful day, but my overriding feeling was one of heaviness and sorrow. When it came time to play the recessional I could hardly see the music through my tears. My mother had taken the day off to come to the graduation. It was my good fortune that my father was home and could come too. Eric's mother had prepared a little celebration at her house. I went home with Eric for the rest of the overly warm day, while my mother went home with my father. I'm sure she thought the party at Eric's house would be too much for my father. She would have a graduation dinner for me on Sunday. That night I wrote in my diary: "It was a lovely graduation, but I should have been with my mother more."

nine

"Great Is Thy Faithfulness"

JUST BEFORE MY FRESHMAN year at Wayne University, on one of the hottest days of the summer—the mercury had topped out at 95 degrees—my mother and I arrived home from our jobs at Hudson's Department Store to find my father was not there. At this time of day he was always in the kitchen putting a delicious dinner together. His cooking was one thing besides reading the *Detroit News* he put a lot of thought and effort into, always telling us how healthy his hamburgers were with all the fat broiled out of them. My mother asked me if I had noticed that he had been talking a little fast at breakfast that morning. I hadn't wanted to alarm her, but I had noticed that he was talking faster and more than usual at breakfast. "Yes, he was talking a lot," I agreed. "He's put on weight too, which is not a good sign." We'd come to recognize that my father becoming too heavy was another sign that a hospitalization was in the offing. He always came home from the hospital bone thin, so it was only natural that he would gain weight, but if he gained too much weight we became concerned. Despite his nutritious cooking, his only exercise was his two block walk to the store two or three times a week.

Danny arrived home from his job at Cunningham's Drug Store a few minutes after we did. When we told him we didn't know where dad was his face lost its color as it usually did when anything was amiss with our father. He sank down in a chair in the kitchen. Right away he got up and suggested that he and I go outside and ask our neighbors Tom and Dorothy Mohan who were sitting on their front porch, seeking relief from the heat, if they'd seen him. Dorothy said that she usually saw him going to the store, but today she hadn't seen him at all. They were fond of my father. Sometimes they sent their two young children over in their pajamas for my parents to babysit them when they went out. "We'll keep an eye out for him if you'd like to have your supper," Tom said.

We made a cold supper of sliced tomatoes and some left over meat-loaf we found in the refrigerator.

"You'd think he'd have left a note telling us where he went," I said.

"But he never goes anywhere," Danny said. Danny seemed even more affected by this sudden disappearance than my mother and I did. He didn't want any supper—only a glass of milk. My mother often said, "Danny is not a talker." Instead, when anything troubled him he busied himself working on his car or on a drafting project for school.

Between sips of hot tea my mother said that we must go out and look for him. Even in the hottest weather she drank hot tea. I think it was a Canadian custom that especially when anything worrisome happened, you made a pot of tea. Then she said, "But first I'm going to phone Aunt Daisy and Uncle Doc to see if he might have gone to see either of them." He used to visit them all the time when Danny and I were younger and he drove a car. The phone calls gave us no further clues to where my father might have gone. They both said to let them know when we had word. I thought they should have offered to come and help us find him. But they had never offered help of any kind. I could imagine Aunt Daisy holding one of her séances and asking the spirits to tell her where my father was; but she wouldn't do anything concrete to help anymore than she would straighten up the clutter in her big house. None of his brothers or sisters ever visited my father in the hospital—or sent him as much as a carton of cigarettes. I found that a strange way for a family to behave.

My mother changed into a cotton dress. I put on some tan shorts, a light blue tee shirt, and sandals, the coolest clothes I could find. In this heat it felt good to get out of my nylons. The three of us walked down to the grocery store on Grand River Avenue—thinking that since this was the only place he ever went, if something had happened we might find some information along this route. Even though my father shopped at Kroger's super market several times a week, no one would know him well enough to remember whether he'd been there that day or not. It was too large a store. Perplexed, we came home.

Darkness fell and still no word. My mother called the police, who came and made out a missing person's report. We sat up late trying to talk, but we were really listening for the phone to ring. When we did give up and go to bed, the heat kept us from sleeping. In the morning all three of us called in to say we were taking the day off—another blistering day. We combed the surrounding streets in the used black Oldsmobile Danny had bought with his earnings from Cunningham's. Each time we saw a man in a white shirt our hopes rose, only to fall again when we came closer and the man in the white shirt was not our father.

"In all the years of your father's illness he's never disappeared like this," my mother said. She sat in the front seat where she alternately cried and then sat up straight and put her handkerchief away in a resolute manner—as if to say, "We must keep on searching." I'm sure each of us silently feared that in this heat my father could be dead. After about two hours we gave up our search by car. In the relative cool of our upper flat we called all the likely hospitals and even the City Morgue. Then, after a bite of lunch, my mother waited at home in case a call came in—this was before answering machines—while Danny and I went out again to drive around looking. We drove in ever increasing circles around the area and then retraced our path as in a labyrinth. At sixteen Danny was a good driver. I still hadn't learned to drive. After a near-accident when Eric tried to teach me, I decided that perhaps I didn't have the right temperament to drive a car.

The next morning, Thursday, my mother thought she must return to work, leaving Danny and me to continue our search. But Friday, her day off, she came with us again. Each day of waiting and searching in the heat wave that hovered over Detroit made the outcome our minds conjured up more and more chilling. We knew that suicide was a major risk with manic-depressives, but usually in the very depressed phase. We felt quite certain my father had been heading into mania two mornings ago, which in a way was reassuring. He had never become deeply depressed while he was at home—only in the hospital. We pressed on, becoming more tired and despondent by the hour.

Early on the fourth day, a Saturday, a phone call came. My father's sister-in-law in Ohio was calling. "Dan is here with Arthur and me," she said. "He came by bus." Arthur, one of my father's several older brothers, had visited us once or twice with his wife Mae, so we knew them slightly. When my mother got off the phone the three of us sat in the dining room near the phone and talked. Why would they wait so long to call us, we wondered? Our relief that he was alive and in a safe place outweighed any anger we might have felt, at least for the moment. We imagined that when he first arrived my father was able to carry it off that this was just a visit, but that as his condition worsened, Mae could see that he was seriously mentally ill and called us. She had intimated to my mother that he was "pretty high." As it turned out, he had arrived without a suitcase which should have been a clue to his state of mind.

My father's family had always found it hard to accept that he was truly mentally ill. To me they each seemed a little fragile—the ones I knew—and they were probably afraid to acknowledge that an illness of this proportion could occur in their family. Those I knew had left their Methodist upbringing and turned to the occult and other new age beliefs—the séances for Aunt Daisy, miraculous cures in his chiropractic practice for Uncle Doc, and for Aunt Kathryn, Divine Science, a group which taught that God is love and there is no sickness or evil in the world, much like Christian Science. I didn't know Uncle Arthur that well, but that he waited so long to call us suggests that he too didn't want to see the situation for what it was—that his brother was mentally ill.

My mother's job was the most important, and she had to work that day, a Saturday; so Danny and I got ready to drive to Ohio. Would Danny's car make it, we wondered? Tom Mohan had been worried that it wouldn't. Since he didn't work on Saturday, he decided he would come with us. The three of us set out in Tom's car, a much newer blue Chevrolet sedan. He was nervous about how disturbed we would find my father when we got to Ohio. "Do you think he'll come back with us willingly?" he asked my mother before we left. All the way there Tom talked of different strategies for getting him to come home. I felt relief that he'd been found. If we needed to phone the police to take him to a hospital, I knew how to do that.

Aunt Mae's directions led us to the deli-like luncheonette Uncle Arthur owned on a main street in Canton, Ohio. We opened the door and there stood my father talking to Arthur who, shorter than my father, was almost hidden behind a high counter. My father, in a wrinkled white shirt, looked glassy-eyed, flushed and sweaty, but glad to see us. In a loud voice, and with great aplomb, he introduced Tom to his brother and sister-in-law. Then he ordered coffee and pastrami sandwiches for everyone. "They're the best," he assured us. I was a little alarmed to see him so elated. Aunt Mae sent worried, sympathetic glances in my direction. Tom, who was tall and rock-jaw handsome, appeared tense as he turned his baseball cap around and around in his hands. Behind the counter Arthur silently made sandwiches for us and looked a little sheepish, or so I imagined, about waiting four days to call us.

We sat at one of the two tables to have our sandwiches and coffee. My father never sat down and ate nothing. He talked to everyone who came in—proudly introducing each customer to, "my son and my daughter, and my neighbor, Mr. Mohan." When we finished our sandwiches, however, he was ready to come home with us. There was a resigned expression on his face now that told me he knew he was going back to the hospital yet again. He gave Mae and Arthur goodbye, thanking them over and over for their hospitality and asking them to come and visit us. I got into the back seat with him and Tom turned the car around toward the highway to Detroit. Mae came to the door and waved to us, but Arthur stayed behind the counter.

On the way back my father became quiet. He looked tired. He thanked Tom for coming after him then he closed his eyes. I think he even slept a little bit. I looked out the window at the dry brown fields we passed and hoped that this hospitalization would be short. The last one had been only two months. In a couple of weeks my classes at Wayne University would begin and I had hoped he would be there when I came home so I could talk to him about my studies. Current events and intellectual issues interested him more than they did my mother and I liked to have discussions with him.

We never did find out why he took a bus to Ohio without telling us. We had become accustomed to a certain pattern in my father's illnesses. We knew that if his elevated mood went beyond a certain point, it would not turn around and another hospitalization was inevitable. As painful as this process was to us, we knew what to expect and how to handle it. His running away introduced a new element of unpredictability. We weren't sure now what other turns his illness might take.

My mother saw to it that life went on as scheduled. She made sure she kept her job at Hudson's by selling more dresses than any one else in her department. She kept our home running as smoothly as ever with clean sheets, church, and white-table-cloth Sunday dinners to which you could bring a friend. My brother began his junior year at Chadsey High School where he could study architectural drawing not available at Cooley, and I began a major in elementary education at Wayne University.

During registration at Wayne I found that subscriptions to the Detroit Symphony were available to students at very low prices. I bought two of the least expensive ones hoping Eric and I would go to the concerts together. As opening night approached, as I feared, Eric said he was too busy between studying and working at his father's gas station to even think about going to a concert. Eric did not share my love for classical music, nor had he enjoyed the double date to a play at the Schubert Theater I once arranged. Eric's chief enjoyment was fishing off his father's cabin cruiser on Lake Erie. After giving it several tries, even with him gallantly baiting my hook, I knew I would never be passionate about fishing. I told myself these differences were not important, but I *was* disappointed that he didn't enjoy music. On the morning of the concert, I told my mother I'd be late coming home because I was going to the symphony. She asked if Eric was going with me. I told her that he had too much work, that none of my friends were interested, but that I didn't mind going alone. And at that point I didn't.

"It's going to be a wonderful concert," I told her, "All Beethoven, with Zino Francescotti playing Beethoven's violin concerto."

"Sarah, I'd be glad to go with you. Just meet me downtown after work and we'll have a quick supper and go." Since I enjoyed my mother's company just as much as I enjoyed any of my friends' company, I was delighted. "I'll phone Danny and tell him," she added, "I'm sure he won't mind. He can probably have supper at his friend Dale Brown's."

That night after a supper of baked scrod, steamed spinach, and baked potatoes at Stouffer's Restaurant on Washington Boulevard, we picked up my tickets at the box office of the Masonic Temple Theater. The Symphony had been forced to move there from Orchestra Hall in 1939 because of the Depression. It was a beautiful, ornate space on Temple Avenue—and it was huge. When we went to our seats we discovered that my least expensive seats were on the side in the second row from the back of the uppermost balcony. We were early, so we were almost the only ones in this elaborately decorated concert hall that held almost two thousand people. I settled in, but I noticed that my mother seemed a little jittery. She told me that she had always had a fear of heights, something I'd not known. I looked down at the row upon row of empty brown wooden seats that stretched in front of us at a steep pitch. It did give the illusion that you could fall out of your seat and tumble right down onto the orchestra floor. After a few minutes she said, "You know, Sarah, I don't think I'm going to be able to sit here. It's such a long way down." Her voice sounded tremulous.

"I know what you mean. Do you want to leave?" I asked turning toward her. She, who had never seemed frightened of anything, had now gone completely white and was clenching the arms of her seat with both hands.

"No, I don't want you to miss this concert. Let's see if we can get orchestra seats. Since it is opening night we'll be able to see the women all dressed up." We gingerly left our seats, trying not to look down, and found our way back to the lobby. The young man in the box office told us that the orchestra seats were sold out; but then he said to wait—there might have been a cancellation. He came back with two tickets on the aisle a third of the way back. The price was higher than we had expected, but we said we'd take them.

A large number of people were now pouring into the lobby, women in long silk dresses with fur capes or stoles over their shoulders, many of the men in tuxedos. There was an excitement in the air. "I'm interested to see how the women dress for opening night," my mother whispered to me. I looked at my mother dressed in the black crepe dress she'd worn to work. With her three-string pearl choker, pearl earrings, and not a hair out of place, she looked remarkably dressed up. I wore a new purple corduroy dress that looked dressy enough, yet was one I could wear on campus all day. I decided we would pass inspection even for an opening night.

Before the concert began we whispered about which of the elegant gowns we liked, the jewelry and hairdos, trying not to be too obvious. It was well worth the price of admission to see this fashion show. Detroit's elite were all around us, I'm sure, the Fords and the Dodges, but we couldn't recognize them. Then the lights lowered and the fashion show ended with the familiar three dots and a dash of Beethoven's "Fifth Symphony."

From this seat on the aisle I had a good view of my violin teacher, Jack Bosen. His seat on the outside of the fourth desk in the first violin section told me he was now high up in the hierarchy of violinists. He had charged me only three dollars for my once-a-week lesson. I began to feel my usual pangs of guilt that I hadn't spent more time practicing with such a great teacher. This time I told myself, "Stop that and enjoy the concert." After intermission, Zino Francescotti began to play Beethoven's violin concerto. A hush fell over the audience when he came to the credenza at the end of the first movement and his fingers moved with such speed and ease up and down the neck of his violin that I could hardly see them. The program notes said that Francescotti first performed this difficult concerto when he was ten years old. In the second movement when the violin moved into a minor key, his tone was almost like a human voice. He and the conductor, Karl Krueger, had to come out three separate times for bows. I was absolutely thrilled to be there.

On the way home on the bus my mother continued to exclaim about the clothes—we both said our most favorite was the emerald green gown worn by a young woman with blond hair. "Did you notice that comb that held her hair?" I asked. "I think it had both diamonds and emeralds." As she watched all those women dressed so elegantly and usually on the arm of a man wearing a tux, my mother would have had every reason to be envious; but I didn't see any hint of that. The music had to be the best I had ever heard, and as much as it thrilled me to hear such gorgeous music, I think I enjoyed even more watching my mother have such a good time.

A few weeks later it was time for the next concert on my subscription and again I had no one to use the other ticket. The tickets were so inexpensive I didn't consider it a huge waste; but at the last minute my mother said, "Sarah, I want to go with you. I need to prove to myself that I can sit in that seat. It's ridiculous for me to be afraid of sitting there." Then she added, "Besides, we had so much fun the last time." And that is what she did. We took care not to arrive too early so that we were not the only ones in the upper balcony. This alone made it much less scary. My mother did not see herself as a fearful person. I knew, though, that a big part of her motivation to be able to sit in that seat was her desire to be with me. Our relationship—the fun we had together—seemed to give her so much pleasure. She could have fun just going for a cup of coffee with me.

During my first year at Wayne I was, so to speak, "imbedded" in my family and my "extended family." Ever since I was in tenth grade we had lived in the upper flat of the house owned by the parents of my friend Pat. Mr. and Mrs. Forbes had long known about my father's illness and did not see it as a problem—they would never ask us to move, which was a great comfort. There was constant interplay between the two families. Pat had a brother two years older than me and at the time we moved in another baby, Cathy, was born to the Forbes's. At two and three Cathy came upstairs almost daily to visit with my father, usually saying, "I smell bacey," meaning bacon. He enjoyed her visits.

On any given evening you could interest someone from the two families in going to the movies with you, or get up a group to play pinochle on the dining room table. On Sundays my mother, my brother, Pat and I always went to Calvin Church together, sometimes joined by Mrs. Forbes and even by my father on rare occasions. After church, Sunday dinner at our house was now open to whomever wished to come—my friend Ann Tittl, my brother's friend, Dale Brown, or one or more of the Forbes family. My boyfriend Eric came often. It no longer seemed to upset my father to have more people around the dinner table. He enjoyed moving quietly around the kitchen with my mother and bringing in a full gravy boat for the roast beef he'd just carved.

Wayne University soon came to feel like an adjunct to my own home. Even though I had chosen to go to Wayne largely under the pressure of my mother's need of me, I never doubted that I would like it there. How could anyone not like college? Wayne's original building, unofficially named Old Main, dated from 1894, and had a long history before becoming Wayne University. It had once been deemed an architectural marvel with its Ludowici glazed tile roof, a magnificent vestibule, terra cotta arches, maple floors, oak doors, ornate stairways and a tower clock. By the time I arrived there in 1948 the orange-yellow brick had been darkened by urban grime, and the interior showed many scuffed up signs of wear. Still I loved the wide corridors, classrooms with high ceilings, and other traces of its 19th-century beginnings. My favorite place in Old Main was a coffee shop in the basement where I would buy a cup of coffee for a nickel and a Lorna Doone cookie for a penny, find a broken desk-chair nearby and sit and read *The Detroit Collegian* or study for an exam. This spot had a cave-like quality with large metal pipes running overhead. Its charm was that it *had* no charm.

The two other classroom buildings, State Hall and the Science Building, were brand new, but to me they seemed cold and uninspiring compared to Old Main. A block further down Cass Avenue was Webster Hall, a rundown hotel the university purchased to serve as a Student Center. The outside was still rundown, but the interior had been renovated and now housed a cafeteria, a student health center, departmental offices, several comfortable lounges that made good places to study, and a few meeting rooms. On the upper floors were Wayne's only dorm rooms for out-of-town students. In the basement of Webster Hall was Wayne's only swimming pool, lined and surrounded with ornate jade green tile, elegance of a bygone era. On most days I found time to go for a quick swim. This mismatched assortment, spread over four city blocks, with a few grassy patches around the two newer buildings, and some nearby mansions the University purchased for extra office and classroom space, comprised the campus. Never having seen the glories of the University of Michigan campus and the lovely college town of Ann Arbor, I thought Wayne's campus was just fine.

From the first day of classes at Wayne, however, I began to notice something I had never experienced at Cooley High School. The note in my diary reads:

> September 20, 1948. I went to my classes for the first time. My Sociology teacher talks like a Communist, but isn't. My English teacher looks my age, and my German teacher is a nice big German man. Eric is in my German class.

Wayne was sometimes referred to in the Detroit newspapers as a "hot bed of Communism." Two faculty members had been dismissed for supposed Communist leanings. Students protested their dismissal, but not outrageously. As for me, the political unrest didn't worry me. Like my parents I was a liberal Roosevelt-Democrat, and agreed that speakers from all political perspectives should be allowed to speak on campus. But the anti-religious views that often went hand in hand with the liberal political views did trouble me. It was subtle, but in little side comments, or perhaps in what they didn't say, I began to realize that most of my instructors and professors were either agnostics or atheists. The instructor in sociology appeared to agree with Marx about religion being an "opiate of the people." In my psychology course the young instructor was a behaviorist, and religion had no part in that system. He could explain everything about human nature with stimulus-response theory. In a speech someone gave in my persuasive speech class I first learned that Freud viewed religion as "an illusion," and felt that a mentally healthy person would abandon such beliefs. That many of my teachers shared the views of Marx and Freud and disparaged religion came as a bewildering surprise to me. I feared that the people I considered the "Intelligentsia," the smart people of this world, considered the Christianity I had grown up with on a par with a fairy tale.

I still found time to go to all the services at Calvin Church and to the Christian Endeavor group. That there were many highly intelligent people at Calvin was of some comfort. Our young minister, Roger Mc-Shane, whom I considered an intelligent man, was a graduate of Princeton Seminary. In his sermons he sometimes contrasted the atheistic beliefs of Communism to Christian beliefs, so I knew he was aware of Karl Marx. But I saw for the first time that a large part of the culture, at least at Wayne University, did not share my belief in God—Luther's Mighty Fortress, who had become my fortress too—and this posed some difficult questions. Who was right? They couldn't all be right.

My teachers' agnosticism or atheism opened up other questions. I didn't lie awake at night over these issues, but I'd be brushing my teeth and find myself wondering, "If there is no God, then why *are* we here?" Or, I'd ask myself, "What is the purpose of life if God does *not* exist?" In my persuasive speech course I gave a speech arguing that a belief in God was essential to finding purpose in life—only to be rebutted the following week by a student from the newly formed state of Israel who argued just as ably that God was not necessary to his finding a purpose in life—building the state of Israel gave him purpose enough. I wouldn't say my security was crumbling, but it felt extremely threatened. All the hymns I sang with such confidence, all the prayers to God to bring my father home, all the sermons I had heard, were they all about nothing? Throughout this year at Wayne there were things I had always known, that although I made no conscious connection to them at the time, I'm sure heightened this inner turmoil—I would call them "the un-thought known"—things such as, *My father said he became an agnostic at the University of Buffalo.*

By spring there had been several student demonstrations protesting the administration's refusal to allow certain Communist-leaning speakers to speak on campus. The administration feared that too much public disapproval would undermine community support. The University was growing rapidly and it desperately needed public funding. The demonstrations were peaceful. A group of students would gather around a spokesperson standing on a box with a megaphone in one of the few green spaces on campus. The protesters made banners and carried signs. Articles in the *Detroit Collegian* argued that students' rights were being violated by these refusals to let them bring certain speakers to campus, also First Amendment rights. In response the Political Science Department sponsored an essay contest on Students' Rights.

When my English instructor made the contest an option in place of one of our themes, I decided to give it a try. I went to the library in Old Main and looked up what I could find on students' rights—there wasn't much. But at a meeting in Webster Hall where both sides debated, the issues became much clearer to me. That night when I sat down at the desk in my room with a cup of coffee, the essay practically wrote itself. A few weeks later I rushed into English class late. My instructor, a very young-looking witty woman with blond curly hair, was sitting on top of her desk in a bright red dress, swinging her legs. I got there just in time to hear her say in a coy voice, "I suppose by now you've read in the *Collegian* that someone in our class won the essay contest." I stumbled into my seat and was astounded to read in the *Collegian* of the person sitting next to me that I had indeed won the first prize of $35 for my essay. "Congratulations," she said, pointing to me, and the class applauded.

That afternoon I swam in the jade green pool and relished most of all the thought of telling my mother about winning the essay contest. When I got home that night and told her, she was happy for me and said she was proud of me, but I'm not sure she ever read the essay. My father was still in the hospital. He for sure would have read it.

On Sunday our friend Mony came for dinner and asked to read my essay. I had argued that a university had to balance preserving its purpose as a source of truth and enlightenment with the need to secure enough public funds to stay afloat. The real question, I said, was how many degrees of freedom can you give up before you undermine your purpose as a source of truth and enlightenment altogether? I must have been aware at some level of the balancing act going on in my own life—balancing my obligations to my mother, to Eric, and to myself. How many degrees of freedom could *I* give up without sinking myself altogether?

"This is well-written," Mony said. "And I agree with your thesis." Coming from Mony, who ran the board meetings for the Student Aid Foundation on which sat seven or eight high-level Detroit executives, those words were important to me. Mony was indeed an intellectual, which is the only thing my mother was not. My mother was extremely intelligent, but I couldn't share much about what I was studying with her. She didn't have time to read or she might actually have enjoyed discussing what I was learning. I recalled how she used to like to read from her huge volume of poetry, the book with Gray's, "Elegy Written in a Country Church Yard."

Along with my mother, Eric was still a constant in my life. One night we had studied German until late in the evening in the library at Wayne and then he drove me home. We sat in his car in front of my house. He was talking about the long hours his father worked and how he worried about his mother being alone so much.

"Don't I know! You work a lot too," I said. "What will it be like for us?" He ignored my little dig, and moved out from behind the steering wheel, turned to me and said tenderly, "Oh, it will be totally different. We'll be some place like Northern Rhodesia and we'll be working together to help the people there." Eric's eyes took on that dreamy look they always had when he talked about his future as a missionary doctor. He put his arm around me and kissed me softly on the mouth. I kissed him back and nestled my head into the firm muscles of his shoulder. "Of course you'll be taking care of the little ones, but I'll help you when I finish doctoring." In the light shed by the streetlight I saw the mischievous grin on his face.

"While you're doctoring, I'm going to be teaching. Remember?"

"Not when they're small you won't. That wouldn't be good for them." He tweaked my nose, but I knew he was serious. I didn't want to hear again what Saint Paul said in Ephesians about wives being submissive to their husbands. We had debated that issue and I totally disagreed with him. I let the matter drop and asked how many little ones he saw in this vision of the future. I told him I had always wished there'd been more than just Danny and me.

"Two's not nearly enough," he said. We kissed again.

"As a kid I sometimes picked out names for six girls and six boys before I went to sleep," I told him.

"Twelve's a bit much. I was thinking more like—oh, maybe five kids?"

"Our kids will be so great, Eric. Let's try for seven." I'd been born on the seventh day of the seventh month and weighed seven pounds and seven ounces, so I liked sevens.

He thought a moment. "Seven sounds good." And with that we settled into some serious necking. I wasn't sure how we were going to resolve this question of wives being submissive to their husbands. And the idea of my not working while the children were young—that was a problem.

Yet I don't think it was these differences that made me catch my breath whenever Eric spoke seriously about our being married. It was something more—but I couldn't grasp what—something frightening—another unthought known, perhaps—*When I grow up I'm going to have babies, but no daddy.*

Out of the blue during spring semester Mony invited me to have dinner with her at the the Women's City Club, a private club downtown where she had a membership. I loved being with Mony, and this would be the first time we ever had dinner alone. When we met in the lobby she was wearing a pale blue suit that matched her eyes. She looked beautiful with her prematurely white hair framing her face in short fluffy curls. To me Mony was like a thoroughbred race horse—light, quick, high spirited, and exquisitely sensitive. She was also very smart. We went up a flight of stairs to an elegant dining room—tables with ivory colored tablecloths, each with a little lamp that made for a warm, quiet atmosphere. A hostess showed us to a table on the side. Mony looked over the menu and ordered the turkey dinner, so I chose the same.

For a time we chatted about my classes at Wayne. I figured there must be a reason Mony had wanted to talk to me and I was right.

"How do you feel now about not going to Michigan?" she asked me. I told her that I felt okay about it, that Wayne was great, and that I was totally enjoying it.

"Your mother's a wonderful woman, Sarah, but with working and taking care of your father, she's had no time to develop her own life." I slowly buttered my Parker House roll before I told Mony that I had never thought of it that way before—that she had no life of her own. Inwardly I thought that my brother and I, and my father, were her life. And her job—she enjoyed her work—she did have a life of her own.

"She enjoys being with your father when he can be home, but they don't go out as a couple and have friends over the way they used to. I went to some very good parties at your parents' before your dad became ill."

"I know. Do you remember how I wouldn't go to bed until the last guest had left?'

"I do. You were a party-girl at a young age." Mony smiled as if remembering those parties. Then her voice became serious again and she went back to the point she was making. "Your mother's life has changed so much. I'm afraid she's come to depend on you and Danny as her main source of companionship."

"Isn't that only natural?" I asked her. I felt I needed to defend my mother. I couldn't bear to think there was anything she did wrong. To me she was perfect.

"It's understandable. But it would also be understandable for you to feel some resentment about the way she kept you from going to the University of Michigan. It wouldn't mean you don't love her, you know." Mony looked at me very intently, as if trying to find something she couldn't find.

"I honestly don't resent it, Mony. It was what she had to do. She's had a hard time with my father's many hospitalizations, and yet she's been so good to Danny and me. I can't imagine how she does all that she does."

"Why shouldn't she be good to you? You're her daughter!" There was something in the definite way Mony said this that just for an instant made me want to cry. Yes, I am her daughter. Why does that seem like a new thought to me? "The way she has managed everything is admirable, Sarah, but it doesn't mean you owe her your life."

"I guess I never thought about it that way. I honestly don't feel resentful though."

"I just wanted you to feel free to express it if you did."

"I do feel free, honestly. I would tell you if I had regrets about not going to Michigan." We went back to our turkey dinners. which were getting cold. I was hungry and ate every bit of my turkey and the dark red cranberry sauce.

The waiter took our plates and we ordered dessert—blueberry pie ala mode, small servings, and coffee.

"Do you think you want to marry Eric?" Mony asked—second topic.

I was pretty sure I did, and I told her that.

"The reason I'm asking is I hope you don't wait until he's out of medical school. That's just too long."

"That sounds wonderful, not waiting that long," I said, but my inner thought was, *that would be impossible.* I looked around. The dining room was completely filled with well-dressed professionals, mostly women. We finished our coffee. It had been a wonderful evening for me. Mony, who lived downtown, walked me to my bus.

At home that night I recorded the whole conversation with Mony in my diary, and ended with, "I had such a good time tonight. Mony is so understanding and makes everything seem very hopeful." Was I saying, she seemed to understand the complicated relationship I had with my mother, and still she felt hopeful that I could leave and marry Eric? But why did I have that immediate inner thought, "*that would be impossible*"? I didn't know—but my unconscious must have known that, *If I can't go 40 miles away to the University of Michigan how can I go to Africa?*

On a Friday towards the end of this first year at Wayne I was studying in a lounge on the fourth floor of the Student Center, a place with soft comfortable chairs and couches. I had spread out my books on the coffee table and was curled up with my sociology book when all of a sudden I was aware of a hymn being sung—a group of people were singing a hymn. Hymns—in this Godless University? It was not a hymn I knew, but it was unmistakably a hymn. I gathered up my books and followed the sound around a corner and down a corridor to where I found a group of students in a conference room, identified by a sign outside as "Wayne Christian Fellowship." A nice-looking young fellow at the door smiled and handed me an open hymnbook. I went in and took a seat. "Great is Thy Faithfulness" is the hymn they were singing. It was stirring:

> Great is Thy faithfulness, O God, my Father.
> There is no shadow of turning with Thee.
> Thou changest not, Thy compassions they fail not;
> As Thou hast been Thou forever wilt be.

The group sang the chorus with so much strength and conviction.

> Great is Thy faithfulness! Great is Thy faithfulness!
> Morning by morning new mercies I see;
> All I have needed, Thy hand has provided.
> Great is Thy faithfulness, Lord, unto me.

Next they sang an even more beautiful hymn, "O the Deep, Deep Love of Jesus," designated as an old Welsh melody by the young man leading the singing. I later learned his name was Gil Hunter. This hymn was in a minor key and I loved it—another one I had never heard before:

> O the deep, deep love of Jesus,
> Vast, unmeasured, boundless, free;
> Rolling as a mighty ocean
> In its fullness over me.

Underneath me, all around me,

Is the current of Thy love;

Leading onward, leading homeward,

To my glorious rest above.

This group clearly loved to sing—there must have been forty or forty-five students here. A few announcements were made about when the small group Bible studies were meeting the next week, and then the speaker was introduced, a physician in the area who looked to be in his fifties. He spoke on how to balance one's spiritual life with one's academic life and stressed making time for prayer and the reading of Scripture each morning, telling how he found time to do this in his busy schedule as a physician. I was pleased to see that he seemed to have a very good mind, and still believed in God. The thought of a small group Bible study appealed to me too. I had been given a Bible when I was confirmed in the Lutheran Church, but I had never read much of it. I found the King James Version difficult to understand when I started with Genesis and soon gave up. After the meeting several students introduced themselves to me and invited me to come back. I had already decided I would return the following Friday.

In what remained of the semester, on Fridays I found myself returning to the Wayne Christian Fellowship meeting. I loved the hymns they sang from the Intervarsity hymnal, *Hymns*, compiled by a wonderful hymnologist, Paul Beckwith, and I liked the students. The speakers too, some clergy but mostly lay people, were unusually good. Eric came to one or two meetings, but he was usually too busy trying to get As in all his courses so he could get into medical school, and still meet his father's demands at the gas station.

I became friends with one young woman in the group, Muriel Hunt, and we sometimes talked about religious questions. She was a very serious Christian. I counted myself a serious Christian too, but the students in this group were even more serious. They spoke openly about their faith, whereas even at Calvin Church it would be unusual for a young person to speak very personally about his or her faith.

I came to like these students in Wayne Christian Fellowship more and more. It puzzled me though when some of them talked about Christ as though they actually knew him—as if they had just had a conversation with him. When I was a small child I used to talk to Jesus all the time, but

I had not been in the habit of doing this as an adult, although I did pray to God. One boy in the group, for example, said, "I have to choose a major soon and I'm praying for the Lord to show me whether it should be history or philosophy. I think he wants me in the ministry eventually." I was astounded that he thought God could give him guidance in such specific choices. Most of these students seemed to be on an inside track with God that I couldn't get on. This troubled me as much, or even more, than the agnostic professors troubled me. I wondered if perhaps they were the real Christians and I wasn't a Christian at all. Still, I never missed a meeting on Friday where I could sing hymns such as "Be Still My Soul," written by Katharina von Schlegel and set to Sibelius's stirring music:

> Be still, my soul: the Lord is on thy side;
> Bear patiently the cross of grief or pain;
> Leave to thy God to order and provide;
> In every change He faithful will remain.
> Be still, my soul: thy best, thy heavenly Friend
> Through thorny ways leads to a joyful end.

I was both comforted and disturbed by these meetings where I found such unwavering faith. What did it say about me—and my faith?

ten

1949—When the Music Stopped

MY FIRST YEAR AT Wayne University had ended and I had a respectable 3.7 grade point average. Academics were fun for me as long as I avoided math and science. As I began my sixth summer working at the J. L. Hudson Company, I was able to advance from a lowly stock clerk to the lofty position of salesperson. Selling carried the incentive of a 1 percent commission and was infinitely more interesting than stock work. My mother and I still took the bus together downtown every day, most mornings stopping at Greenfield's for a second cup of coffee and our beloved French crullers. We then competed to see who could sell the most merchandise by the end of the day. Usually she won. Unless I went to the outdoor symphony concert or went out with friends from work, we rode home together.

That summer my mother and I took a week's vacation and went by bus to visit her brother John, who had become so depressed that he was in a mental hospital in Lindsey, Ontario. I was shocked that anyone in my mother's family could need a mental hospital. They had always seemed so hardy. This was my mother's only brother, the one who inherited both of their father's farms, and who made her leave her home on one of these farms as a young woman. My mother was convinced that John's wife, Aunt Maggie, had forced him to do this. Maggie could be quite cruel to John from what my mother had observed. For my part I had always liked Uncle John. Seeing him now, gaunt and thin, and so depressed he could barely speak to us, I felt very sorry for him. We stayed with my mother's favorite cousin, Gilbert—a warm bear of a man—who with his wife Mamie still farmed and had adult children at home around my age, Ross and Betty Jean. They made sure I had a good time.

During our visit celebrations were underway for Canada's Independence Day on the 1st of July. The night of the 1st I went with two of my second cousins, Mary and Betty Jean, to a street dance in Fenelon Falls, the small town nearest the farm where my mother had grown up—a picturesque place I had known my whole childhood. Uncle Harve, married to my mother's sister Flora, had a butcher shop on the main street and several times our family had stayed at their comfortable white frame house just off the main street that had enough bedrooms for everyone.

We hadn't been at the street dance long when a tall, very Canadian-looking young man—that is, tall, slender, clean-cut, and serious—asked me to dance. He was actually very good looking. Between dances I learned that his name was Don Milne, that he'd just finished his first year at the University of Toronto's School of Social Work, and that he was counseling for the summer at nearby Camp Kagawong.

This was a square dance and with the many square dances the Christian Endeavor group had held at Calvin Church, I'd become an accomplished square dancer. So was Don Milne. We danced together the entire night, the "swing your partners" and "do-si-dos" becoming more wild and jubilant as the night wore on. Several times his fellow counselors tried to drag him away, but he refused to leave. When the dance was over, he asked for my address, which I gave to him. A chance meeting with someone I'd probably never see again did not seem a disloyalty to Eric. Two days after we arrived home I received an eighteen-page letter from Don, which I answered in a friendly way, not giving it much more thought. I had to admit that I'd had a lot of fun with him. I did enjoy his letter, which recounted in interesting detail his social work studies, his cello and piano playing, and his family life with his parents and two younger brothers. Like me, he lived with his parents and commuted to his courses at the University of Toronto.

The remainder of the summer, working at Hudson's, I spent as much time as I could with Pat, since she was going to leave in September for Alma College in upstate Michigan. I had a twinge of jealousy over her going away. I even talked with Mony mid-year about possibly transferring to Alma, a small Presbyterian College, but Mony thought I'd receive a better education at Wayne and advised against it. Mostly I feared I would miss Pat terribly. We'd been the closest of friends for seven years now. With Eric working so much at his father's gas station, I had more than enough time to do things with Pat—we went to movies and outdoor symphony concerts, just hung out and talked, or played violin and piano together. She had a sense of humor that kept me from taking things too seriously. I could talk about anything with Pat, and I would miss that.

For reasons I don't understand, after keeping a diary for five-and-a-half years, in early August, August 9 to be exact, I suddenly stopped writing anything in my diary. On September 11, the day Pat left for college, I wrote one last entry—and after that nothing. This last entry was cheerful enough. It was Sunday. I hugged Pat goodbye, gave her a gift of some jazzy stationery to write letters home and to me, and helped put all her stuff in the car. Pat and her mother took off for their long drive to Alma College and I went to church with my mother and Ann Tittl, a good friend from Cooley High School who had begun coming to Calvin with me. I noted in this diary entry that Roger McShane's sermon was on "Christian Optimism," then wrote, "I could use some of that," but I've no idea what I meant by that. The rest of this entry recounts a particularly fun-filled day. We had the usual Sunday dinner my parents always prepared, with Danny's friend Dale, Mr. Forbes, and Pat's little sister Cathy as guests. That afternoon I went to a Student Aid Foundation tea at Wayne's Student Center where I talked to Mony. At the Christian Endeavor meeting that evening I agreed to be co-chairman of the worship committee for the coming year, and after the evening service the Christian Endeavor group had a party at Bob Alexander's, my former boyfriend's, where we made milkshakes and played charades. Of this party I say, "We had loads of fun,"—then no more entries after that.

By all accounts, until this point in time that summer, I seem to have been my normal self—outgoing and able to have a good time as witnessed by the street dance in Canada and the enjoyable evening at Bob's house. But why did I did stop writing in my diary?

Then just after Labor Day, but before classes began at Wayne, Eric took several days off from his job at his father's gas station to go fishing with a couple of his friends and invited my brother to go along. The afternoon they returned, I found Danny sprawled on the studio couch in the dining room, his head on one of the backrests he was using as a pillow. He looked particularly glum. I asked him what was wrong. Never one to complain, Danny just shrugged his shoulders and gave me an unconvincing grin. "You don't look like someone just back from a great vacation," I pressed him.

He gathered his long slender body into a sitting position. I sat down beside him. "Okay, it wasn't great. I didn't know these other two guys at all, and Eric spent all his time out in a row boat with this girl—but it's not a big deal."

"I'm sorry—and surprised. Normally Eric is pretty sensitive to people's feelings." I put my hand on his shoulder.

"I know he is. I was surprised too. But don't worry, I'll get over it. It just wasn't the vacation I thought it would be, and I needed a good vacation." He stood up, replaced the backrest, and said, "I'm going to take a shower." That ended the discussion. Danny was such a sweet kid. He'd been a tease when he was younger, but as a teenager I can't think of him ever doing anything mean. He loaned me money, he drove me places since I still didn't drive and he had a car.

That evening Eric came over. When he came up the stairs I saw that he was dressed up—shirt, tie, blazer, his blondish brown hair combed back in its attractive pompadour—as if he planned for us to do something special after his four days away. His soft brown eyes looked happy to see me as he gave me a long warm kiss and seemed not to notice me stiffen. I led him down to the front porch, a place we often went to talk because it was private. The glider belonging to the Forbes creaked with age as we settled into it. Normally I'd be snuggled up next to him, but this night I sat at the far end of the glider. Immediately I brought up the story of the girl in the rowboat, and in a voice I hardly recognized as my own because it sounded so firm, I said, "I don't want to see you again—ever."

In the remaining daylight I saw his look of shocked disbelief. "You can't possibly mean that. That girl's fifteen years old. She's a kid. She wanted to learn to fish. There was nothing romantic about it, I swear." He held up his hand as if taking an oath.

"I don't care *how* old she is. I don't want to see you anymore." I sounded even more adamant.

"I'm really sorry Danny didn't have a good time. I want to apolo—"

"This has nothing to do with Danny," I interrupted him. "It has to do with us. You've been distant for some time now—this just clinches it."

He put his head in his hands. Through his fingers he said, "Sarah, please don't do this. I love you. Don't throw away all that has happened between us." I said I was sorry, but that my mind was made up. I didn't actually *feel* sorry as I looked at him hunched over on the other side of the glider. I didn't feel anything.

Then Eric sat up. His voice sounded pleading. "I feel closer to you than I've felt to anyone in my life. Think about all our plans for the future, our talks about children and going to Africa."

I pushed the glider slightly with my foot and it creaked as usual. He was right. I hadn't thought about these things at all. I was as surprised as Eric at what I was doing—that I was turning away from all the warm exciting feelings I had had for him. All I knew was: *I simply had to do it.*

He moved closer and put his arm around me, but I pushed it away. What I was doing didn't make any sense. I knew that. But I also knew that nothing he could say would change my mind. I believed Eric about the girl—that he wanted to teach her to fish. He was such an avid fisher-man he would gladly teach anyone to fish. The girl in the rowboat was a trumped up reason I was using to break up with him because I didn't have a real reason.

After an hour of trying to talk to me, Eric stood up. He looked completely bewildered as he felt for his car keys, then he walked down the front steps. I thought I saw tears in his eyes but I couldn't be sure. By now it was dark. I knew I was hurting him, perhaps dreadfully, and yet I couldn't even feel bad about that. The whole scene had a feeling of unreality. It happened suddenly, unexpectedly. I didn't plan it. Everything about if felt strange. It was unlike me to seize control in this way. It was as though I were an actor in my own play and these were the lines I was compelled to say, but I didn't know why I was saying them. At the same time I felt very strong. I had no doubt that what I had just done was the right thing to do. *I simply had to do it.*

After Eric left I sat on the porch for a little while—thinking. The girl in the row boat was a ruse. That was clear. Even his neglect of my brother wasn't reason enough to abruptly end a relationship that had been this good—especially on a first offense. It's not as if I'd been thinking about breaking up with Eric. I hadn't—at least not consciously. But suddenly I knew it was something I had to do. It wasn't like me to make snap deci-sions. I remembered when I broke up with Bob, my first high school boy-friend, in order to see Eric. I had anguished for weeks beforehand, and for months afterwards it troubled me that I had hurt him. But I couldn't even feel bad about doing this to Eric. I felt a coldness I'd never known before. I went upstairs, but avoided my parents who were still in the kitchen finishing the dinner dishes. I would tell them about Eric later.

Eric came to my house every night for the next several nights—almost a week—to try to persuade me to change my mind. The two of us sat on the studio couch in the dining room while I repeated over and over what I had said before, that I didn't want to see him. Each time he gave up after a few minutes and left. Finally I asked my mother to go to the door and tell him I didn't want to talk about this any more, and for a time he stopped coming. I'm not sure how my parents viewed this sudden change of direction. Eric had been very good to them. Many times he had taken them with us for a picnic when he and I went swimming at one of the nearby lakes. They'd become fond of him. But they didn't try to offer an opinion on this, if they even had one. My stance was so strong it would have intimidated anyone who tried to dissuade me.

A few days after I broke up with Eric it was time to register for classes. I went down to Wayne University and changed my major from elementary education to pre-med—Eric's major. Since I wasn't going to go with Eric as a missionary to Africa, then I would be the doctor and go myself. I was afraid the adviser I spoke with would look at my high school transcript and see that math and science were not my strong suit. He was a pleasant, efficient young man, however, who never inquired about my reasons for this radical change. In minutes I was registered for the full pre-med requirements: chemistry, zoology, math, and a second year of German. Chemistry and physics were the only subjects in high school where I couldn't count on an A. In pre-med, I would need those As to get into medical school, but this didn't worry me. I was riding high on my decision to go to medical school. I'd never known any women who had done this, but I was sure I could succeed. I felt proud of my decision to go to Africa alone. In fact, I felt very powerful.

Feeling powerful did not last long, however. Before classes started I received an invitation to a picnic that the Wayne Christian Fellowship was holding in a park outside Detroit. I had been glad to find this group of devout Christians on campus last spring and had made several good friends there. Now, all of a sudden, I felt uneasy about going to this gathering. I didn't feel like talking to anyone. Had my friend Muriel Hunt not phoned me and offered to pick me up, I would not have gone. On the long drive to the picnic I could think of hardly anything to say to Muriel. Normally she and I could talk endlessly. We arrived at the park where some members of the group were already roasting hot dogs over a fire. The air smelled of fall and burning wood. It had been a chilly, overcast day and the fire felt good. Steven Friend, a fellow I had come to like very much, came up and handed me a freshly pared stick for roasting a hot dog.

"Did you have a good summer, Sarah?" he asked me, his voice full of good cheer. In a muffled voice, even though I had had a very good summer, I just told him. "It was all right." I felt frozen. He started telling me funny stories about things that happened at the camp where he'd worked all summer, but I couldn't concentrate long enough to catch the humor. When I didn't respond with more than, "uh huh," a few times, and didn't laugh at the appropriate places, he looked puzzled. Finally, he gave me a friendly pat on my shoulder and walked off. The whole night was like that. I was weirdly quiet. When someone offered me a cup of hot cocoa I could barely say, "Thank you."

We sang hymns around the fire and I could blend in a little better, but as much as I had always been crazy about group singing, this night I experienced no pleasure in it at all. Music had always thrilled me or comforted me, especially hymns, but this night, it was as if the music had stopped for me. I couldn't hear it over the din of my own thoughts. All I wanted was to get home to my own room where I could try to figure out what was happening to me. My experience at this gathering was altogether foreign to me. My whole life I had enjoyed being with people—almost above anything else—now suddenly I could barely stand it. Something inside me had begun to unravel—and this was the first time I was fully aware of it. When I was breaking up with Eric and changing my major, I felt extremely confident; but tonight I felt frightened. It felt like when the summer sky suddenly turns dark and you know a bad storm is coming and run for cover. I wanted to run to the cover of my home, my room. I couldn't tell anyone about any of this. I didn't have words for it. Muriel and I drove home in almost complete silence. When I got out of her car I managed some words of apology for being so quiet. I told her I hadn't been feeling very well.

Classes began and I attended all of them—but by now it was not surprising to me that I couldn't concentrate in any of them. In zoology lab we were identifying different organisms under a microscope. To me they all looked the same. I couldn't focus long enough to see the difference between the cross-section of an earthworm and say—protozoa. Even while I was looking through the microscope, my mind would slide off into some frightening thought—such as, "I don't seem to really care about anybody." I was trying to memorize the symbols for elements in chemistry when that same thought came again, that I really *didn't* care about anyone—not Eric, or Pat, or my brother, not even my mother and father. The more I thought about it the more I knew I really didn't love *anyone*. I seemed incapable. A few days later I was reviewing some German vocabulary in the library when I found myself thinking that if I can't love anyone, I must be a particularly bad person who will never be able to do any good in the world. I tried to learn just three German verbs, *bedeuten, besuchen,* and *bezahlen*, to signify, to visit, and to pay, but these meanings became all jumbled up with the thought that I'd never ever do any good in the world. My life would never have a purpose.

My blue and white bedroom at the back of the house was a serene quiet place. At night I sat at the small mahogany desk I had purchased with my first paychecks from Hudson's and tried to force my mind to stay on the subject of chemistry. The new thick textbook with its sterile white letters on a hard black cover felt heavy in my hands as I held it open to the first chapter. Chemistry had never interested me in high school, and now it was torture to try to understand it.

I finished reading the first paragraph and realized that I had comprehended absolutely nothing. I reread the paragraph and the same thing happened. I had been thinking about Eric the whole time and how I didn't feel anything for him. I knew this same feeling of indifference now extended to my mother and father, and to Pat and Danny—all the people closest to me. Initially this was the problem that frightened me the most—my lack of feeling for those I used to love so passionately. But soon this led to the added meaning that I was therefore a very bad, or even an *evil* person.

When I couldn't shake these thoughts long enough to read a single paragraph in a textbook, it made me wonder *what is happening to my mind*. I could no longer control my thoughts or direct my attention to anything else. At dinner with my parents and Danny, my mind was still focused on my lack of feeling for other people. To me this meant that I was not a good human being. All I said at dinner were things like, "Please pass the salt." Before now I had been the most talkative person in the family. Yet nobody remarked on my being so quiet. I'm sure my family just didn't know what to make of these changes in me, or how to respond, so they said nothing.

Eric made another attempt to see me. By then my feelings about the breakup had changed significantly. We sat in the living room, I on the couch and he in a nearby chair. I whispered because I didn't want my parents, who were in the kitchen, to hear me when I told him, "You must save yourself, Eric. Don't you realize that I will never be able to be anyone's wife, or even anyone's girlfriend, because I just can't love anyone?" He looked completely confused, so I tried again. "Breaking up with you had nothing to do with the girl in the rowboat. It's something much deeper than that. It's simply that I'll never be able to marry you or anyone because I can't love anyone."

All he said was, "Sarah, I don't understand what's come over you. You're not making any sense." He got up to leave. What I told him made perfect sense to me. It was what I knew to be true. I walked him to the door. I had a feeling he wouldn't try to see me again. *If I can't go 40 miles away to Ann Arbor . . .*

My feeling that I couldn't love anyone, and therefore was a totally bad person, began to make me wonder if I might go to hell when I died. The more I thought about it, and I thought about it all the time, the more convinced I became that when I died I would for certain wind up in hell. It seemed inevitable. In class I tried to appear as if everything was all right, but it was very hard to smile in the face of this new certainty I'd come to have about hell. I ran into my friend Ann Tittl in the hallway of State Hall one day and managed a quick, "Hi," then rushed on as if I were in a great hurry so I wouldn't have to talk to her. In zoology class that afternoon I was looking through the microscope when my mind slid off into the frightening thought, *what is it going to be like in hell?* I had never heard anything about hell at Calvin Church, or even at the Lutheran Church. At Calvin they talked about God only as a loving being who welcomed everyone into his care. I wouldn't have liked a church that preached hell-fire and brimstone, although I knew these churches existed—probably from brief snatches I heard while surfing radio channels.

The fears I had now were totally different from the religious confusion I had known the year before at Wayne University. Back then I was raising questions people usually asked at my age: "Why are we here?" and

"What is the purpose of life—especially if there is no God?" Those questions were unsettling to me, but not frightening. I knew I wasn't alone in asking them, and felt sure that in time I would sort them out. These new concerns had to do with me, the kind of person I'd become. They haunted me. In a sermon once, I had heard that Saint Paul wrote in one of his epistles that he was the chief of sinners; but I knew now that he was wrong. I was worse than he ever thought of being. I knew Saint Paul had become a good person who wrote large sections of the New Testament, but I could not find any good in me.

Every night after supper I sat at my desk and tried to study, but it was always the same. I couldn't get through the first paragraph without my mind going to these inescapable thoughts. When I gave up and went to bed the thoughts kept me awake. I lay with my blue chenille bedspread pulled up to my chin, staring into the darkness. Eventually I saw the first gray light of dawn begin to filter through my sheer white curtains. Then I got up and went to school. After a few nights of lying awake, I thought perhaps it was good that I couldn't sleep. With the whole night ahead of me, surely I should be able to *think* my way out of this problem—the problem of going to hell. I began with what I called the basic premise, "I am a bad person," and then tried to find some logical approach to altering this or to disprove it. I tried to remember the way we learned to use logic in my philosophy course the year before to prove or disprove a thesis. When morning came I hadn't reached a second step in my attempt at a logical solution. My thinking was too fragmented for me to remember anything I had learned in my philosophy course.

Two-and-a half weeks into the semester I still went to every class, but it was becoming more and more difficult to hide how detached I was from it all. The only thing I thought about now was how to get out of going to hell. Nothing else mattered if I couldn't figure this out. I avoided talking to classmates and professors, especially in lab where the teaching assistant tried to help us with our microscope and our drawings. My drawings were so inaccurate I hid them when the TA came around. Still, nobody knew. I just looked tired from not having slept—and very distracted.

My remaining common sense told me I would never pass my courses under these conditions—no sleep, unable to take in anything that I read or heard. I must have slept some, but it felt like I was awake all night, for several nights. Only my own thoughts seemed real to me—that is, seemed at all important. I had to figure out how to get out of this pit of badness. Hell loomed as an ever present threat. But in the meantime, I knew I would have to drop out of school for a while—maybe forever. I couldn't imagine myself ever returning to school and enjoying it as I had in the past.

My parents were still drinking their tea in the kitchen after supper when I went to tell them I wanted to leave school. Our kitchen was a cheerful place. Autumn sunlight still filtered through the white curtains flecked with red on the windows behind my parents. I had to tell them that night. Tomorrow was the last day I could withdraw from my courses without penalty and I did not want to waste the tuition. I was on a scholarship from the Faculty Wives Club this year, which made me feel doubly guilty about withdrawing. I thought about that day last June when I went for the interview—as I crossed Cass Avenue on my way to Webster Hall I knew I looked like a probable winner in my powder blue dress with white eyelet sleeves. I had always looked like the proverbial "girl next door" with my long brown hair and blue-green eyes—the sweet young thing you'd want your son to marry—but it was so deceptive, I realized now. How I wished the Faculty Wives had chosen someone else.

In the kitchen I told my parents as casually as I could, "I've decided not to continue in school just now." I knew my father wouldn't object, but I was surprised that my mother didn't even question this decision. They had to have been aware that something very strange was going on with me—something was seriously wrong. My mother said only, "What will you do instead?" as if I had just said I wasn't going to the movies that night, but her eyes looked tense and her thin lips formed a straight line—her worried look. My father didn't say a word. I felt relieved that they weren't going to try to persuade me to stay in school.

After thinking a few seconds I said the first thing that came to mind, "I think I'd like to work at Hudson's full-time for a while."

My mother's face relaxed a little. "Why don't you speak to Mrs. Murphy? She could see that you get your job extended to full-time."

I hadn't thought of talking to Mrs. Murphy. "It might be good to talk to her," I said. "Maybe I'll go tomorrow after I withdraw from my courses." Back in my bedroom I closed my heavy black-covered chemistry book that lay open on my desk with a relieved sense of finality. That night in the bath tub I held my hand under the hot water faucet for a few seconds to get some sense of what hell would feel like. The water was very hot. The minute I felt pain I pulled my hand away.

Elaine Murphy directed the Employees' Consultation Service; her position was similar to a head social worker. It was unusual for a department store to have a social worker in these years. Several times Mrs. Murphy helped us get my father hospitalized when we couldn't do it on our own. When I was younger my mother took me to see her a few times—to show me off, I think.

"Mrs. Murphy will see you now," the secretary announced. Elaine Murphy came out to meet me wearing a pastel tweed suit and a rose colored blouse. Small and trim with wavy dark hair framing a lively face, she looked to be in her mid-forties.

"Sarah. How nice to see you. Come on in." Her voice sounded warm, welcoming.

"Thank you," I said as I followed her. I remembered her now. She was one of those people who smile with their eyes. Her spacious office was furnished in Danish modern, the upholstery and carpets in shades of green and turquoise. The room felt calm and inviting. She motioned to a chair across from her uncluttered desk and I settled into it. I liked that the lights were low.

"What brings you to see me?" she asked without further preliminaries. To my surprise I felt at ease. I told her I wanted to take some time off from school and wanted to work full-time if I could. She looked very attentive, but waited for me to say more.

"You know—just some things I need to think through."

"Something in particular troubling you, Sarah?"

I thought yes, there are big things troubling me, but I can't tell her about *those*. So I said, "Not really. Just things like what to study? What to be? I've changed my major to pre-med. It's hard to concentrate. Too many other questions."

"Other questions?"

"Last year at Wayne some of my professors made it quite clear that they were atheists or agnostics. My father says he's an agnostic, but I don't think I'd ever met an atheist before. I guess my life's been pretty sheltered." For a moment I was back at Wayne University the year before where these *were* the things on my mind.

"It's confusing to hear opposing views at times," she said, nodding her head.

"I mean, well, if there's no God, maybe there's no purpose to life at all."

"And that's an uncomfortable thought."

Something made me want to continue. "Then, to make matters worse, I found this student religious group on campus. I went a few times. The kids in that group are great, but they seem so sure about their faith. It was unsettling." I took a tissue from the box on her desk to wipe a tear.

"That made things more confusing?"

"It did."

Mrs. Murphy just waited, her head cocked to one side. My lack of sleep must have affected my judgment, for in a few seconds I told her, "You may think this sounds strange, but it's very clear to me now that I really don't love *anyone*, my boyfriend, my parents, not anyone. I just realized this in the last few weeks." Mrs. Murphy just nodded understandingly, so I went on.

"This means I'm really not a good person. In fact, I'm a very bad person." I even told her about St. Paul thinking he's chief of sinners when in fact I was. "The worst of it is," I was leaning closer across her desk now and whispering, "no matter how long I live, I know that when I die I am going to go to hell."

"How frightening to live with that thought," she said. Still she just sounded sympathetic, not shocked as I feared she might be. Suddenly I realized that for someone who wants a full-time job, I was being much too open. I tried to pull myself together and sound more matter-of-fact.

"It's mainly the religious questions. These are things I have to think through, and why I need to work full-time just now. Do you think you can help me?" I waited uneasily to hear her answer.

"You're struggling with some difficult feelings right now," Mrs. Murphy looked at me intently. She was quiet for a few seconds as though she was thinking about what to do. "This is what I *can* do. I'll see that you get a full-time job, but only on one condition," and here she sounded very firm, "and that is that you agree to see the firm's psychiatrist. I think he can help you understand these feelings that are troubling you." My immediate thought was that I wished I could continue to see Mrs. Murphy instead of the firm's psychiatrist. She struck me as a truly wise person. But maybe a psychiatrist knew more about these kinds of questions. I wished I didn't have to wait a whole day to see him—or even more perhaps.

I told her that I would see the firm's psychiatrist, since I wanted to work.

"It's a good decision. I'll make the appointment, Sarah, and call you at home this afternoon." She took my phone number. Thankfully, back when I was fourteen we had again been able to afford a phone. She got up to walk me to the door. I thanked her and left.

Suddenly I felt so tired I wondered if I could make it home. My legs felt shaky—as if they could buckle under me at any second. My mother would want to know what happened with Mrs. Murphy, though. I stopped on the sixth floor and found her racing around her department as usual, waiting on several customers at once, so we only exchanged a few words. When she heard that Mrs. Murphy wanted me to see a psychiatrist, I saw a flicker of that tense expression her face always had whenever my father was heading into another hospitalization, but then that look left. She said she trusted Mrs. Murphy's judgment. I said goodbye to her and started for the bus. The walk to the bus felt like a crawl. I reached home, mumbled "hello" to my father, went to my bedroom and got under the covers taking off only my shoes. I slept so soundly I didn't hear the phone when Mrs. Murphy called, but my father took the message. I had an appointment on Monday at two o'clock with Dr. Frank Sellars.

That night when I took my bath I didn't put my hand under the hot water again. That wouldn't tell me what hell is like. I couldn't know until I got there.

eleven

"The Day Thou Gavest, Lord, Is Ended"

MY MOTHER WANTED TO go with me for my first appointment with Dr. Sellars. She had begun to treat me like a much younger person, but her protectiveness felt comforting. After a morning spent slowly packing my textbooks and school papers away in a box to store in the basement—sad to be giving up on school—I sat down with my father and shared a can of Campbell's chicken soup which he had heated. He knew this was the day of my appointment. "Good luck, honey," he said as he watched me put my green hooded raincoat on to go downtown to meet my mother at Hudson's.

The rainy weather matched the way I felt. We walked to the clinic a few blocks away, sharing an umbrella but saying very little. I wondered what Dr. Sellars would be like. Would he be an older man with a beard like pictures I'd seen of Sigmund Freud? I hoped he'd be a male counterpart to Mrs. Murphy. We found the clinic and took two seats in the crowded waiting room. Magazines covered the round coffee table. I looked through them—several *Saturday Evening Posts*, some fairly old issues of *Life Magazine*, a *Good Housekeeping*—none of them interested me. A woman came over to my mother, introduced herself as a social worker, and invited my mother to her office. I knew my mother would tell her what a happy outgoing person I'd been all through high school and last year at Wayne University; and how sudden and mysterious this depression seemed to everyone who knew me. I had heard her say this to other people. She said it to our minister, Roger McShane, on the phone. I could understand how perplexing this change in me must be for my mother.

A prim looking woman in a navy blue suit called my name from the doorway and I followed her into her office, puzzled because I had thought

Dr. Sellars was a man—Frank Sellars. She told me she was a psychiatrist, and that there was some uncertainty as to whether I would see her or Dr. Sellars for psychotherapy. She asked me many questions: When did I first begin to feel depressed? Did I have trouble sleeping? Were there any changes in my eating?—all the time taking notes on a lined yellow pad. She seemed cold and mechanical, so I told her as little as possible. When she had asked all her questions she walked me back to the waiting room and said in her curt way, "Wait here for Dr. Sellars." There were people of all ages in the waiting room, even a little girl with a man I assumed was her father. After a few minutes Dr. Sellars came out and introduced himself. He was tall and angular with brown wavy hair and deep set brown eyes— a little stooped over in his tweed jacket, although he looked to be only about thirty-five. As distraught as I was—and I was very distraught—I still noticed that he was ruggedly handsome.

I followed him down the hall to his small cluttered office where his huge desk was piled high with papers. Two swivel chairs were pushed against the bookcases that lined one wall with another in front of his desk. A big window with no draperies took up one end of the room. He offered me one of the chairs and sat opposite me turning his chair away from the desk. I liked that I could move around a bit in the swivel chair—I could face the window if I wished and not look at him directly. Still, I pulled my raincoat around me a little tighter as if for protection.

Dr. Sellars leaned back and intertwined his fingers over his trim waist. I found his brown eyes calm and safe. I was glad he had no note pad like the woman psychiatrist. He looked at me for what seemed like a full minute and then he said,

"I understand you've decided to take a break from university for a while—can you tell me about this?" It was such an open-ended question—where to begin? I decided to tell him my more normal sounding worries first—the way I had with Mrs. Murphy.

"My first year at Wayne shook things up a bit. I met up with all kinds of beliefs that were new to me. That started me thinking," I told him.

"Oh? What about, Sarah?"

"Well—like what I could believe about life. I mean is there any meaning to it all? Is there a God? Things like that." He just waited for me to go on, but I detected some discomfort in the way he twiddled his thumbs—his hands still clasped on his waist. I went on. "You see my church had been very important to me—but at Wayne I met so many intelligent people who did not believe anything I had learned at church."

"What church did you grow up in?"

"Mostly Presbyterian. My mother's Presbyterian. But for a few years my brother and I went to a Lutheran church because it was close. They're quite similar." Dr. Sellars leaned back further and clasped his hands behind his neck. It didn't take me long to see that psychiatrists really didn't deal with questions about the purpose of life—or why we are here. Instead of talking about these questions I was raising, Dr. Sellars asked me, "Can you tell me a little more about your growing-up years, Sarah? Maybe going as far back as you can remember?"

"Well, sure. I have lots of memories of my childhood. It was a happy childhood, especially the first few years before my father became ill." My mind went back in time to when my father wore a white pharmacy coat—and how eagerly I waited for him to come home every night. I told Dr. Sellars a little about this. He looked more relaxed.

Turning to the present again, he asked me, "What is troubling you the most right now, Sarah?" I decided to tell him about my deeper problem—of not loving anyone, of being a very bad person, and being condemned to hell. I felt I might as well. But he didn't say anything about these things I told him either. I concluded he would be no help. I would have to keep coming to see him, or that woman, in order to keep my job, but he couldn't help me. Of that I felt certain. I could tell he thought my problems had to do with my childhood and didn't see how important the religious questions were to me. At the end of the time, after he had asked a few more questions about my family, Dr. Sellars took me back to the waiting room.

In a little while he asked me back to his office again. I assumed he'd been talking to the woman in the navy blue suit. He told me he was going to be my therapist and that he wanted to see me three times a week, Monday, Wednesday, and Friday at one o'clock. Hudson's would give me an extended lunch hour, he said, and would cover the cost of my therapy. I was glad I would be seeing him and not the woman. He had a looser feel to him than she did—a sort of young Abe Lincoln tweedy feel. He walked me back to the waiting room where I saw my mother was waiting. Dr. Sellars introduced himself to her and told her about the plan—three sessions a week at one o'clock beginning next Monday.

"I'm not sure Dr. Sellars can help me," I told her on the way back to Hudson's.

"Please give it a try, Sarah," she said. "It's awfully good of Hudson's to pay for your therapy."

"I'll give it my best try," I said and gave her a good-bye kiss on her cheek. She went back to work and I went to the bus. I felt even more desperate after meeting Dr. Sellars. I had had a vague hope that he might know of a solution to these problems, but I saw he didn't at all. He had said nothing about my problem of being an extremely bad person—or about how I could avoid going to hell when I died.

Many years later I learned from Mrs. Murphy that Dr. Sellars had called her back after he saw me that day and told her, "I'm not sure this one is going to get better." He may have thought I had inherited my father's illness, or that my strange thoughts signaled the onset of a schizophrenic process that often begins around this age. I never for an instant thought I had inherited my father's illness. I didn't see it as an illness at all, but as the truth about the way I was—a totally bad human being. In fact, however, it was an illness, but a different more treatable illness than my father's.

Mrs. Murphy also set up an appointment with an internist to rule out any physical cause for these sudden changes in my mood and thinking. I went to see the doctor she had chosen, who never said anything about the purpose of the examination. In a routine fashion he listened to my heart and checked my blood pressure. A technician drew several vials of blood. When the nurse weighed me, I was surprised to see I had lost twelve pounds. In these past turbulent weeks I had been eating more than ever, or so I thought. Another significant change was that my appearance no longer mattered to me. Since I was only going to die and go to hell, I had begun putting thick layers of butter on my bread at dinner—something I would never have done before. Still, on this doctor's scale I weighed only 113 pounds instead of my usual 125. As I was putting my clothes back on, the thought occurred to me that if I'm never going to do any good in the world, I shouldn't use up unnecessary food. I decided to cut back on what I ate and eat only what I absolutely needed. In two days when I went back for the test results, the only abnormal finding was a slightly low metabolism for which the doctor wrote a prescription for a low dose of thyroid.

My father had said nothing about these changes in me, but I knew he had to be worried about them. On a Saturday morning the two of us were alone in the kitchen finishing up the breakfast dishes. My full-time job wouldn't start until the following Monday. My mother had left for work and my brother was out somewhere. When I dried the last cup in the dish drainer, on an impulse I asked my father if he would go for a walk with me. I just felt like getting out somewhere away from everything. To my surprise he said, "Sure honey. Where would you like to go?"

"Somewhere in the country," I told him, "but that would be hard without a car." He had a solution, though.

"We could take the Schoolcraft bus to the end of the line. It's still much like country out there." Normally anything that energetic would not appeal to him.

"Let's do that," I said with a shade more enthusiasm than I had felt in a long time. I could picture that area from driving there with Eric. It was beautifully rural with country roads and meadows off of Schoolcraft, a main artery.

"I'll get my jacket and tie," he said. He had on a white shirt and navy blue suit pants. My father still dressed quite formally—the same way he had dressed when he went to work except for his white coat. I was wearing my usual school garb, a plaid skirt and a sweater, and took my corduroy jacket for warmth. We left the house almost immediately and walked the two blocks to Schoolcraft and then up a block to the bus stop. We barely spoke beyond noting that it was a beautiful fall day.

"Thanks for doing this," I said when we reached the bus stop.

"Don't mention it," he said. I felt some awkwardness between us. I used to spend hours talking to my father when I was younger—asking him questions about things we studied in science class or what was going on during the war in Europe. Like my mother, I believed he knew everything. But in high school and my first year of college we hadn't talked as much, unless to discuss what he read in the newspapers. I was usually too busy with my own activities to chat with him for very long. Every day I had something—a music lesson, choir practice—or I spent time with Eric. When the bus came, he paid the fare. Ever since my father stopped working my mother made sure he always had money in his pocket. He must have found it demeaning to have to accept it from her, but he was never without money.

Out of the window of the almost empty bus I watched the few stores on Schoolcraft slip by, interspersed with houses. There was Jean Showler's house, my friend from grade school and high school. I used to stop by to pick her up to walk to high school. My days at Cooley High seemed a world apart now—all that took place in a different country, lost to me forever. It felt good that the bus was taking us farther and farther away. We crossed familiar main arteries—Greenfield, then Southfield, and on past Telegraph Road. There were hardly any stores and fewer houses the farther we went. We were the only passengers when we reached the end of the line.

The day seemed even more beautiful out here with the leaves almost at their peak of color. Brilliant red maples and yellow oaks were everywhere. The fields were still green.

"Let's go this way," My father said, pointing to an unpaved road across from the bus stop. I looked. It seemed to have the most foliage and the most open green meadow of any of the possible directions. Glad that he was taking the lead, I followed. We started down the road he had chosen, then after a few minutes I raised a fear I had had.

"Are you disappointed that I dropped out of Wayne University like this?" My voice was wavering—close to tears.

"I could never be disappointed in you, honey. You were working too hard last year. That was all."

"I was working hard," I acknowledged. I had long been accused of having too many irons in the fire.

"I hope you'll try to relax now and not take everything so seriously. You know what they say, 'life is just a bowl of cherries.'" He laughed a droll little laugh and I tried to laugh too. He had used this saying as far back as I could remember to minimize any unsettling event. I never knew exactly what "life is just a bowl of cherries" meant. Except for when he was manic my father was by far the most patient, understanding person in the family. Any time my mother and I quarreled, and we did quarrel—especially when I was in eighth grade and wanted to go to roller rinks she deemed unsavory places—he was the peacemaker urging us to make up.

"You're right, Daddy, I probably do think too much." I picked a tall piece of alfalfa growing beside the road and began to chew on the end of it. "Right now I'm feeling bad about the Faculty Wives' Club giving me their scholarship. They were so good to me and I blew it." I couldn't let go of that.

"But you withdrew in time. You'll use that scholarship again next year."

"Maybe, but maybe not." In my wildest dreams I couldn't imagine going back to the university. I felt sure that I would always be this way—and I could never go back unless I had solved the problem of going to hell.

The two of us fell silent for a while. Perhaps to break the silence my father held out his package of Camels and said, "Would you like a cigarette?" I was shocked. My father had to know that I didn't smoke. He never wanted my mother to smoke and she didn't. I figured he was trying to help me in one of the few ways he could think of, so I took the cigarette. We stopped walking long enough for him to light my cigarette, and then one for himself. I was sure I would choke if I inhaled, so I just puffed on it carefully. We walked for a long time with our cigarettes, neither saying much. My fear about hell was now the only thing I thought about—and it wouldn't be a good idea to worry my father with that. We always tried so hard not to worry him. Besides, this time alone with him out here in the country was so peaceful I didn't want to spoil it with my dreadful thoughts.

The sun was high in the sky now. This felt like a safe oasis walking here on the outskirts of Detroit with my father. I wished we could just stay here and not go back—keep walking like this forever. I so appreciated that he was not asking me why I left school—or why I broke up with Eric. I knew he wouldn't ask me about these things. He was the least intrusive person I knew.

"The trees are beautiful," he noted looking up at them, "but I've always hated to see the leaves turn because it means winter is coming."

"And I like fall the best. The air is so crisp. This summer was too hot." As I said this I thought of how I had always liked the fall—when school started up and everything got going again. But this fall was different from all the others. We were silent again, a comfortable silence now. We walked for an hour-and-a-half, making only small comments about things we saw, and then we came to a dead end in the road.

"We could go left or right, or turn around," he said.

"I guess we should go back, although I wish we didn't have to."

"I know what you mean. Aren't you hungry?"

"Not really. We can have lunch when we get home."

"Another cigarette?" We had already changed direction.

"No thanks." I took his arm. "I do feel better though. Walking like this helped a lot." I said this even though I knew nothing had changed; but this had been a peaceful time—the only time in these past few weeks I had felt a little relief from my tormenting thoughts. A wind had come up. It was getting colder, so we walked a little faster. We reached Schoolcraft Road and he said once more,

"Just try not to let things bother you, honey. I've learned it doesn't pay."

"I know, Daddy. I will try." We got on the bus that was waiting in the bus stop and rode home.

The next day was Sunday. For the first time in my life I was not going to church. It had been several weeks now. Ann Tittl, who had been my good friend all through high school and then at Wayne, must have heard at church about my dropping out of school. She phoned me to see if I'd like her to come over. I really didn't want to see anybody—then again, Ann was someone I felt comfortable with—so I told her she could come if she would like. When Ann came in, we went to my room to talk. I think it was because I had so little to say that she suggested we go to a movie to "take my mind off things."

We went to the familiar Tower Theater on Grand River, but as I watched the film the same thing happened as when I read my chemistry textbook—I comprehended nothing—absolutely nothing. My eyes were on the screen the whole time, but when we walked out I had no idea what the film was about—or even what movie we had seen. The entire time my mind had been on the problem of being a bad person and the inevitable consequence of hell. Since my one aim was to try to figure out a way to change this disastrous situation, I didn't even fight these thoughts. I tried to work on the problem—continuously, so the movie became another good opportunity. I turned these new revelations about my character over and over in my mind, hoping I would discover some way to overthrow these grim truths, but nothing ever changed in my constant ruminations. I just repeated the same sequence of ideas—I don't love anyone, therefore I'm a bad person, as a consequence I must go to hell when I die.

Outside the movie theater Ann said, "Why don't we go to the evening service at Calvin?" Ann had been coming to my church quite regularly for some time now. "We just have time to get there by seven-thirty."

I was so unaware of everything that I hadn't realized until she said this that Ann had missed the Christian Endeavor meeting at six o'clock to go to the movie with me. That was good of her, but made me feel bad. I told her that I wasn't sure I could handle the evening service, but I would try. We got as far as the door of the church. Christian Endeavor had just let out and several of our friends were milling around in front of the church before going in for the service. I couldn't go inside. There was just no way.

I could hear the congregation beginning to sing the first hymn. I could picture Jack Phlieger leading the singing. They were singing "The Day Thou Gavest, Lord is Ended." Standing as we were on the steps of the church, I could even hear the words:

> The day Thou gavest, Lord is ended,
> The darkness falls at Thy behest;
> To Thee our morning hymns ascended,
> Thy praise shall hallow now our rest.

"That's one of your favorite hymns, isn't it?" Ann said. "Let's go in." They were singing the second verse now:

> We thank Thee that Thy Church un-sleeping,
> While earth rolls onward into light,
> Through all the world her watch is keeping,
> And rests not now by day or night.

"I know you're trying to help me, Annie," I told her, "And that *is* one of my favorite hymns—it's so fitting for an evening service, but right now it wouldn't make any difference, believe me." She saw I wasn't going to be able to go inside and walked me home instead. We were silent most of the time, but I felt her presence a friendly, understanding one.

What I couldn't explain to Ann was that this feeling of impending doom had nothing to do with church. No minister at Calvin, or at the Lutheran church for that matter, had ever preached about hell and damnation. I wouldn't have been at home in a church like that. I loved the quiet dignity of Calvin Church. It had been my larger family for several years now and had always been a comfort to me. The thoughts I had now were terrifying to me. But they didn't come from Calvin Church. That's why I didn't think the church could help me with them. I felt I had to work them out on my own.

It was Monday already. I had to start my full-time job at Hudson's, though I was not looking forward to talking to customers. My mother and I took the Grand River bus downtown. On the way over to Hudson's we stopped at Greenfield's, as we had always done if we had time, for a second cup of coffee. Normally we each ordered a French cruller as well. This morning I was careful to say I would just have coffee. It was part of my new plan not to eat more food than I absolutely needed.

"They're light as air," my mother said. "Are you sure you won't have one?"

"No, I'm not that hungry," I told her. Before this my mother and I used to have so much fun having coffee together—chatting busily about plans for this and that—a birthday gift we needed to buy, or a dress in her department she thought I might like. I had been buying my dresses from her for a while now. I knew it was hard for her to see me this way. I was no fun at all. I even refused to have a piece of *her* French cruller.

At Hudson's I went, as I had done before, to the office that gave out assignments for salespeople who were floaters to whatever department needed them. There I discovered that I was not going to be selling. Instead I would be a stock clerk again or check merchandise in and out of the fitting rooms—the things I had done before I turned eighteen. It was definitely a step down but I wasn't disappointed. I understood that no one would foist anyone who looked as forlorn and melancholy as I did on the public. My clothes were already loose from the weight I lost. I wore lipstick to try to counteract my drab appearance. But if you looked in my eyes, as I had in the mirror that morning, they were dull and lifeless, and there didn't seem to be anything I could do to change that. I went to Miss Clancy's office. She was still in charge of stock clerks and checkers. I had known her ever since I began working here the summer I turned fourteen—that was five years ago. I found her standing as straight as ever behind the counter where she gave out assignments.

"I'm glad to have you back, Sarah," Miss Clancy told me, "although I know this is only temporary." She was doing her best to console me about the demotion.

"I'm glad to be here," I told her, and it was true. I used to be a little scared of Miss Clancy. She could be stern. But today I experienced her as most kind. She told me I'd be in Misses' Inexpensive Dresses, a department I knew well on the same floor as my mother's. I knew all the people there. The stock work would keep me busy, I figured, so I wouldn't have to talk much to any of them. Besides they were all very friendly and had known me a long time. I felt relieved to be going there.

"This will be your assignment," Miss Clancy added, "until I need you somewhere else, Sarah, and then I'll just call down. By the way, I know about the extended lunch hour so don't worry about it—whatever time you need will be fine." I thanked her and went down to the sixth floor. I found the assistant buyer, remembering my first day of work at Hudson's when Miss Shinkman was the assistant buyer—now she was married and had two children. Dresses had just come in that needed to be unpacked and hung up. I felt relieved to have this solitary, mindless activity. It gave me time to think my own thoughts. I needed to do that—needed to figure a way out of going to hell.

At twelve thirty my mother came looking for me. Since this was the first day I would go to see Dr. Sellars on my own, she thought I should take a taxi to make sure I was on time. We went out to Woodward Avenue together. I got a cab and she handed me a paper bag, a lunch she had bought for me. As the cab pulled away I opened it and found a thick liverwurst sandwich on rye bread and a huge chocolate chip cookie. It was more than I could ever eat—or wanted to eat. I ate two bites of the sandwich in the cab. It tasted good with mustard on the liverwurst. The rest, and the cookie, I put in a waste bin on my way into the clinic. In the waiting room I saw a rack for coats, but I kept mine on and took a seat.

Promptly at one o'clock Dr. Sellars came and nodded for me to follow him. We settled into the same chairs we had taken the Monday before for my interview.

Dr. Sellars asked me another of his open-ended questions, "What do you remember of how this depression began, Sarah?" That was the name they were giving my condition—"a major depression." I told him about my two abrupt decisions, breaking up with my boyfriend and changing my major to pre-med. I told him how after that I had come to realize that I didn't love anyone, and that I was a bad person, and that soon after that I began to feel deeply sad and frightened about going to hell. He asked why I felt I was a bad person.

"Well, if you can't love anyone you can't be a very good person," I told him.

From his next series of questions I began to suspect that Dr. Sellars thought I might feel guilty about some sexual feelings or activities. I had no problem telling him all there was to tell about my sex life to date—it had consisted of a lot of necking with first one boyfriend and then the second, and that was all. I think we both agreed there wasn't much to feel guilty about there. The time was up. He walked me to the door and said, "I'll see you on Wednesday."

I walked back to work. It wasn't that far. I wished I could make Dr. Sellars understand what I was struggling with, but I didn't think I'd ever be able to do that. My feelings sounded illogical, but they weren't. It made perfect sense to me that if you didn't love anyone, you couldn't be a good person. It wasn't a matter of anything you had done or said, not done or not said. It was what you were inside. I wanted to be a loving, kind person—the kind of person my mother was inside, but I couldn't be that kind of person.

Later in the week Roger McShane, our minister, came to see me. He was an extremely sensitive young man who was sincerity and gentleness personified, not as robust and jovial as our previous minister, Tom Lindsey. His sermons were thought-provoking and had usually received high ratings in my diary. Not long out of Princeton Seminary, Mr. McShane had come to our church only a year or so before with his attractive, fashion-conscious wife. They had no children as yet. He had known me only as one of the leaders in the youth group.

We talked quietly in the living room while my parents disappeared into the kitchen. Like my parents, Mr. McShane appeared mystified by my preoccupation with hell, the little bit I told him about that. Wisely, he didn't offer any theological explanations, or attempt to assuage my fears. He just listened. As he left I thought I heard him say to my parents something to the effect of, "It's hard when someone becomes so self-absorbed." The comment might as well have been a dagger. He had inadvertently pointed to what I was most ashamed of, my self-centeredness—my inability to feel anything for other people. Inwardly I protested, *but you don't understand how helpless I am to be otherwise—how trapped I am in my own self-absorption and evilness.* Later I wondered if I might have misheard him. It wasn't the kind of thing Roger McShane would normally say. I probably heard what I was afraid he *thought*.

I felt I needed to find out more about hell so I could know what to expect. "Dante's *Inferno*" was a phrase I had heard in one of my literature courses at Wayne. On Friday, my day off, after I saw Dr. Sellars I went to the Detroit Public Library and found *The Divine Comedy*, which included

The Inferno. I checked it out. I had thought there was something about a "lake of fire" in this book, but I couldn't find that part. The book seemed much too complicated for me to understand in my present state of mind. Back at home, sitting in a special corner of the couch I had adopted as my refuge, I read in one section about an old man in a boat who said,

> "You need not hope that you will ever see heaven.
> I have come to take you to the other side, into eternal darkness,
> fire and ice."

Was there ice in hell too, I wondered. Just then both my father and mother came into the living room. My mother saw the page heading, *The Inferno*, in my book.

"I don't think it's good for you to read this, Sarah. It will only make you feel worse. Please let me take it."

"But it might help," I said, as I handed the book to her. The words of the old man, "You need not hope that you will ever see heaven"—those stayed with me as if he were speaking them directly to me.

On Sunday Mony, the friend who tried so hard to persuade my mother that I should go to the University of Michigan, came to see me. With all these visitors, Ann, Roger McShane, and now Mony, I felt as if I had just been in a terrible accident and everyone was coming to visit me in the hospital to cheer me up. They were being kind, but no one could undo the damage the accident had caused. No one could change the unalterable facts I had discovered about myself. Still, I was glad to see Mony—as glad as I could be about anything. We sat on the studio couch in the dining room. After a while I told her some of my tormenting thoughts. Mony took my hand. She said, "I think all the hell we experience is right here on earth and that what you are going through right now is hell." I didn't agree with her that there was no real hell after death, but I felt that Mony understood better than anyone how bad this felt—not to be able to shed the idea of hell even for a moment *was* a little like being in hell already. I didn't say anything more. I sat there holding Mony's hand. I wanted to hold on to her comforting presence as long as I could.

twelve

"Come Ye Thankful People Come"

DR. SELLARS WAS ALWAYS interested in what happened to me as a child. I told him as much as I could remember about those early good years, singing hymns with my mother, the way she read to us and taught me poems, took us to the park—and then I told him about my father becoming ill. "That's the way my father's manic-depressive psychosis began. He started preaching from the balcony in Shettler's Drug Store where he filled prescriptions," I summarized.

"You were five years old?"

"I was five." The afternoon sun was beginning to shine through Dr. Sellars' one large window showing up the dust particles rain had left on the outside. The window definitely needed washing.

"That must have been very hard for you—and your mother." He leaned forward and his voice sounded tender. I kept looking out the window. I was thinking about the emptiness in our apartment when there were no more sounds of my father's laughter, when he no longer brought friends home and came home ready to romp and play with Danny and me.

After what must have been a long time—I was so into my own thoughts, I said, "It was. I missed him a lot." I checked my watch. There were still ten minutes left.

"Your father was in the hospital a long time that first time?"

I knew exactly how long. "Eight months in Ypsilanti State Hospital."

"That's a long time for a child." Dr. Sellars leaned back in his chair again.

"Our life changed. But my mother was such a strong person. I always felt secure." I wasn't going to agree that my childhood was unhappy, or the cause of what was happening to me. There were unhappy moments to be sure, but for the most part our life was good. My mother made it that way. I felt deeply indebted to her. This was Monday and I had talked more than usual. When the clock on the wall said 1:50, I got up before Dr. Sellars this time and went to the door. He walked me to the waiting room as usual.

By Wednesday I had something much more important on my mind and didn't want to talk about the past. My father was back in the hospital again and I hadn't even seen him go. He had had at least eight or nine hospitalizations since that first one I told Dr. Sellars about, and I could describe each one vividly. But this time I was so fogged in by my distracting thoughts that I had no idea how this one took place—whether the police had to be called, as was so often the case, or even *when* this happened. And where was I? I didn't know. I felt sure that what was happening to me caused him to have to go back to the hospital. Maybe he had my brother drive him to Ypsilanti. After a period of silence, I shouted at Dr. Sellars,

"Can't you see that I'm killing my parents? It would be kinder to take a gun and shoot them than to kill them by degrees this way." He was taken aback at my vehemence and sat straight up in his chair.

"What do you mean, Sarah?"

"I'm sorry. You couldn't know. My father is back in the hospital again, and it's all because he was worried about me. On top of that, every day the lines in my mother's face grow deeper—all because of me. Now do you believe me when I say I'm a terribly bad person?"

Dr. Sellars never answered my questions directly—and only rarely asked questions of me. Later in the session I managed to engage him in some conversation, but it was short lived. I was trying to get him to understand how evil I was. I told him, "In the past, even when I did something that *looked* as if I cared about someone, I only did it to look good, or for the satisfaction I got in return. It wasn't genuine."

In one of the few times Dr. Sellars ever debated anything with me he argued, "Well, of course there's satisfaction that comes with being of help to someone, but that doesn't negate the goodness of the act of kindness or generosity." We were actually having a philosophical discussion and I felt pleased. I surmised that to reveal his own feelings in this way went against his psychoanalytic principles. But I felt he still didn't understand what I was saying.

"You see I'm not really talking about deeds. I'm talking about the whole nature of my being that is behind the deeds—that my whole being is not good. I have no love inside of me for anyone."

Dr. Sellars let it go at that. We both fell into contemplative silence. I was deeply troubled that my father was back in the hospital—that I didn't even see him go this time, and didn't know how he got there. I had always felt terrible when he went to the hospital, but this time it was my fault, so I felt infinitely worse. I began to weep silently and took a white handkerchief from my coat pocket. We sat in silence a long time.

"My parents would be so much better off without me," I said shaking my head in despair as the session ended—I said it more to myself than to him.

Dr. Sellars got up and opened the door. "I'll see you Friday, Sarah." His brown eyes looked distantly compassionate as I left.

"See you Friday," I repeated, and hurried back to Hudson's Department Store. The streets outside had an unreal appearance walking back— I was still cloaked in my own thoughts about what I was doing to my parents. They felt like a big gray hood over my head.

I was working in the College Shop that week, checking merchandise in and out of the fitting rooms. It was not my favorite department—a bustling place full of college-age young women. When I saw these girls come by my desk carrying colorful skirts and sweaters to try on—usually there were two or three of them shopping together, having a wonderful time—it made me deeply envious. It was hard to believe that this time last year I had been one of them. I felt sure I would never be numbered among that happy bunch again. That wasn't a major concern, however. My main concern still was that I hadn't figured a way out of going to hell when I died. Hell was inevitable, hell was eternal.

My weight was dropping. Every day before meeting my mother for lunch in the cafeteria I went to the Employees' Health Service on the same floor and stepped on the scale near the door. It was a doctor's scale accurate to the quarter of a pound. If I couldn't slide the balance bar down a little further than the day before, I ate even less. Already my menstrual periods had stopped because of my low weight. My mother watched anxiously as

I took only an orange for lunch or a half slice of bread—saying nothing because Dr. Sellars had told her not to draw attention to my eating.

At home in the evening, our five-room flat had become something of a haven, particularly the couch in the living room. After supper—there were only three of us for supper now—I put on a night gown and a long lavender housecoat, tied the sash tightly around my waist, and curled up in a corner of the couch, my feet tucked under me. I curled up as small as possible and felt relatively safe for the time I could stay there. I had begun doing this even before my father went back to the hospital. This was the same brown mohair sofa from my childhood, only my mother had covered the worn upholstery with slipcovers made with a fabric that had cheerful pink flowers on a leafy green background. The new fabric felt much better to the touch. *If only I could just stay here where I feel safe*, I thought. I felt like a little girl snuggled there, protected. I could cry there if I wanted to—and I did. Usually I cried silently. I didn't want my mother to hear me crying. I wiped my eyes and blew my nose with Kleenex I kept on the end table. I usually ended up with a whole pile to take to the garbage. The couch had taken on a different meaning than I had ever attached to it before. It had become an island of safety—like the oasis walk I took with my father. Sometimes I sobbed silently here for an hour or more.

With my father in the hospital I moved into the double bed in my parents' room with my mother. I felt less alone there, and my mother didn't mind. Apart from the time I spent curled up in a corner of the sofa, the only other time I felt any relief from my fears about death and hell was when I went to bed and could lay these fears down for a few hours in sleep. When I got into bed and pulled the covers up over my shoulders, I had a fervent wish that morning would never come. I dreaded waking to yet another leaden day with no hope of change. I thought about people waking up each morning after a terrible event—such as the death of a child, or becoming a quadriplegic. I imagined them hoping, as I did, that the situation was a bad dream from which they could awake—then waking to find it was not a dream. Waking was the worst part of the day.

Although I slept better now that I slept with my mother, one night as I lay awake thinking about what it means to be a bad person, the thought came to me so clearly, *you were born this way.* It didn't come as a shock, but more as an explanation; I was absolutely certain it was true. I sat up in bed wide awake. Until then I hadn't realized this. No wonder I wasn't able to make a dent in my badness—it was because I was born this way. It would be like trying to change my green eyes to brown. At least now I knew the reason, but it made my situation even more hopeless. Now I knew I would never be able to change and be able to love other people. It all depended on the way you were born.

Having made this discovery, I began to develop my own theology. The church had it wrong, I was certain. It wasn't a matter of faith in God, or believing in Jesus Christ as God's son and following Him. It was a question of whether you were born a good person or a bad person. Most people don't know which they are, I was sure. It was my misfortune that I figured it out.

During the day at Hudson's, after this, as I walked around the store, did my stock work, or checked merchandise in and out of fitting rooms, I felt I could tell which people were born good and which were born bad. Riding down the escalator I saw a floor manager who had spoken to me curtly the week before when I worked in his department. He was definitely one of the people who were born bad. He didn't know it yet, but when he died he would go straight to hell—like me. It became my secret knowledge. I took a little pride in having figured it out even though it carried such terrible implications for me—that I was one of the bad people slated for hell. I would spend eternity with people like this floor manager.

Time seemed interminable to me now. A day felt like a week—given the excruciating monotony of my job checking items in and out of fitting rooms, or buttoning up dresses and finding missing belts—then going home every night and crying silently on the couch a good part of the evening in which I read no books or newspapers and paid no attention to the news on the radio. It seemed unfair. I hadn't asked to be born after all—and now there would be no escaping my fate. This was what I cried about now when I cried—the unfairness of it all. Then I went to bed hoping against hope that morning would never come—only to wake and start the whole routine all over again. The sameness would have been even more deadening were it not for the constant fear of eventually going to hell. The terror I felt was not boring. The terror was . . . there is no word for it.

Now that my father was not there, I felt totally dependent on my mother. We did everything together—went to work, met at the employees' cafeteria for lunch, rode the bus home together, had dinner, went to bed. I lost track of Danny although he was in and out, trying to get through his last year of high school. My mother was my lifeline. When we got on an empty elevator together after lunch one day, I had the thought that my mother was the only one in the world I could rely on. I looked at her and said pleadingly, "Please don't leave me. Don't ever leave me." She had never given me the slightest reason to think she would leave me, but I knew I was not easy to be with the way I was.

"Sarah," she said, "you couldn't beat me away with a stick." I smiled at the image this conjured up. She still had a sense of humor.

"I just needed to hear you say that." I told her. For the moment I took comfort in seeing that she still loved me.

There was a ritual to the meetings between Dr. Sellars and myself. I was always in the waiting room a few minutes early and he was always exactly on time coming to the waiting room to take me to his office. He would nod silently that I should follow him. I sat in the same swivel chair opposite his desk with my green gabardine coat wrapped tightly around me. It would be months before I could take it off. He had his chair over to one side, so I could choose to look at him or be more with my own thoughts—as one is on an analyst's couch. Although he did not use a couch, after the initial history-taking, Dr. Sellars began to use the orthodox approach of always waiting for me to speak first. If I didn't speak, he didn't speak. Sometimes I didn't speak at all for the entire session. At those times I was thankful Dr. Sellars didn't push me to talk. I appreciated his willingness just to sit with me and say nothing—he could tolerate being with me in my despair.

On the day before Thanksgiving—we would be off Thursday and Friday— I went to meet my mother in her department to go home. I was glad to have the next two days free, although I didn't know how I would fill the time. Mrs. Brown, a salesperson in my mother's department everyone called Brownie, came over to talk to me. Brownie, who seemed always to wear a brown dress, had known me from when I was a child of five or six. Tall, with white hair and penetrating dark brown eyes, she walked with a lumbering gait. With one of her long arms encompassing me she said in her warm authoritative voice,

"Now Sarah, I know you've been having a hard time, but tomorrow I want you to sit down with pen and paper and write down ten things you are thankful for—will you do that for me?" I appreciated Brownie's concern for me, but my immediate feeling was here is still another person who wants to fix what is wrong with me and it's not going to work. I wanted to tell her that; instead, I was polite and said,

"I'll do that, Brownie. You have a good Thanksgiving." She gave me a firm hug.

"Do that now—ten things—and you'll feel better." My mother came from the locker room with her coat and purse and we left among the many holiday good wishes flowing back and forth between the departing saleswomen. The people my mother worked with were good souls. They had worked together for years and years, most of them, and truly cared about each other. I left thinking, *If only it were as easy as you think, Brownie. It's so much more complicated than that.* Then I thought *how fortunate Brownie is. She was definitely born good.*

That evening Mrs. Forbes, our landlady and mother of my friend Pat, came up the back stairs to visit us. My mother and I were in the kitchen finishing up the supper dishes. My brother had missed dinner that night so we had saved his on the stove.

"Have you fallen in love with your psychiatrist yet, Sarah?" Mrs. Forbes asked teasingly. She took a seat at the kitchen table. I drew in my breath. Did she really think this was a joke? And who told her I was seeing a psychiatrist? I continued to dry the dishes and said, "Not yet. He is good-looking though." Somewhere I'd heard that people do fall in love with their therapists but I didn't understand what purpose that served. "Have you heard from Pat?" I asked, uncomfortable that I hadn't answered any of Pat's letters.

"She phones once a week. She's not going to make it home for Thanksgiving—too much work. She decided to wait till Christmas." I sensed Mrs. Forbes had come to talk to my mother, so I hung up my dish towel and retreated to my room to change into my night clothes. From my bedroom, just around the corner from the kitchen, it was hard to avoid hearing bits of their conversation. "With all your attention going to Sarah . . . ," I heard her say, then something about, "senior year is hard for anyone." Mrs. Forbes was absolutely right. We rarely saw Danny. He flitted in and out like a shadow. All this had to be hard for him—his father becoming ill when he was so young, and now his sister. Danny and I had been very close during our teen years. In the youth group at church he used to begin so many sentences with "My sister says . . ." I had to caution him not to do that. But my poor mother—this was just one more thing to lay on her. When I heard Mrs. Forbes go down the back stairs, I went back to the kitchen to see how my mother was taking it.

"Would you have some more tea?" she asked as she filled the kettle.

"Sure." I sat down at the kitchen table. Out of the corner of my eye I saw my mother looking at me. I was noticeably thinner and I could see in her face how much this troubled her. "I couldn't help overhear some of what Mrs. Forbes said about Danny."

"She's right. I have been neglecting Danny."

"You can't be everywhere. And it's my fault you have had to be with me so much."

"It's not your fault. But did you know that Dr. Sellars called me the other day and told me I wasn't to let you out of my sight?" I felt my throat tighten at these words.

"No. What would make him do that?" Had he read my thoughts, I wondered.

"Something you said—something about your father and I being better off without you."

"Well, it's true. And now I'm messing up Danny's life too—but I didn't mean anything serious."

"Are you sure, Sarah? Much of the time I *have* to let you out of my sight."

"Of course I'm sure." The kettle boiled and she poured the water into the teapot over fresh tea leaves.

"Let's use the new china cups you bought me in Canada last summer." She got them down from the cupboard. We both thought tea tasted better in English bone china.

"I'm worried about Danny," I told her.

"I'm going to spend more time with him. He's very close to two of his drafting teachers at Chadsey. I think he's getting a lot of encouragement from them."

"It does help when your teachers like you," I said, remembering how important teachers had been to me. All that had changed now. All that studying had been for nothing. We heard the front door open and close. It was Danny.

"Danny, come and have something to eat with us. You must be starving," my mother called to him. When he came into the kitchen he had a forlorn, weary look on his face I'd not seen there before. Still he mustered a grin. He set down the big bag of books he was carrying.

"Thanks—I could use some good food," he said rubbing his hands together as though to warm them. My mother got up to heat up his dinner. Danny dropped down in the chair next to me with a sigh. "How are you doing?" He looked in my eyes. I knew I looked pretty miserable. You can't make sad eyes shine no matter how hard you try to rev up your energy. I told him I was doing okay.

My mother brought Danny's plate to the table and announced, "I'm roasting a turkey tomorrow even though there will only be the three of us."

"With sweet potatoes, green beans, and mashed potatoes and gravy?" Danny listed our usual Thanksgiving fare. He had gone to the sink to wash his hands.

"Everything. Sarah and I picked up a pumpkin pie at Awry's Bakery on our way home."

Danny grinned again and dug into his food. I thought of how my mother always kept holidays, even in the worst of times. I wasn't sure where I'd get the energy but I told them I would make the cranberry sauce—something my father always did.

We sipped our tea while Danny ate his dinner. I felt sure my mother would have invited company for Thanksgiving except she knew that I wasn't up to that. I wouldn't have minded having Mony, but she always went to Spokane over Thanksgiving to see her nieces. It would be fine. The three of us were used to being alone together. The hard part would be imagining our father spending Thanksgiving in Ypsilanti State Hospital with not even a visit from my mother. She must have thought that would be too much for me, and she couldn't go because she'd been told not to let me out of her sight. All of this was my doing.

After Danny finished his supper my mother went into the living room and slid back the cover on the piano keys. This cover used to be kept open all the time, but now it was closed to keep the keys from gathering dust. She began to play the Thanksgiving hymn, "Come Ye Thankful People Come."

"Danny, Sarah," she said. "Let's sing some Thanksgiving hymns." I realized I hadn't sung hymns with my mother for the longest time—ever since these thoughts began to occupy all my waking hours. I hadn't had my violin out of its case either. But I couldn't summon up any desire to sing.

"I'd rather just listen while you play," I told her. I came into the living room and sat in my special corner of the couch. Danny had taken the table cloth off the dining room table and laid his drafting sheets out to do some work. He said he was too busy to sing. My mother continued playing and sang the words by herself:

> Come, ye thankful people, come,
> Raise the song of harvest home:
> All is safely gathered in,
> E're the winter storms begin;
> God, our Maker, doth provide
> For our wants to be supplied:
> Come to God's own temple, come.
> Raise the song of harvest home.

She sang a couple more Thanksgiving hymns, "We Gather Together to Ask the Lord's Blessing," and "Now Thank We All Our God." I thought about Brownie and the list she wanted me to write—ten things for which I felt thankful. I felt thankful for my mother and that she could sing even when everything in her life looked bleak. But it was hard to be thankful about anything else now that I had discovered that I had been born a bad person. Why had this happened to me? Why couldn't I have been born a good person like my mother? Or like Brownie? Like Danny? Like my father? It seemed so unfair. There must be some way out, and yet I couldn't see one. If you are *born* bad, how can anything change that? I took off my slippers and pulled my feet up under me on the couch. I liked the sound of my mother's singing, but it made me heavy-hearted to think of how many times we had sung together—and to know that I could no longer even do that. I had no desire. I took a tissue from the Kleenex box and cried silently for a few minutes. I couldn't feel thankful. I couldn't write the list for Brownie—and worst of all, I couldn't even sing.

thirteen

"Hark How the Bells"

DR. SELLARS' OFFICE WITH its walls painted an institutional green, his roll-top desk cluttered with stacks of papers, had begun to feel comfortably familiar. But as I sat in the swivel chair I still kept my coat, now my winter coat, wrapped securely around me. I'd been coming here three times a week for almost three months, and my certainty that Dr. Sellars would be of no help had not changed in the slightest. Still, I liked that his behavior toward me was so predictable. I could set my watch by his appearance at the door of the waiting room at one o'clock any Monday, Wednesday, or Friday. I knew too that if I happened to be saying something at the end of the fifty minutes, which never happened because I said so little, he would still get up and go to the door at ten minutes to two o'clock to see me out. He always wore the same kind of tweed jackets with a tie that was a little askew—it could be the same tweed jacket—I didn't look that closely. His thick wavy hair was always a little tousled, and a wordless kindness emanated from his serious brown eyes. I marveled that he could sit through these long periods of silence with me without fidgeting, although once in a while he played with his unlit pipe. Sitting there I had the thought that if I knew him as a real person outside this office, I would like him. But he was powerless to change my darkness, the evilness that would inevitably take me to hell. I said nothing the whole session. There seemed to be no point.

Precisely fifty minutes from the time I had entered the office, Dr. Sellars walked me to the door. It was a Monday, so as always he reminded me, "I'll see you on Wednesday."

"Yes, Wednesday," I mumbled, even though I knew I wouldn't be here by Wednesday. By Wednesday I would have taken the only logical course. I left the clinic, pulled my coat around me more tightly—the December wind felt cold—and walked the few blocks back to Hudson's Department Store. Tomorrow on my lunch hour would be the best time. For weeks now I had known how I would do it.

On days I didn't see Dr. Sellars my mother and I always had lunch together. That Tuesday morning I phoned her department and told her I couldn't meet her at eleven o'clock because I'd been assigned a one o'clock lunch hour.

"I'll try to change mine," she said

"Thanks, but I've made arrangements to go with Jerry," I lied to her. I didn't like lying to her. I couldn't remember ever lying to my mother, but I had to carry out my plan.

"Sarah," she hesitated. "You know—that is—Dr. Sellars feels we should take our lunch hours and our breaks together." I told her I'd switch with someone and see her at the usual time. Dr. Sellars had alerted her that I was "seriously suicidal," although I didn't know how he knew that. I had never talked to him about my plan. I felt I had to let her follow his instructions or she might think it was her fault. Besides it would be good to have lunch with my mother one more time. I could still carry out my plan.

We met at the employees' cafeteria. My mother had learned not to say anything when I took only a dish of Jello or an orange for my lunch. Even though I wouldn't be alive much longer I wanted to stick to my diet, so I took a half a grapefruit. The one thing I could take pride in was that I weighed only 90 pounds.

We found a table near the window that looked out on downtown Detroit from the fourteenth floor. It was a gray winter day on the verge of rain or snow.

"It's been a slow morning," my mother said. "There are no customers there at all." I told her that I was sure her sales would pick up in the afternoon. We didn't have much to talk about. I felt totally flat and dull. One would think I'd be sad knowing this was the last lunch I would ever have with my mother, but I wasn't. I was sad down to my bones about the awful predicament I was in and the terrible choices open to me, but I didn't feel much about anything else. It was the thoughts—cold calculated thoughts—that possessed me. I knew that what I was about to do would benefit my mother too. The strain and fatigue from months of living with me in this state were taking their toll on her. It was torture. For me to get off the scene was the right thing to do. It was the only *decent* thing to do.

We took our trays over to the sliding belt that would carry them to the kitchen and caught a down elevator to the sixth floor, her stop, where I said goodbye to her. Her lined smiling face still looked beautiful to me. It struck me as the door was closing that this was the last time I would see that face. I looked longingly after her and saw the quick step she took to be sure she would not be late getting back. "Fifth floor," I told the operator. I was in the College Shop again checking clothes in and out of fitting rooms—boring, boring work. The person who relieved me expected me back at twelve o'clock, but that hardly mattered now. They'd figure out that something had happened when I didn't show up. I got on the next up elevator and took it to the top floor, the 23rd—where I was the only one left on the elevator. I glanced at the elevator operator in her crisp gray uniform with white cuffs—worried she might think it strange that I was going to this floor that had no one there, but she said nothing.

I had never run into a soul on the 23rd floor. There were a few unused offices up there but it was mostly storage area. I knew the exact location of the chute that ran the full height of the building and had an opening on each floor. In my years as a stock clerk I had thrown many empty boxes down this chute from various merchandise floors to the incinerator below. More than once in the last few weeks I had come up here to look down the chute with the thought of jumping—but never with the certainty I felt this day. I had gone over the problem in my mind so many times. I knew it was the only logical solution, and the sooner the better. Every day I lived I was making matters worse for myself and everyone around me—my mother, my father, and now Danny too.

I entered the little room that housed the door to the chute. They were exactly the same on each floor—a barren space, about four by six feet, painted a gun-metal gray, dimly lit by a bare light bulb hanging from a cord, and empty except for a dustbin and a wide push broom. It made me think of a room where the death penalty might be administered. The door to the chute was on the left wall as you entered—an opening about two feet square. I had checked it out and knew I would have no trouble fitting through the opening. After losing 35 pounds I was not very big—not nearly as big as some of the boxes I had thrown down there.

The door to the chute creaked from disuse when I opened it. Looking down I saw only blackness. No fire from the incinerator burned at the bottom as I always expected—only an impenetrable darkness. I closed the door again. There was a fire at the bottom actually—a Dante's inferno that

I knew was inescapable for me. Even though I had been over this so many times, I stopped to review my logic once more to make sure:

First of all I feel nothing for anyone, no love or compassion, so I know I am a bad person. As I look back, even when I did something good, it was only because it made me feel good or I wanted to look good—but basically I never cared about anyone but myself. In the last few months I've come to realize there are good people and bad people. It's the way you are born. I just happen to have had the misfortune to be born a bad person. Contrary to what I learned at church, I know now that if you're born bad no matter how hard you try, you can't be good. It's all a matter of how you were born. If you were born a good person you will go to heaven when you die, but if you were born a bad person you will go to hell. Now that I've figured it out, that the reason I couldn't love anyone was that I had been born bad, I can see that the smartest thing I can do is to die now and have fewer misdeeds on my record. Every day I'm alive I make more people miserable. Because of me my father became manic again and had to go back to the hospital. My mother looks worse every day, and my brother is having a hard time in his senior year of high school. It's an open and shut case. Dr. Sellars can't change it. Our minister Roger McShane can't change it. The kindest thing I can do for everybody, including myself, is to die now. They will soon forget about me and go on with their lives.

I opened the door of the chute again and looked down. Dying itself didn't frighten me and for certain the fall down 23 floors would kill me. But that I would wake up in some nether world engulfed in flames—that terrified me. And the thought that once I jumped, there would be no turning back. It was permanent, eternal. I stood with the door of the chute open and went through my reasoning one more time—still hoping to find another way—but the logic was flawless. It was the only thing to do.

Still I knew that once I climbed into the chute and let go I would have passed the point of no return. My thinking shimmered with clarity, however. The longer I lived the more harm I was doing and the more I would have to answer for in hell.

I hoisted myself up to the open chute by sitting on the side of the large dustbin. Should I go in feet first or head first? Feet first, I decided. I put my right foot into the opening. I looked at my foot—my low-heeled black pump and nylon stocking. I knew it was my foot, but it didn't feel like my foot. I felt detached from my body. When I put my left foot into the opening I was seized by a different thought. The thought was: *Wait! There could still be something you haven't thought about!* But what I am doing is so completely logical, I argued with this thought. But the thought came again: *There may still be something you haven't considered. What would it hurt to wait one more day?* I suppose it couldn't hurt to wait one more day—not that much at least. Okay, I said in answer to the thought, I would wait one more day. One at a time I removed my feet from the opening. Nearly tipping over the dust bin, I lowered myself to the floor, closed the door to the chute and then to the room itself and took the elevator back to the fifth floor. I was fifteen minutes late getting back from my lunch hour. The girl who had relieved me to go to lunch was checking her watch. "Now I'm way behind in my schedule," she said. I told her I was sorry. In my mind I still saw the image of my feet in that chute and wondered what it might be that I had not considered.

That afternoon on my break, walking with my mother on the seventh floor, we heard music—voices singing. I recognized them as the Hudson Carolers who went throughout the store singing in various departments at Christmas time. After what felt like a narrow brush with death and hell that morning, the voices sounded strangely like those of angels—singing this light, fast, ethereal carol I had learned in high school:

> Hark how the bells,
> sweet silver bells,
> all seem to say,
> throw cares away.

My mother and I walked in the direction of the sound and found the Carolers, about forty in number. They stood on risers wearing black choir robes in the middle of the Green Room, the most expensive dress department. I'm not sure what had taken us to the seventh floor. My mother sometimes went there to look at the "Better Dresses," one way she had of keeping up with the fashions. The music continued:

> Christmas is here,
> bringing good cheer,
> to young and old,
> meek and the bold.

The Ukrainian carol begins softly and then gets louder and louder:

> Oh, how they pound,
> raising the sound.
> o'er hill and dale,
> telling their tale,
>
> Gaily they ring
> while people sing
> songs of good cheer,
> Christmas is here.

Then, more quietly, more slowly, gradually fading away:

> Merry, merry, merry, merry Christmas,
> On, on they send,
> on without end,
> their joyful tone to every home
> Dong Ding dong ding, dong Bong.

Until that moment I had been unaware that Christmas was coming soon. The carolers sang other carols, but I was glad not to have missed this one—I had loved it so in high school when I first heard the student choral group practice it for the Christmas concert. They sang it every Christmas. For the duration of the carol, I was carried back to a joyful time when I played in the orchestra at Cooley High School. How I had loved those concerts at Christmas. Soon the carolers were singing their closing, "We wish you a merry Christmas," and filed off the risers. When the music died away, so did my memories. I was back in the present, still with my problem of finding another solution than the one that seemed the only one possible when I had stood at the chute on the 23rd floor earlier in the day. How I wished I could "throw cares away," as the "sweet silver bells, all seemed to say." But the welcome respite the music had given me was gone.

That it was almost Christmas and I had not even noticed shocked me. My preoccupation with hell had even wiped out God—and the birth of Christ. Hell was real to me every minute of every day, but God was not. Convinced that God would not hear people as bad as I was, I didn't pray any more. I sang no hymns and did not go to church. All the comfort I had drawn from growing up in a Christian church and from observing my mother's faith—this was lost to me. It wasn't that I had ceased to believe in God, but a big black curtain had come down and I couldn't see beyond it, or around it. Yet those few moments of listening to the "Carol of the Bells" brought something back to me—something of the joy and beauty of God—but only for an instant.

On Wednesday I saw Dr. Sellars as scheduled. I didn't tell him about going to the chute on Tuesday. I hadn't carried out my plan, but I knew that if another solution didn't occur to me soon, I would. My sessions became more and more silent. I was afraid to tell Dr. Sellars my thoughts about suicide. If he had any idea of how close I came to jumping down that chute, he would hospitalize me—of that I felt sure. From what he had said to my mother, I sensed he knew he was taking a risk with me. I did not want to go to a mental hospital; and I was in danger of that on two counts—the risk of suicide, and my weight. So I bided my time in my sessions all the time waiting for "something else to occur to me" as an alternative to the chute. Dr. Sellars was incredibly patient. I did not detect the slightest criticism from him when I remained silent. He just stayed with me. I was grateful for this, although I never told him that either.

Dr. Sellars never questioned me about my eating habits, but I'm sure he was in contact with Dr. Watts at the Employees' Health Service. Some time ago Dr. Watts, a tall kindly man with a bald spot surrounded by his black hair, had started giving me vitamin B shots twice a week to bolster my nutrition. One day while waiting for my vitamin B shot, I overheard him talking to another physician. They were discussing the advisability of hospitalizing me for malnutrition. My weight had dropped below 90 pounds. Hearing them talk about a hospital frightened me into eating a little more. I didn't want to go to a hospital, but I didn't want to re-gain my weight either. It was the only source of self-esteem I had left—that I could exercise self-control over what I ate. Still, it drove my mother crazy when I didn't eat. I hated hurting her, but I had to do it. I had never opposed her in much of anything—except, as I've said, in eighth grade when I put up quite a fight to go with my friends to the roller rinks—a fight I never won. A good friend of mine had a very bad experience there—actually became pregnant—so my mother had been right. But about my eating, I knew I was right. I was not going to give in.

On Fridays, our day off, before I went to my appointment with Dr. Sellars, my mother and I cleaned the house together. Dusting in the living room one Friday my hands trembled slightly as I dusted the pale blue and white china tea set with its delicate gold trim. I acknowledged to my mother that I was always afraid of breaking one of these. "If you did break one of them, Sarah, it would be all right," she assured me. "I've come to see that people are much more important than things." This was a child's tea set her oldest sister, my Aunt Annie, brought back from western Canada as a gift for my mother when she was a very little girl. I knew she treasured it—two little cups on saucers, a slender teapot, a creamer and sugar bowl, all on a little china tray. As a child I was told repeatedly to be careful of the tea set, which sat on the long library table in our living room. I knew better than to ask if I could play with it. But I believed her now when she said, "I've learned people are more important than things."

My mother finished her vacuuming the living room carpet and took the vacuum to do the rugs in the bedrooms. I folded my dust cloth, relieved that the house cleaning was finished for another week. I was so tired. If only the house would stay this way and never need to be cleaned again. It took so much effort for me. I felt the same way when I took a shower and washed my hair—if only I would never have to do this again. I had never felt so tired in my whole life. I sat down in my father's big green chair to rest a few minutes. I heard the vacuum shut off. My mother must have finished too.

"Time for lunch?" she called carrying the vacuum to its place in the front closet.

"I'm not very hungry," I called back.

"Please come and have something. You've been working all morning on half an orange." She stopped herself. She'd been told not to make an issue of my eating. But how could she not make an issue when I was getting thinner by the day?

I could hear her in the kitchen preparing lunch. This was going to be a problem. When I weighed myself the day before, I weighed 86 and ½ pounds—up half a pound. It was a dilemma. I didn't want Dr. Watts to hospitalize me, but I didn't want to gain my weight back either. I was still too heavy by my standards. This day I planned to limit myself to half an orange and a half-a-slice of bread. In the kitchen I saw my mother had made scrambled eggs and rye toast, and, as always, a pot of tea.

Faith and Madness

"I'll just have toast," I said firmly. "And some tea. I'm just not hungry yet." It was painful for me to sit on a hard-backed chair, and yet I didn't think I was too thin. As the sole source of any self-esteem, I clung to losing weight as to a life raft.

Our kitchen was a bright sunny room at the back of the house. My mother had set the table with our usual red and white checkered table cloth, ivory stoneware plates and white paper napkins. She served herself half of the scrambled eggs and left the portion intended for me in the pan. I took a piece of the unbuttered toast, cut it in half, and by taking imperceptible bites made the half slice last until my mother was finished with her eggs and toast and had drunk a cup of tea. It had to be infuriating to watch me. In her effort to follow Dr. Sellars' advice—not to make an issue of food—she hadn't said a word about my refusing the eggs. We ate in silence.

She took her plate to the sink and then went to the refrigerator and took out a quart of peaches she and my father had preserved the summer before. She opened the jar and placed two dessert dishes on the table with two teaspoons and a serving spoon.

"I know you'll have some of your father's peaches, Sarah. I think this year's were the best we've ever made." The peaches were beautiful, full bright orange halves perfectly nested inside each other all the way up the jar and floating on clear light syrup.

"No thank you, I'm really full."

"But these are your *father's* peaches," she pleaded.

"I know. Later perhaps, but not just now."

"Just one half? It's only fruit, guaranteed not to put weight on you." She put a half a peach and a little syrup in my dish.

"Mother!" I felt irate. "I just don't want any!"

"Sarah, you're so thin. Do you know what it does to me to see you this thin?"

"My weight went up half a pound yesterday," I said. "I'm really fine."

"Please have some of your father's peaches," her eyes were filled with tears now. "Your father would want you to have his peaches."

I burst into tears. It was dirty pool to make me feel guilty over turning down something my father had made. It was so important to me not to eat, and I knew she couldn't understand that.

"Daddy would never force me to eat if I wasn't hungry." I got up to leave the kitchen. "I just don't want them."

158

"I'm so worried about you. What am I going to do? What am I going to do?" My mother was really crying now with her head in her hands. She had never broken down like this.

"Just leave me alone. I don't mean to make you feel bad, but you have to understand. I just don't want them."

"Just one! It wouldn't hurt you to do this for me." Her face was contorted with anguish and her eyes were red from crying so hard.

"But it *would* hurt me when I just don't want them." This was the strongest stand I had ever taken against her. Eventually I went over to her and put my hand on her shoulder.

"I'm sorry, I'm really sorry," I said. Then I took my plate with the remaining half piece of toast to the sink and threw the toast in the garbage. I left for my appointment with Dr. Sellars and tried to put that image of her sitting there crying out of my mind, but it followed me all the way to his office.

While totally focused every day now on suicide, I also worried about the future and having enough food to survive in the event that I never had the courage to take my life. I worried about what would happen to me after my parents died and there was no one to provide a home for me. I pictured myself picking food out of garbage cans to stay alive—literally a bag lady. The image horrified me. I didn't think about my brother taking care of me. I had always been the big sister and had enjoyed Danny's looking up to me. But he was totally lost to me now. He could have been on another planet. I envisioned myself going around the streets looking for food—maybe even begging because I was afraid to die.

My sessions with Dr. Sellars were still very quiet—mainly because I didn't want to talk to him about suicide. Once in a while, though, I felt compelled to ask him a question. I'd begun to feel that I looked less human than I used to look—more like an animal. I took my eighth-grade graduation picture to him, a large 8 x 10 photograph, and asked him,

"Don't you think I look different now than I did in this picture? More like an animal?" In the picture I had an impish smile. I even looked intelligent—or so I thought. We had each had to make our own graduation dress, so in the picture I was wearing the dress I made—a complicated princess style dress of white eyelet material with blue velvet ribbon laced into the edging of the square neck and around the short sleeves. It had been difficult to make and I had felt proud of it. Now I felt totally removed from the girl in the photograph. When I looked in the mirror my face looked different to me—almost feral—the way I thought a child raised by wolves might look. Or was it just the long-term effect of living in constant dread and of being so thin? Dr. Sellars looked at the picture for quite a while. He sidestepped the animal part and said simply,

"You do look a fair degree happier in this picture."

I looked at him and wondered aloud, "What is going to become of me? What could I ever do?" Inwardly I was thinking about my parents dying and picturing myself eating out of garbage cans to keep alive because I was afraid to die.

In marked contrast to these inner imaginings, which I didn't share with him, Dr. Sellars handed me back the photograph and in a very serious tone said calmly, "Well, before we can decide whether you should be a lawyer, or whatever, we have to find out what's troubling you."

A lawyer? Did he say lawyer? I said to myself. *How in the farthest reaches of his imagination could he think I might ever become a lawyer? Yet he had said "lawyer."* It was a male profession in my mind then—a prestigious profession. How could he look at me and say that? I was a mess. Bone thin, I looked like someone out of a concentration camp. Surprisingly however, I felt a twinge of hope. I thought, *He must see me differently than I see myself,* and it all hinged on his saying "lawyer." The time was up and Dr. Sellars walked me to the door. Carrying my eighth grade graduation picture I walked down Woodward Avenue back to Hudson's, but the words that kept reverberating in my head were *lawyer, he said lawyer.*

fourteen

"Will Your Anchor Hold in the Storms of Life?"

MY MOTHER MUST HAVE celebrated Christmas with a tree and presents if only for my brother's sake. New Year's Eve might go by without much notice, but she had never failed to celebrate Christmas and Easter no matter how grim the circumstances. Yet Christmas escaped me altogether. Except for the carolers at Hudson's there was for me no Christmas—no Christmas shopping, no Christmas Eve service at church. I barely noticed that the Forbes family had sold the house and moved to northern Michigan to run an inn, or that Pat, my best friend, did not return to this house at all—nor anything else that fell outside the circle of my preoccupation with death and hell. My mother worried that the new owner might ask us to move, but I had deeper worries.

All through January and February and March the days passed like a series of gray dead turns of a wheel, or muffled beats of a distant drum, with their slow rhythmic sameness. I was on a treadmill of agony. From time to time I received a letter from the young social work student I had met in Canada the previous summer, but since I had nothing to say to him, the letters went unanswered. They piled up on a corner of my desk as reminders of the happy person I had once been. Every night after supper I sat in the same corner of the green and pink flowered sofa, weeping over the same sorrows—my despair that I could never hope to be a loving, good person because I had been born bad—and the fear that never left me, the enormous fear, that when I died I would for certain find myself in a fiery hell. At nine or nine-thirty I crept into my mother's bed, glad that I could avoid these terrifying thoughts for a few hours. But in the minutes—sometimes an hour—before sleep came, I lay there dreading the morning when I would wake to yet another torturous day with no hope of change that I could see, another day of fastening belts and buttons on dresses to make the racks look neat and tidy, of trying to eat as little as possible, sometimes making a trip to the chute and deciding as before to "wait one more day," all the time knowing that my mournful state was painful to everyone around me, especially my mother. I knew nothing of John Calvin's theology, but my certainty that I was doomed was much like Calvin's doctrine of predestination. To my way of thinking this had all been preordained. If only I could have been among those preordained to be good.

Sessions with Dr. Sellars carried the same deadness. I began to wonder why he didn't give up on me. Instead, he appeared at the door of the waiting room exactly at one o'clock three times a week as though the therapy was progressing as it should. I never saw any sign of discouragement in him, but in my view we were on a hopeless mission—psychotherapy could never help someone like me. On a particularly beautiful April day, a Friday, my mother decided to come with me to my appointment to keep me company and perhaps to enjoy the good weather. As we left the clinic she paused for a moment, as if to absorb the sunshine, and then looked up at a blossoming tree that managed to grow on this busy city street. She turned to me, and seeing the same sad expression on my face, said, "Oh, Sarah, how I wish you could enjoy a day like today." She almost never said anything about how pitiful I looked, but her comment made me feel worse than I already felt. I was ruining the beauty of the spring day for her. Yet to feign better spirits seemed beyond my power. How I too wished that I could enjoy the beauty all around me. I told her I was sorry. We walked to the bus in silence.

April came and went, then in early May, Dr. Sellars and I were sitting in his cramped oblong-shaped office. The building was ancient and the high ceilings made the room seem even more long and narrow than it was. The one window at the end still needed washing. He played with his pipe— then scratched his chin as if he were ruminating. I had been silent for at least ten minutes when Dr. Sellars put his pipe down on his desk, leaned forward in his chair with his elbows on his knees, hands clasped in front of him, and said, "Sarah, I think I know what your unforgivable sin is."

I was jarred to attention by the words "unforgivable sin." That Dr. Sellars was about to tell me something came as a miraculous event. He never said anything except in response to what I said.

"You do?" I murmured—anxious at what he might be about to say.

"You see, it is a sin against your mother—and it is the sin of growing up and leaving her. You weren't supposed to do that." His words were slow and deliberate. Then he paused while his thoughtful brown eyes searched mine for a reaction. But I didn't have one immediately. I just soaked in his words.

Actually, I hung onto every syllable of those words since this was the first time Dr. Sellars had said anything about my problem of being a bad person—let alone acknowledging that I had an unforgivable sin.

Much later I learned that this was what psychoanalysts call an "interpretation," and that he was telling me something he had ferreted out about the unconscious conflict that underlay my illness—except he never used the word "unconscious" or any psychological terms whatsoever. Silently I repeated what he had said so I wouldn't forget.

I think I know what your unforgivable sin is. You see it is a sin against your mother. And it is the sin of growing up and leaving her. You weren't supposed to do that.

Somewhere in a place I could locate only as way down inside me I knew Dr. Sellars had just said something deeply important. *My sin wasn't against God? It was against my mother? How did he come to know this? I had told him so little. And what does it all mean?—I wasn't supposed to grow up?—I wasn't supposed to leave? I wasn't supposed to do any of these things—go away to the University of Michigan, marry Eric and go to Africa? I had no right. But everyone grows up—everyone leaves eventually.*

"How did you figure this out? I told you so little."

"I don't know for sure, it's what I think," he said. Neither of us said anything more. But the words he had spoken stood out all the more sharply against the silence—*the sin of growing up and leaving her—you weren't supposed to do that—you weren't supposed to do that—you weren't supposed to do that.* At the end of the time he walked me to the door the same as always, and said he'd see me on Wednesday, the same as always. Yet something felt different. I felt I *wanted* to come back on Wednesday. I had never felt that before.

A day or so after Dr. Sellars made his statement about my unforgivable sin, I had lunch with my mother in the employees' cafeteria as I always did when I wasn't seeing Dr. Sellars. We finished lunch and went to Hudson's basement store to buy a piece of fudge for my mother to have on her afternoon break. She was convinced that a piece of chocolate fudge gave her energy for the rest of the day. Sometimes she chose maple walnut. I, of course, did not eat fudge—my weight still hovering around 86 pounds. As we rushed through the aisles on the way to the candy department we passed a square display table that had a sign on a metal stand that caught my eye. It read:

SALE

Irish Linen Handkerchiefs

10 cents apiece

I stopped to look at the handkerchiefs. They had perforated edges, and I remembered that I had several spools of different colored crochet thread at home I had bought a couple of years before during a short-lived enthusiasm for crocheting. My mother, who'd been forging ahead of me toward the fudge counter, came back to look for me.

"Look at these handkerchiefs for ten cents apiece," I said to her. "I have all that crochet thread at home. Maybe I should buy a few of these and use up that thread." My thought was a practical one—that the crochet thread shouldn't be wasted. But when I looked at my mother's face for a response, I saw a flicker of awareness that told me she saw a larger significance to my interest in the handkerchiefs. This was the first time since I had dropped out of university nearly nine months before that I had shown an interest in anything except my brooding thoughts. She quickly endorsed my idea.

"At ten cents a piece they're a bargain. How many would you like to buy?"

"I think six would be good," I told her.

We found a salesperson and I made my sixty-cent purchase, less my 20 percent employee's discount. We still had time to buy a piece of fudge for my mother.

That night after supper I found the little spools of colored thread and my crochet hook. There was a pink spool, a bright green one and three or four others. I gathered up the spools and the handkerchiefs and sat on the studio couch in the dining room. Choosing the green spool I began crocheting a small border of green lace on one of the handkerchiefs. The shiny silver crochet hook moved rhythmically in and out between my fingers. I liked the look of Kelly green against the snow white linen. A sense of enjoyment I had not felt for a long time came seeping into me. When

I finished the green edged handkerchief, I folded it—later I would iron it. Right then I wanted to crochet a light blue edge on a second handkerchief. It felt good to be doing this. For the first time in months I had something to show for the time spent. When I ironed them the finished product had a freshness that pleased me—the filigreed lace, both the green and the light blue, against the high quality linen, looked delicately beautiful.

From that evening on, gradually, I began to pick up the threads of my life. A week or so later I wanted to see the movie, *The Father of the Bride,* with Elizabeth Taylor and Spencer Tracy, playing at our local Tower Theater. My mother was more than happy to go with me, relieved to see these signs of my former self emerging. This time I followed the plot of the story with no difficulty, unlike the last film I had seen with my friend Ann Tittl when nothing registered. I enjoyed the humor—and even laughed out loud at times. I thought Spencer Tracy was terrific.

I began to eat again, slowly. At first my shrunken stomach wasn't ready for a full meal, but over a period of three or four weeks I became able to eat a half of a tuna sandwich or a small plate of spaghetti at lunch. My mother had to be beside herself with relief and joy to see me eating again, but she managed not to comment. After five or six weeks of eating, my appearance changed dramatically. Although I was still careful about what I ate, not wanting to gain back *all* the weight I'd lost, I began to resemble the happy person I used to be. I could now acknowledge what I couldn't see before—that at 86 pounds I was emaciated—not at all attractive.

Once I began to look better, I wanted to go back to church. My mother and I had begun singing hymns together again and it made me aware of how much I missed church—the sermons, and even more the music. Going to church would mean getting together with my friends there and I wondered how they would react—how I would react. The first Sunday back at Calvin Church, however, my re-entry felt quite comfortable. The kids in the Christian Endeavor group seemed overjoyed to see me—my friend Ann Tittl especially—and asked very few questions about my long absence. Had our minister, Roger McShane, or the youth minister, Stacy Roberts, coached them? I doubt it. I think it was just their Christian warmth and tactfulness. Showing kindness was a strong suit of this whole group. I had shared so many good times with them that it made me almost giddy with happiness to be back. When questions did come up I just said, "Well, I was a little depressed, but I'm better now." Much,

much later I learned that Roger McShane had counseled the members of Christian Endeavor not to contact me during my depression, explaining to them that what I was experiencing was too complicated for them to be of help. I think he was wise in doing this.

A few weeks after I returned to church I was leaving the Christian Endeavor meeting one night when I saw a familiar figure standing by the door. It was Eric. I hadn't seen him since I broke up with him at the start of my slide into dark waters. I figured he must have heard from friends that I was getting better. Later I learned that he had called my mother from time to time the whole nine months of my absence to see what was happening with me—so she was probably the one who told him I was "back." When I reached the place where he was waiting he smiled and said, "Hi. I thought I'd like to go to the evening service with you. Would that be okay?"

"That would be very much okay," I said. I felt truly glad to see Eric. He smiled again and looked relieved. Christian Endeavor met in the church basement. We walked up the steps, entered the front door of the church, and took a seat in a pew filling up with other young people. Sitting next to Eric in church, as I had so many times before, felt good, although I knew I wasn't the same happy-go-lucky girl I had been back then. Much had changed in me. I had met a vulnerable side of myself I hadn't known was there; but I had also found an inner strength that felt different. I knew for sure that I would never be that vulnerable again.

Jack Phlieger was asking for requests of favorite hymns during the hymn sing before the service proper began. I decided to make a request. "How about number 36, 'Will Your Anchor Hold in the Storms of Life'?" This hymn was usually requested by an older person, but I felt I had been through a few storms now, and I had always loved this hymn. Mr. Phlieger said that this was one of his favorites too. The pianist played a few bars and the congregation began to sing.

> Will your anchor hold in the storms of life,
> When the clouds unfold their wings of strife?
> When the strong tides lift,
> And the cables strain,
> Will your anchor drift or firm remain?

And the chorus:

We have an anchor that keeps the soul
Steadfast and sure while the billows roll,
Fastened to the rock which cannot move,
Grounded firm and deep in the Savior's love.

We sang one more of the four verses. This hymn sing before the evening service at Calvin Church was something I dearly loved. I was so glad to be back. Eric reached for my hand. The touch of his strong, athletic palm with its calluses from pumping gas felt warm and familiar.

Afterwards Eric and I went for a Coke. Like my other friends, he did not ask for explanations, even of my strange behavior toward him, but I sensed a slight wariness as we sat sipping our drinks. He was choosing his words carefully. After we chatted for a while—about our parents, about our brothers, and his little sister—the uneasiness diminished. He told me that his second year of pre-med had gone well.

"I had more time to study than I had the year before," he joked. It had been a point of contention between us that he spend more time with me. Then he said shyly, "I'd really like to see you again—even if it means I can't study as much." I told him that could be arranged. He looked pleased and smiled. When he drove me home he asked, "How about next Friday, or Saturday?" I told him Friday would be good.

Soon we were enjoying each other's company as much as before, but without the same degree of commitment. We didn't talk about marriage or the future, but more about everyday things—the Korean War, that was frighteningly imminent, or the television set his family had just bought ahead of almost everybody else. For the first time we just had fun without the former seriousness—went swimming at our old high school, or at River Rouge Park when the weather was warm enough, went to the movies where we saw double features and newsreels. We didn't try to plan what would happen next.

Something had shifted after Dr. Sellars made his single interpretation in which he told me that I suffered from feeling I had no right to grow up and leave my mother. After he said that the thoughts about hell and about being a bad person were shed as though a black shawl I had been wearing was now left behind on the floor or out in the street. I could remember having these thoughts—vividly, but I no longer believed them—or thought about them much at all except to wonder *how could I have had such crazy ideas?* That puzzled me, but more as an oddity or a curiosity than anything I needed to worry about.

Could that one "interpretation" Dr. Sellars made about my unforgivable sin have caused these persecuting thoughts to leave? The timing suggests that is exactly what happened. I couldn't fit all the pieces together at the time but in retrospect, expecially while writing this memoir, I could see that his interpretation identified the overwhelming sense of obligation I felt to stay and help my mother with my father's illness—perhaps for the rest of my life—and that unconsciously I believed I had no right to grow up and leave her. I had not been aware of feeling an obligation of that magnitude. But reviewing what I have written in this memoir, I believe Dr. Sellars was incredibly accurate—that my unconscious mind felt it was wrong, ungrateful, *sinful* even, to want to be free to leave and chart my own course when my mother needed me so much. Carried to an absurd conclusion, as the unconscious mind can do, I felt deserving of hell for such a selfish desire.

I never told my mother that Dr. Sellars felt I believed it was wrong to grow up and leave her. She would have felt she had caused my depression. And she hadn't caused it—it was the way I perceived the situation of my father's illness and my responsibility. One could argue that my mother was wrong to dissuade me from going to the University of Michigan. For certain that's what Mony thought. But I thought, and still do, that my mother literally had no control over her actions in this matter. I believe her excessive need of me was as unconscious to her as my outsized sense of obligation was to me.

Wayne University turned out to be a stimulating place. I'm sure I had more full professors as teachers at Wayne than I would have had as an undergraduate at Michigan. I don't think giving up the University of Michigan was a problem for me. Giving up Michigan is important for what it showed—that my mother could not part with me, at least not yet. So when Eric and I talked about marrying and going to a far away country, my unconscious mind, I believe, condemned this as traitorous. It wasn't until Dr. Sellars lifted all this to consciousness that I could see the fallacy in my harsh judgments of myself. My relationship with my mother did not change outwardly after this—we still did as many things together as ever, and I knew her love for me was as enormous as mine for her. But inwardly I now felt free. I knew that when the time came for me to leave home, I would be able to do that.

In the weeks following Dr. Sellars' interpretation, from time to time I had a mental image of having come from behind a penumbra, a shadow that had enveloped me, out into the light. Even though I didn't understand until much later why I had been in that shadowy place—I knew for certain that this depression would not return. It left almost as suddenly as it had come but the months in between its coming and departing had seemed interminable. For me now, I understand this year as a moratorium in which an imbalance in my relationship with my mother was set right. When I came out from behind the penumbra, something felt finished—I would never be in that pit of blackness again.

Time proved me right. Unlike my father's illness that returned again and again, mine never has. My father had a very different kind of illness than I had. His manic-depressive psychosis was probably in large part genetic—triggered by the stress of losing his drugstore during the Depression. I *could* have inherited this illness from him. It is my good fortune that I did not. Who knows the ways of genes—researchers are trying to identify genetic markers of a predisposition toward manic-depressive illness, although results still appear inconclusive as to just how heredity takes place. Had my father been born fifty years later there would have been medications that could have stabilized his mood swings, enabling him to continue in his profession and live a normal life. I've since known several people with this illness who do live a normal life. My illness I believe can best be described as a late adolescent crisis that is usually responsive to good psychotherapy—if one is fortunate enough to receive that. In retrospect I feel it was God's grace mediated through generous, capable people like Mrs. Murphy, Dr. Sellars, and the J. L. Hudson Company that I received this help—which in all likelihood saved my life.

In the months that followed I felt an extraordinary feeling of joy, as if my life had been returned to me fuller and richer than it had been before. This joy reached an even greater peak when my father was discharged from the hospital and could be home with us again. This had been one of his longer stays at Ypsilanti State Hospital. While I had felt guilty about causing his return to the hospital, now I could concede that though it probably was my illness that provoked this episode, I couldn't help becoming ill.

I was enormously glad to see him. This time he did not look thin and sad as he always had before after a hospitalization. His walk even had a little spring in it as he came toward me. He was smiling and there was good color in his face—I think because he was so glad to see me enjoying my life again and back to my normal self. We hugged each other with a hug that carried enormous meaning—*I'm glad you're well—I'm glad to be home—I'm glad we're both well.* We sat in the kitchen and had coffee and angel food cake—my father, my mother, Danny, and I. That we were all together again felt like God's enormous gift.

My brother, meanwhile, graduated from Chadsey High School that June, and took a pretty blonde girl named Amy to his senior prom, stopping at our house on the way for pictures of Amy in her formal and him in his rented tux. For the first time in a long time our family had a celebration with no cloud hovering overhead. My parents made Danny a festive dinner the Sunday after his graduation. Our friend Mony came, Danny's friend Dale, and my boyfriend Eric, and Amy. Once again the smell of my father's baked chicken filled the kitchen and filtered out into the dining room. As I set the table I breathed in that wonderful smell that signified my father was home and well. My mother brought out the graduation cake from Awry's bakery, decorated in Chadsey's school colors, and we ate cake and watched Danny open his presents. My mother's face was almost radiant—her worry wrinkles barely visible. When her incredibly blue eyes met mine for a moment, my joy was like a song rising inside my heart. The music was back.

Dr. Sellars felt we should continue our sessions even though my mental state had taken a 180 degree turn. I was content to do this. Now that I wasn't depressed, I could appreciate more fully how ruggedly handsome Dr. Sellars actually was, and began to dress as attractively as I could for our sessions. I now had an inkling of what Mrs. Forbes asked me about falling in love with my analyst. I did like him a lot. We no longer talked much about the past or my dark thoughts, which had entirely disappeared. We talked about the future and my plans to go back to Wayne University in the fall—something I thought would never happen now seemed easy. In one of these sessions, however, Dr. Sellars did bring up the past. He asked me, "Whatever happened to those religious or philosophical questions you were asking when you first came to see me—'Why are we here?' and, 'Is there a purpose to life?' Do you think about them at all?" I was surprised that he remembered—and even more surprised that this was a subject that interested him.

"I know I haven't dealt with those questions—and sometime I must," I told him, "but for now I want to enjoy this new freedom from all those fears. To tell you the truth, I mainly want to have fun."

"Then that's what you should do," Dr. Sellers said, playing with his pipe, his brown eyes twinkling. "You'll get back to those questions when you're ready."

"I know I will—probably before too long. Right now I've been trying to decide what major would be the most enjoyable when I return to Wayne in September. It's not practical, but I was thinking of Art as a major—drawing and painting, although I've never done anything like that before."

"Why not give it a try? And, Sarah, perhaps it's time for us to consider going to two sessions a week or even one. You can think about it and we'll talk about that next time?" I said I would.

He rose to see me to the door. When he said he'd see me on Wednesday, I had a fleeting memory of the time I had said I would see him on Wednesday but fully planned not to be there—the time I had been the closest to jumping down the chute at Hudson's. A chill came over me and then a feeling of deep relief that the idea of "waiting one more day" had kept me from jumping. I would have missed out on so much—the whole rest of my life.

"Yes, for sure," I said and left the clinic. It was a beautiful day. I hurried back to my work at Hudson's. I wanted to get more sales on my book to make up for my long lunch hour. By now everyone had recognized my recovery, so even my position of salesperson had been restored. I enjoyed waiting on customers and trying to find the dress that would look best on them. I especially enjoyed working in the College Shop where girls were buying clothes for school because I'd soon be one of them again. I too was buying some new clothes from the College Shop. I enjoyed the sunshine and the rain, and having a French cruller with my mother at Greenfield's coffee shop. I enjoyed waking up in the morning to a whole new day.

fifteen

"Lead Kindly Light"

In September I returned to Wayne University and again changed my major—this time to Art. I thought art would be the most fun of any major I could imagine—and for now I really wanted to have fun. Instead of the heavy pre-med courses with which I began the year before, this time I had a schedule filled with studio courses in drawing and painting, and sculpture, along with my second year of German. I felt excited buying large pads of drawing paper, oil paints, brushes, and canvases—entering a world entirely new to me. Mimicking the other art students, I changed the way I dressed as well. My friend Ann Tittl ran into me on Cass Avenue in front of the Science Building one day and doubled over with laughter.

"Sarah, what on earth are you doing in that getup?"

"Come on, Ann. This is my new look," I told her, but I was laughing too. I wore a long rust-colored corduroy skirt with hat to match, a dark green corduroy jacket over a black turtleneck, horned-rimmed glasses, black tights and boots. The outfit went together almost too well to be truly Bohemian, as I intended, but it was fairly off-beat for 1950. Ann was wearing a pleated skirt and saddle shoes, the norm. As an art major, I wanted to look the part. Whether or not I had any talent remained to be seen.

Along with my art courses, I resumed my former activities at Wayne. My old beat reporting on women's sports at the *Detroit Collegian* was still available to me. I had never been remotely athletic, but I enjoyed meeting with the women's teams and knowing their world from the sidelines. Walter Poole, the director of the Wayne Symphony Orchestra, welcomed me back to my place in the second violin section and even gave me a music scholarship. On Fridays at noon I again went to the Wayne Christian Fellowship meetings.

In my exuberance over being a joyful person again I joined Wayne University's chapter of the American Youth Hostel that met once a week and went on outings in the area. I believe I was the only woman in this outdoorsy group who wore lipstick, so the group chose me as their nominee for Homecoming Queen, a frivolity that panicked me at first. I went to my friend in the Wayne Christian Fellowship, Muriel Hunt and asked if she thought this a fitting activity for a Christian. "Why not a Christian Homecoming Queen?" was Muriel's calm response. To my amazement I landed among the last ten contestants who had to sit for professional head shots. The head shots were placed on a large bulletin board in the Student Center for the final round of voting. When I didn't make it into the last five, the queen and her court, I had to admit to real disappointment. By then I had come to think the festivities would be fun. Considering the skinny sad creature I had been just the previous spring, to be a contestant for Homecoming Queen in September showed quite a transformation. Dr. Sellars seemed pleased.

I truly missed Pat now, and the whole Forbes family who no longer lived downstairs. Mrs. Dawson, the new landlady, lived there alone and was no substitute for the lively back and forth we had enjoyed with the Forbes family. Mrs. Dawson complained about my typing late at night, so I couldn't do that anymore. A true deprivation for this night owl.

Over a weekend I drove with Bob Alexander, my first high school boyfriend, to northern Michigan to visit Pat. We stayed at her parents' newly acquired inn. As three long-time friends, Bob and Pat and I spent hours reminiscing about our shared histories. Each of our lives had changed dramatically the year before. With her family's move, Pat had left behind all her friends in Detroit and gave up a major city for this rural area where she knew no one. Bob had grown restless at Wayne and enlisted in the Air Force. He was now on leave from cadet school, where he was training to be a pilot. In the future he would graduate first in his class and then fly 30 bombing missions over Korea. My life, of course, had been turned upside-down. After Bob and I had stopped dating each other in high school, he dated Pat for a time; but now the three of us were simply good friends. In between swims off the dock, we lay in the sun and talked about our days at Cooley High School, and the pranks we had played at weekend Christian Endeavor conferences—such as the time we stole the speaker's notes just before his talk. We eventually gave them back. We talked too about the year ahead that awaited us in very different settings—Bob learning to fly a plane, Pat back at Alma College, and my expansive switch to an art major at Wayne.

That fall, my brother was studying architecture at the Lawrence Institute of Technology, my mother still ran rings around the other salesladies in her department at Hudson's, and my father again cooked delicious dinners for us. On Sundays the three of us, and occasionally my father, went to Calvin Church. My brother and I still took part in the Christian Endeavor group there, which extended to college age. We luxuriated in this period of calm even more than usual. The traumas of the previous year made this present good fortune seem like Eden.

Eric and I were spending several evenings a week together—as much time as he could spare from his studying. We often studied together— more often we went to a movie or went swimming at one of the local pools. We were going steady again and our affection for each other was reaching a new peak of delicious feelings I had never felt before. The romance itself was sweet. I felt sure we would marry some day, but that day was a long way off, which was a comfort. The thought of marriage still activated some hidden nerve I didn't quite understand because I knew now that I was free to leave.

When I began my sophomore year for the second time, I knew, as Dr. Sellars had pointed out, that I had not addressed any of the confusion about my religious beliefs that had plagued my freshman year. As I thought about these issues, it seemed more plausible to me that a greater intelligence had created us than that we somehow emerged from a random confluence of molecules, so I did believe in the existence of God. From all that I had known about Jesus Christ, I believed that He was indeed the Son of God, so I counted myself a Christian. Having been exposed now to some of the other possibilities (atheism and agnosticism) I was reaffirming the faith with which I'd grown up and felt at peace about that—almost at peace.

I still puzzled over the way many of the students in Wayne Christian Fellowship had an inner closeness to God that eluded me. I concluded that they were more advanced in their Christian faith than I was—especially in their knowledge of the Bible. That many people I respected—my father, probably Mony, several of my professors, and some fellow students—did not believe in God didn't trouble me now. No one could know for certain, so it came down to what each person deemed the best hypothesis about what lay behind this complicated arena of human existence. I felt there was more mystery behind this wonderful creation, the universe, than we could ever fully plumb. For the time being at least I was content to believe in God and in Christ being God's son and live with any other uncertainties.

The students in Wayne Christian Fellowship were planning to host a week of lectures on campus in February. That fall and during January I worked on the committee that planned this event. We put up posters, placed notices in the *Detroit Collegian*, and secured meeting rooms. Leith Samuel, an Anglican priest from England, would lecture on campuses across Canada and the United States sponsored by Inter-Varsity Christian Fellowship, the national organization of which Wayne Christian Fellowship was a chapter. We learned that in England Leith Samuel often spoke to student groups at Oxford and Cambridge. To me this meant that he must be really smart—perhaps an intellectual even. Oxford and Cambridge were at the apex of institutions of learning in my estimation. I looked forward to hearing a truly learned Christian.

On a rainy February day two other committee members and I went to meet Leith Samuel's train arriving from Chicago. The person who emerged was a tall, lean Englishman in his mid-thirties. He looked like a runner. I later learned that in university he *had* been a sprinter. He had lively blue eyes, straight light brown hair, and an appealing, modest way about him. After greeting him as warmly as we could—we were a little in awe of this dignitary from abroad—we piled into a cab back to the Student Center, where a meeting with other members of the Fellowship had been set up. Once we'd settled into chairs arranged in a circle, Gil Hunter, our president, introduced Leith Samuel to the others and asked him to tell us about his plan for the week ahead.

First Leith told us a little about himself. His name "Samuel" he said, came from Jewish ancestry on his father's side, of which he was proud. His father had become a Christian as a boy of seventeen, so Leith had been raised Christian. He was married and had two children. For the past five years he had been a missioner to university students on campuses across England. He said he felt he had a calling to minister to students.

"Have you lectured at American universities before?" Muriel, our vice president, asked him.

"First time I've crossed the pond. I hope my accent and the odd word that differs from yours won't get in the way." Muriel said she was sure we could translate. Samuel laughed and said he thought so too.

He explained that in his five lectures he would speak as though he were talking to someone who had never been to church and try to give a basic understanding of the Christian faith—the truths upon which almost all Christians agree. I began to think about the many sermons I had heard in my life so far, and my two years of Lutheran catechism. My thought was *even with all that exposure to Christian teaching I would be hard pressed to give a basic understanding of the Christian faith to someone—even to myself. Where would I start? What is the basic Christian faith? I really didn't know.* I had already concluded that Leith Samuel was indeed a bright man. Since I had never heard a systematic explanation of the Christian faith, I decided I would go to every lecture. That was definitely what I wanted to hear—the basics.

"The lectures are from twelve to one p.m. Monday to Friday," Gil explained, "with a question period the first four nights from eight to nine thirty. We were fortunate to get the same amphitheater in the Science Building for all the sessions." I decided I would go to go to the question periods as well. I thought it a little ironic that these lectures would take place in the Science Building. Perhaps Leith Samuel will be up to answering the scientific arguments I'd heard against belief in God. I left feeling eager to hear what this energetic young Brit would have to say to the students of Wayne University next week.

When I arrived for the first lecture I was surprised to see so many students there. We had advertised the series as a "Council on Campus Christianity." I hadn't liked this title much, wondering why campus Christianity should be different from any other Christianity, but perhaps I was wrong about the title. As I looked around the large amphitheater I saw it was filled almost to capacity. I took a seat about halfway back in the center section of the curved rows of seats covered in blue velour, each row raised above the one below. There would be no hymn singing because these lectures were aimed at students outside of Wayne Christian Fellowship, not the members. At exactly twelve o'clock our president, Gil Hunter, began the meeting with an introduction of Leith Samuel. Gil was a warm, friendly person. I would be anxious before such a large audience of mostly strangers, but Gil appeared at ease as he welcomed the students and the five or six faculty members who had come. Gil was always at ease—always himself.

Gil sat down amidst applause. Leith Samuel reached the podium with a few quick strides, as though eager to begin. He wore a well-tailored dark suit—almost black but not quite—and a clerical collar. His tall, athletic build was a striking contrast to Gil, who was short and a bit pudgy. When Mr. Samuel started to speak, I was relieved to find his speaking style appealed to me—very sure of himself, but not the least bit arrogant. It took only a few sentences to know he was indeed an intellectual who could speak a university student's language. He made a joking reference to his back to front collar to start with, which deftly removed that barrier. I had hoped that Leith Samuel might convince some of the non-believing students at Wayne of the value of having a faith in God and in Christ. But sitting there in that first lecture, I began to feel glad to be there for me. *Had I missed something in my understanding of my faith, I wondered, that it crumbled so easily when I met with some skepticism my first year at Wayne? And why hadn't my faith kept me from that awful depression last year? Was the depression related in some way to my faith—or was it from a different source altogether?*

Samuel began at the beginning—in the beginning God created the heavens and the earth—and said that, of course, creation did not take place in six days as we count days. I looked around at the audience. *The room was very still. Samuel had captured their attention already.* And God created man to have a relationship with himself, he continued. The biblical story of Adam and Eve and the serpent implied that at one time man knew God, but that something else, sin and distrust, entered into the equation and man lost his former knowledge of God. *With the horrible war and Holocaust we'd just witnessed, no one could dispute that mankind had lost its way.*

The rest of the Old Testament, he explained, is chiefly the story of God's attempt to bring man back to a relationship with himself through his chosen people, the Hebrews, the only people who came to a belief in one God—or monotheism. *It is amazing that no other people or civilization came to a belief in one God except the Hebrews. God must have revealed himself to them in a particular way.* According to Samuel, God did.

After this first lecture I was eager to hear more. I went to lunch with Gil and Muriel and some other members of Wayne Christian Fellowship. We sat around a table in the student center and talked about the lecture.

Faith and Madness

Most agreed they had never heard a lecturer who spoke as clearly as Samuel did. We had begun congratulating ourselves that our efforts had paid off in the large turnout when Muriel, with a puckish grin, said, "Or might this be the work of the Holy Spirit?" Muriel's faith was so deep, and she was the most level-headed person I knew.

I excused myself from the others. I was eager to go to the question period that night, but in the meantime I had some studying to do for my English Education class that afternoon. At mid-year I had changed my major one last time. Art courses had indeed been enjoyable, but without abundant natural talent, and no job waiting at the end of an Art major I worried about making a living. English and literature courses had always been favorites, so I opted for English Education, which would lead to a license to teach high school English, and this at last felt right.

Attendance at the lectures continued to be high. Beginning with Abraham, Leith Samuel told how God had revealed himself to the patriarchs and the prophets on down through history until the coming of Christ. In Jesus Christ God gave the fullest revelation of his nature, Samuel said. Much of what he said about the Old Testament was familiar to me, but I appreciated hearing it in an historical context. *Everyone should have a course in Old Testament, or in the whole Bible, for the sheer educational value of it, I concluded.*

What was new to me came on Wednesday when Samuel talked about Christ as the "Word of God," or the "Logos," the Greek word for "Word" or "Reason." I had not known that Christians believe Christ pre-existed before his birth as Jesus in Bethlehem. "John's Gospel makes this very clear," Samuel said. Then he read from the first chapter of John:

> In the beginning was the Word, and the Word was with God, and Word was God. The same was in the beginning with God. All things were made by him; and without him was not anything made that was made. In him was life; and the life was the light of men. And the light shineth in darkness; and the darkness comprehended it not.

"And a few verses later," Samuel said, "we read":

> And the Word was made flesh, and dwelt among us, (and we beheld his glory, the glory as of the only begotten of the Father) full of grace and truth.

Later in John's Gospel, Samuel pointed out, Jesus himself says, "Before Abraham was, I am."

Samuel described the coming of Christ as the most cataclysmic event in human history, God taking on human form to reveal his nature to man as fully as possible. The main point to which Leith Samuel's lectures were leading, however, was that one could have a relationship with this Creator-God who was eager to show man how to fulfill his role in the continued creation. This astounded me, that I might have a part in God's overall plan for creation—*yet wasn't that exactly what I had been searching for in my questions about purpose and meaning in life—the "Why are we here?" question?*

Samuel brought up another idea that was entirely new to me—probably the most important concept in all of Christian thought—the concept of grace, that God's love for us does not have to be deserved. It's totally without conditions. I had always thought that God's love had to be earned by doing good deeds and caring for others. Samuel made it clear to me for the first time that this is not the way it works—God's acceptance cannot be earned—it can only be accepted. Following Jesus' teachings about caring for others is inevitably an outgrowth of a relationship to God, proof that the relationship exists, but it is not what brings the relationship about. *I never understood that before—that each of us is self-seeking unless God gives us his grace to be otherwise. We all need forgiveness. But we're loved just the same.* I left the lecture pondering all these thoughts about grace.

In his Thursday lecture Samuel explained what it meant to have a relationship with Christ—that it was more than just believing the stories about Jesus, or even believing Jesus pre-existed and is the Son of God. One needed to have an encounter with Christ—like Nicodemus, the Pharisee who came to Jesus by night—and then make him the center of your life. This too was new to me.

In the question period that night, Samuel compared having an encounter with Christ to an empirical test. "When you go into your laboratory," he said, accenting the second syllable, "and read in the chemistry manual that if you put chemicals X and Y together, you will get a specific result, you don't have to take the manual's word for it. You can make an empirical test and see for yourself." *I liked his use of an analogy from science—Wayne University always emphasized science—the students here understand empirical tests.* Samuel continued, "In the Book of Revelation the risen Christ, speaking to the churches, said":

> "Behold, I stand at the door, and knock: if any man hear my voice, and open the door, I will come in to him, and will sup with him, and he with me."

"If you really want to know whether Christ means this or not," Samuel said, "you can make an empirical test—that is, you can test out what Christ says here, if you wish, by opening the door."

It sounds both too simple and too awesome, and what does opening the door mean—opening your heart? Samuel suggested a prayer one might pray if he wished to open the door and ask Christ in. *Again, it sounded too simple to me—too easy. Yet his argument was a reasonable one. If you never "opened the door," how would you know?*

That night after the question period, riding the two buses on my way home from the university, I continued to think about what Samuel had said. *On the one hand it sounds too simple—or is it too scary? Yet, if Christ could be known in this mystical way, and could give meaning and direction to one's life, I would want that.*

I stepped off the bus and unexpectedly found myself in a resplendent world. A blanket of fresh snow had turned everything white. The snow sparkled and glistened under the streetlights as more snow fell in the hushed residential street. Everything around me looked very bright. Entranced by the beauty, I wanted to twirl around and dance. Walking the two blocks to my house in the midst of this magical, silent splendor, my thoughts turned again to Leith Samuel's empirical test, but in an almost playful way. Before I made this empirical test, I wanted to mark the date. It was February 22, and I thought, *Tonight is George Washington's birthday, and since George never told a lie, what you say tonight you must really mean.* I was deeply serious, but there was this jocular attitude about the date as well.

In the second block the snow was still coming down luxuriantly in the bright stillness, creating a silent world set apart. The trees that lined the street were heavy with snow. I could have been in a deep wood—the street practically unrecognizable in its glistening new garb. I decided I did want to make the empirical test. Without pausing in my walk or closing my eyes, I prayed silently the prayer Leith Samuel suggested:

Lord Jesus, I thank you for dying for my sins, and I ask you to come into my life and show me what you want me to do with it.

I did not feel particularly sinful at that moment, but I prayed the prayer just as Leith Samuel had suggested anyway. Nor did I have any set expectation—so I wasn't prepared when immediately after I prayed, I felt a response. It came as a surprise. I did not see a great light as St. Paul saw on the way to Damascus, but I felt responded to by a presence that had to be Christ. The response seemed to come from a space just above me and to my left, but without sight or sound. The feeling of shock or surprise soon settled into a deep sense of peace that was different from my earlier enjoyment of the snowy night. The enjoyment of the night was of my outer surroundings—this peace was inner. It was enhanced by the beauty of the snow, but not dependent on it. The snow formed the setting, like a majestic cathedral, but the response came from deep inside me. *I will come into him and sup with him and he with me. Those were Jesus' words. Perhaps they were true.*

As I neared my house though my skepticism returned full bore with thoughts such as: *This is all well and good when you're out here on this glorious winter night with all this snow—who wouldn't feel peaceful in a mysterious way here? But just wait till you go inside. You'll see that it's just an illusion.* I didn't want to leave the beautiful soft glow of the snow under the streetlights. It looked as though someone had lit a hundred ivory candles to light up the night. I feared that when I went inside my feelings of peace and Christ's presence would evaporate. But it was late—reluctantly I went inside.

My parents were still up watching the eleven o'clock news. "Why are you coming home so late, Sarah, the fourth night in a row?" my mother asked in a worried, impatient voice. Normally, this would provoke an irate, "I'm twenty years old, mother. Don't you think it's time you stopped telling me when to come home?" Only I didn't feel my usual surge of anger. I explained to them that tonight had been the last night of Leith Samuel's question periods and that this had been a special week. My father chimed in with, "Your mother's right, honey. You've got to think about your health." I never felt angry with my father, but I wondered why I didn't feel annoyed at my mother as I would normally. *Could it be that something did happen?* I said goodnight to them and went to my room.

I loved this room with my blue chenille bedspread, light blue walls, and sheer white curtains. I kept it very neat by always putting my clothes away and clearing my desk when I finished studying. Tonight it looked especially serene and inviting. I got out my Bible and sat down at my desk to look up the verse, Revelation 3:20, Leith Samuel had referred to. There it was: "If any man hear my voice, and open the door, I will come in to him, and will sup with him, and he with me." But was that all that was required to "open the door"—the simple prayer I prayed? I remembered part of a passage I had learned in Sunday school, "Seek and ye shall find, knock and it shall be opened unto you." Perhaps I had been seeking all last year in my own misguided way. I didn't know.

It was late and I wanted to go to the eight o'clock prayer meeting the next morning where we prayed for the conference. But I was afraid that if I went to sleep I would lose the peace I had inside of me. That same skeptical inner voice said: *Something feels different right now, but don't expect this to last. When you wake up tomorrow you'll see that this was just an illusion.* I put my Bible on my nightstand, got into my nightclothes and brushed my teeth. When I turned out the light I pulled back the curtain and could see out my window that the snow was still falling. It was darker here between the houses, but the large white snowflakes were still visible—my cathedral was still there.

When I woke the next morning the first thought that went through my mind was, *When I awake I am still with Thee.* It startled me. With the "thee" I knew it was from the Bible but I didn't know where in the Bible—probably from the Psalms. But there are 150 psalms in the Bible, and though I had heard many of them read in church over the years, how did my mind sift through 150 psalms and come up with a line so perfect to allay my doubt, *when I awake I am still with Thee?* It had to be God who put that thought there to reassure me that he was still with me—sleep had not erased his presence. From that moment on I never doubted that the response I felt in the snow that night was Christ's presence. The feeling that something significant took place at that time has stayed with me through my entire life. Later I learned that *when I awake I am still with Thee* is from Psalm 139.

I went to the university that morning and on my way into the prayer meeting I met my friend Muriel Hunt. She looked at me quizzically for a few seconds and then said, "You understand now, don't you?"

"Yes," I told Muriel, "for the first time I do."

I'm not sure how she determined this in her three-second glance, yet that is probably what I had noted in some of the others in the group, the mystery of this peace I sensed they had which I could not experience before. I knew now why they seemed so sure of their faith and had an inner joy I could sense in them. I now felt that joy.

During the year of depression what I had missed most was the music—that I couldn't even sing when I was depressed. In my life at Wayne now, and at home, and at Calvin Church I had music everywhere again. My mother and I played violin and piano together, I sang in the choir at church, and at Wayne my violin was always with me. Most of all I loved the singing we did at Wayne Christian Fellowship. With my father home and well, with Danny loving his architecture courses at Lawrence Tech, and with my mother looking more worry-free than I could remember, I could sing with a full heart. Two hymns in particular expressed the feelings I had then, soon after my snowy night encounter with Christ. The first one is:

> I know not why God's wondrous grace
> To me He hath made known,
> Nor why, unworthy, Christ in love
> Redeemed me for His own.

> But I know whom I have believed
> And am persuaded that He is able
> To keep that which I've committed
> Unto Him against that day.

The "I know whom . . ." is a quotation from Paul's writings. And that it is "whom" and not "what" makes a difference—it is a person, I now understood, not a set of doctrines or ideas.

The other song I loved to sing at that time was the one I heard in the Student Center that led me to find the Wayne Christian Fellowship meeting:

> Great is Thy faithfulness, O God my Father.
> There is no shadow of turning with Thee;
> Thou changest not, Thy compassions, they fail not;
> As Thou hast been Thou forever wilt be.

But if I had to name my most favorite hymn of all, I think I would join my father in choosing Cardinal John Newman's, "Lead Kindly Light." Life inevitably has its darker moments that force us to rely on someone beyond our selves—on God. My father chose well. The first verse appears in an earlier chapter, but here is the hymn in full.

> Lead, kindly Light, amid the encircling gloom, Lead Thou me on.
> The night is dark, and I am far from home; Lead Thou me on;
> Keep Thou my feet; I do not ask to see
> The distant scene—one step enough for me.
>
> I was not ever thus, nor prayed that Thou shouldst lead me on;
> I loved to choose and see my path; but now Lead Thou me on.
> I loved the garish day, and, spite of fears,
> Pride ruled my will: remember not past years.
>
> So long Thy power hath blest me, sure it still will lead me on,
> O'er moor and fen, o'er crag and torrent, till the night is gone;
> And with the morn those angel faces smile,
> Which I have loved long since, and lost a while. Amen.

I loved it when my father got up from his chair, put down his *Detroit News,* and joined my mother and me as we sang this hymn. My brother joined us too when he was home. My mother's faith in Christ had now become a part of me—just as hers became a part of her growing up on her parents' farm where a chapter of the Bible was read every morning after breakfast and the whole family went to Glenarm Church on the Sabbath. Hers was a gradual absorbing of a life lived in Christ, which she observed most of all in her father. For some reason, despite the example of my mother's faith, I needed a Leith Samuel to explain to me how to accept God's acceptance in Christ.

I also shared more fully in my father's struggles now. I had experienced how overpowering depression can be—and often wonder what would have happened to me without the J. L. Hudson Company, Mrs. Murphy, and Frank Sellars—without Leith Samuel? That my father knew I too had struggled with depression strengthened the bond between us—not expressed in words so much as in understanding looks and glances.

When the heavy tranquilizers such as Thorazine became available in the mid-fifties, I could sometimes persuade him to take them when my mother couldn't. Taken in time they could avert a manic episode. My father's agnosticism didn't trouble me. I was sure he was wrapped as fully in God's loving embrace as anyone, and that the Kindly Light would lead him—and anyone who asks.

Epilogue

My studies at Wayne University took on new significance as I tried to integrate what I was learning with my deeper understanding of the Christian faith. That spring semester I had an extraordinary teacher, Milton Covensky, for a course in Western Civilizations. Dr. Covensky was short, balding, rotund, with bulging eyes, and his courses were packed out because he was such a dynamic lecturer, and very funny. Either he left the door to his classroom open or students opened it so they could stand in the hall to hear the jokes woven into every lecture. He carried a long pointer with which he dramatized armies marching, a pharaoh ascending his throne, a scene in a Greek play—everything imaginable.

One day not long after my mystical experience in the snow, Dr. Covensky was describing the Greek theory of tragedy. For the Greeks, he explained, all life was tragic because there is so much pain and suffering in the world and then it ends in death. But there were three kinds of tragedy according to the Greeks: the Tragedy of Ignorance where you are blissfully unaware of all the suffering in the world, but it is still tragic because it ends in death; the Tragedy of Knowledge, in which you're aware of all the suffering and pain but you can't do much about it, and it ends in death; and an additional tragedy, the Tragedy of Desire in which you always desire more than you can acquire, so life is tragic and still it ends in death. He had us voting for which type of tragedy we would choose.

Life did not seem tragic to me at all at that moment—caught up as I was in my new experience of Christ's presence. I was still thinking about the choice of tragedies when I saw the long pointer Dr. Covensky used pointing directly at me. He wanted my vote. Out of my fledgling understanding of Christianity I found myself saying, "Perhaps you could overcome the Tragedy of Knowledge if you knew there was an overall plan, and while you could not change all of the pain and suffering in the world, you could feel satisfied that you were doing what was given to you to change."

For a moment Dr. Covensky said nothing. I wondered if he was offended by my not choosing one of the three tragedies. Then he asked with marked curiosity, "Where did you get this idea?" Just then the bell rang and my comment led to a discussion between the two of us after class. I told him about my snowy night experience and my belief that we each have a purpose we'll be guided to find if we seek it.

A few days later Dr. Covensky stopped me after class and asked if my mystical experience was like Martin Luther's in the thunder storm. I told him it might be similar, but I wasn't sure. I was reluctant to be compared to that giant of the faith. He had asked another professor in the history department, who counted himself a Calvinist, whether conversion experiences like Luther's still happened today. His colleague told him that they did.

Dr. Covensky was Jewish. I never knew whether he was an observant Jew or not, but he obviously had a deep interest in religion. He referred me to some of the early Christian writers such as St. Augustine and Thomas Aquinas, and suggested I buy Kenneth Scott Latourette's *History of Christianity* that had just been published, which I did. When I had read some of these writings, he discussed them with me. One time I outlined a few lines in the Hibbert Journal he'd loaned me, a library copy, so I could discuss them with him. Dr. Covensky was quietly upset with me and let me know that a scholar must never underline books and journals unless they are his own. I considered these discussions with him a major gift. Were it not for Dr. Covensky I might have adopted a much narrower view of Christianity than the one I came to have.

The Christian faith I hold now in terms of beliefs is fairly "orthodox"— I accept the Nicene Creed, the Apostles' Creed, and believe the Bible is divinely inspired and a major way God speaks to us, but that many parts of it are not meant to be taken literally. While beliefs matter, what is more central than beliefs in a Christian life is a sense of the presence of Christ. Whether this comes through an encounter one can point to at a given time, or through a gradual awareness of Christ's presence, one needs to open the door to Christ every day. For me the best way to do this is in a morning time of prayer and reading the scriptures. I can't say that I've never stepped off the path God was leading me on—I know I have. But with God's grace I'm led back on again. Even the times when I knew I was "off the path," the sense of Christ's presence has never left me. With C. S. Lewis I believe that somehow in Jesus' death and resurrection he overcame death for all men, and opened the way to God for all people so that whether they've ever heard about Christ or not, anyone who genuinely seeks to know God through whatever faith or tradition, or even without one, will find him. And within these certainties for me there is still much mystery and many unknowns.

Some time that spring, my boyfriend Eric told me he had met someone in his biology class that he wanted to date, so he had to break up with me. I was surprised, but not devastated. I felt so sure that my life was now in God's hands that it made it hard to feel breaking up with Eric was a loss. The feeling was more, "I guess the road doesn't lie in that direction." In addition, despite the love and respect I felt for Eric, I had serious concerns about his wish to dominate. Soon after our breakup, while standing with my friend Beth Syme in front of Old Main, she confirmed my suspicion for me. Knowing I'd be amused Beth told me, "Eric says his new girlfriend is much easier to manage than you ever were." I broke into a hardy laugh.

"If he wanted someone he could manage, then he's made the right decision because that was never going to be me." I had regained much of the feistiness and self-assurance I had had as a young child, and could see that there would have been huge problems between Eric and me. It also occurred to me that Eric might have feared that sometime in the future my depression could return. Although I felt certain this would not happen, and it never has, in his place I would have been wary.

After graduating from Wayne University in 1953, I took a circuitous though always engaging route to my profession as a clinical psychologist and psychoanalyst in New York City. I first taught junior high school English for two years in Dearborn, Michigan. Thinking I would accept an invitation to join InterVarsity's staff, I studied and obtained a degree at New York Theological Seminary. Circumstances led me to take a position advising foreign students and the religious organizations back at what was now Wayne *State* University for a year. At this juncture I was torn between my developing interests in theology and psychology. We had read widely in psychology at the seminary. The dollar was so strong against the pound in the late fifties that with the money I had saved working one year, I could afford to become a foreign student myself and take courses in psychology at the University of Edinburgh and Oxford University. In September of 1959 I sailed on the Queen Elisabeth I, and did just that. I took all the courses in psychology I could at the University of Edinburgh and some at New College, the Divinity School in Edinburgh, and then spent the spring term at Oxford. Convinced finally that psychology was the field I enjoyed the most, I applied from abroad to PhD programs at three universities and was accepted at all three. But when I returned from England in late August of 1960, I did not feel excited about any of these programs. Since I had found God usually guided me by what excited me or at least interested me, I was confused.

Although I had known that the University of Michigan, together with New York University, had the best programs in clinical psychology at that time, I had not applied to Michigan because I'd heard one needed an all-A record even to be considered for the PhD program in psychology there. My brother's friend, Dale Brown, was driving to Ann Arbor every day for a summer course at Michigan and pleaded with me to drive up with him and at least talk to the people in the psychology department. I told him they would think I was out of my mind to walk in at the end of August for a September admission to such a selective program. For days I resisted. Then I drove up with Dale on what must have been his last day of class.

As I expected, the officious blond secretary at the psychology department informed me curtly, "We've had 750-some applicants and we've accepted 27, so we're not about to open the door to you at this late date." I'm sure my face turned red with embarrassment. I had quickly turned to leave when I heard her say, "Well, since you're here, which program are you interested in?" "Clinical," I answered meekly. Down the hall a younger, sweeter secretary phoned every name on the roster for me, but the faculty members were all away on the break before fall semester. The only person she reached was E. Lowell Kelly, chairman of the department, and he agreed to see me.

Dr. Kelly, a white-haired balding gentleman with deep-set, kind brown eyes, liked the fact that I had studied at the University of Edinburgh. We spoke about twenty minutes. He wanted me to take two tests: the Miller Test of Abstract Reasoning and the Doppelt Mathematical Reasoning Test. I had heard about Dr. Kelly's battery of twelve tests designed to identify highly creative people. He was only asking me to take two of them. The abstract reasoning test didn't worry me, but I hadn't had any math since high school. I told him that, and agreed to take the tests the next day. Dr. Kelly had also said he had no fellowships, so that afternoon I found two jobs on campus to support myself.

The next day was a Friday, which was still my mother's day off. My father was at home, and knowing they would enjoy the ride I took both parents with me to Ann Arbor. I had hoped to take the tests in the morning, but couldn't schedule them until the afternoon—a muggy, hot afternoon. After the tests I went back to see Dr. Kelly. A call to the testing service gave him the results. He wrote them down. Then, studying them, he said, "Well, if you went over to the Ed School you'd be way out in front, but I'm afraid you'll find the competition here a little tough." My heart sank. But I saw that he was still looking at the scores. "You know, there's something wrong here. You did better on the Doppelt than on the Miller and that shouldn't happen if you haven't had any math since high school. I think you just had a bad day," he said. "There are four forms to the Miller. Come back on Monday and take the second form. Then we'll see." I thanked him and left, feeling discouraged. My parents were waiting on a bench in the famous Michigan quadrangle. Walking across the campus, I told them what happened and said I thought I should just forget it and take the fellowship I'd been offered at Michigan State, one of the three schools that accepted me. Then my father in his usual gentle way said to me,

"You know, Sarah, if you don't come back on Monday and take that test you may always wonder what would have happened. I'll tell you what you should do." My heart leapt a little with anticipation. All my life I had wished that my father was capable of giving me some direction. I listened intently. "Come back on Monday. Try to schedule the test in the morning. Don't eat much breakfast. Have two or three cups of coffee, and you will do better."

Now I had no hesitation about coming back on Monday. I wanted to do exactly what my father told me to do.

On Monday I followed his instructions to the letter. By now I very much wanted to get into the program at Michigan. It was a beautifully cool, sunny morning. Walking back to Dr. Kelly's office after the test, I knew I had done better. He called for the results, which showed that my percentile rating on the Miller had more than doubled—which on this test, thought to be highly reliable, was truly amazing.

"Now I've no question." Dr. Kelly said, "And you can forget about those jobs, I've found a teaching fellowship for you."

This was my father's enormous gift to me. He gave me back the opportunity I had passed up when I was eighteen and my mother couldn't handle my leaving, and moreover, he gave me one of the best programs in clinical psychology in the country. For the next four years I exulted in the whole atmosphere of the University of Michigan and Ann Arbor, to me a thoroughly delightful place. There were moments when I wondered if I should be shut away here in a library and not out where I'd be more likely to meet a husband. Still, in my internship the second year the first time I sat with a patient I knew I would want to do this for the rest of my life.

After Michigan I returned to New York City. I wanted the in-depth training in psychoanalysis that at the time was only open to psychologists in New York City and possibly Los Angeles. A requirement of psychoanalytic training is to have one's own psychoanalysis. For me this was particularly fortunate because there was still a major psychological problem I had not solved—my fear of getting married. I'd begun to think I might never marry and have my own children and this would be an enormous sadness to me. I drew much comfort from my daily communing with God and Christ, in prayer and through reading the Scriptures; but God never said he can substitute for a human being in one's life. In fact, in the Psalms it says, "He places the solitary in families." I longed for that to happen for me—to have my own family. In my training analysis I began to work on this problem with Dr. Harvey Dain, another skilled psychoanalyst, as skilled as Dr. Sellars, I believe.

That my fear of marriage came from seeing my father lose control of his mind and become psychotic time after time had never occurred to me, as strange as that seems. There was the statement I had made to my parents at age six, "When I grow up I'm going to have babies but no daddy." I always knew I had said this; but I didn't know how much my unconscious mind was still operating from that premise—that it is dangerous to have a daddy—that is, to have a husband who might become psychotic and pull the rug out from under you as I saw my mother experience. As the years went by there were several fine men I might have married. I found frivolous reasons to turn each one down.

My work with Dr. Dain began to surface the connection between my father's illness and my fear of marriage. I began to have dreams that the person I was dating was going crazy. After two years of psychoanalytic training I took a break from the four-year program to take a job at the Hospital of the Albert Einstein College of Medicine, hoping I might meet an interesting person there. I still continued my analysis with Dr. Dain.

In the meantime intermittently I was still seeing a man I had met at the University of Michigan, a psychiatrist named David, twelve years my senior. At some point, while working at Einstein, I came to accept Dr. Dain's interpretation that my refusal to marry this man was simply because of my fear of marriage. I told David I would marry him and he moved his whole career in psychiatry to New York. Madison Avenue Presbyterian Church, my church, was reserved for an April wedding. I bought a gorgeous wedding gown at Bonwits, and fearing my age—almost forty—we deliberately became pregnant. When a few weeks before the wedding David changed his mind about wanting to marry me, even though I was four months pregnant, I felt curiously free and even happy. I had lived out my childhood decision of "babies but no daddy." This was a time when I was probably "off the path" because I never felt very excited about this marriage. But as with Joseph and his brothers, God seemed to use it for good. Even more than my psychoanalysis with Dr. Dain, having my son Christopher seemed to free me from my fear of getting married. He was the most beautiful child I had ever seen. I had no regrets.

After spending three years at Einstein, and while I was pregnant with Christopher, our psychiatric unit was closing for lack of funds. The chairman of my department, who tried to secure jobs for all of us, introduced me to a doctor named Charles who did research and teaching at Einstein. Although my private practice was full enough that I did not need a job, when Charles asked me to work on a research project, I said I would. In the course of working on his research every Friday and having lunch at the French bistro around the corner from my office, Charles and I became the best of friends.

After a year-and-a-half when Charles asked if I would have dinner with him, I didn't even have to think about the question I knew he was going to ask me. On this cold December night my answer was a full-hearted, "Yes." I was struck by how similar Charles seemed to Bob Alexander and Eric Anderson, my two high school sweethearts. Like Eric Anderson he was a doctor, and deeply spiritual; and like Bob, he was a generous, fun-loving person. How amazing, I thought, that at forty-two I could still marry someone so like the men I would have married in my twenties if

I hadn't been so afraid. In addition to reminding me of my early boy-friends, Charles is remarkably like my two parents. Like my mother he is strong and utterly reliable, and like my father he is gentle, soft-spoken, and likes to cook. The first time we went out together, taking Christopher with us, I felt I had "come home." When Christopher was two, Charles and I married at Madison Avenue Presbyterian Church on a beautiful December day when it snowed. A year later we had another beautiful child, Jonathan.

When Jonathan was two, I was able to go back and finish my psycho-analytic training. Working with patients for more than forty years now, mostly adults and adolescents in private practice, with some teaching and supervising, has felt like a calling. It's hard to remember a day I did not look forward to going to work. In gratitude for the J. L. Hudson Company paying for my psychotherapy as a young adult, I've always kept one or two spaces in my practice for a patient who cannot afford to pay a fee. It would take another book this size or larger to tell of even a small portion of this later period of life which has been filled with more love, purpose, and adventure than I could have ever envisioned.

As to my parents, once my brother and I finished college and were work-ing for a while, we pooled our savings with our mother's for a down pay-ment on a beautiful two-family brick house in a lovely neighborhood. This meant that when I finally did leave home at age twenty-five to attend New York Theological Seminary, my parents had a home from which no one could make them move. Also, the arrival of the heavy tranquilizer, Thorozine, in 1953 had made my father's manic episodes a lot more man-ageable. This was a much better time for me to leave than if I had left after high school for the University of Michigan in 1948. That, "All things work together for good to them that love God," is really true. My leaving was still hard for my mother, but before long she began to visit me in New York and came to love New York City as much as I did. Thanks to my father's advice, I was still able to enjoy four years at the University of Michigan, and receive a much more important degree, my PhD in psychology. My parents had seventeen good years together in this house where my father grew outstanding roses in the back yard.

My father continued to have manic episodes until he died of heart disease at age seventy-five. At his funeral the minister said something I had never thought about. He said, "In all my visits with Dan, he never once complained about this terrible illness that took away so much of his life. He bore it graciously." That was true and it was noble.

My mother retired from Hudson's at age seventy-one. Everyone thought she was sixty-five, not knowing until years later that when she immigrated from Canada, she managed to shave six years off her age. This made her five years younger than my father instead of a year older—something that would never do in that era. At seventy-one she bought a car, took driving lessons, and began to drive for the first time ever. She and my father were able to go on picnics and long drives as they had when I was a child. They could visit my brother's family, now on the outskirts of Detroit, and visit me while I lived in Ann Arbor.

My mother lived to be two months short of ninety-seven, in good health. She stayed in her own home for ten years after my father died and missed him terribly. Her once lovely neighborhood in Detroit was changing radically by then and was no longer a safe place for her to live. At my husband's urging she sold her house and came to live with us in Scarsdale, in a rambling house that had room for all of us. For nine years she was a much-loved grandmother to our two school-age sons and enjoyed with her grandsons things she had missed with my brother and me—such as being there to make their lunch. For the last ten months of her life, feeling she was alone too much at our house with our sons off to college, she lived in a residence near my brother. I felt sad that she died so far away from me until my brother told me that if he had not had those last ten months with her, he would have felt greatly cheated. Danny and I loved to talk about what a great lady she was.

Danny had become a person of deep faith in his late teens, influenced as I was by experiences in InterVarsity Christian Fellowship. All his life he supported Christian missionaries. He married in his early twenties, had three sons, and worked as an architectural draftsman, having chosen not to finish his degree at Lawrence Tech. He nevertheless designed and oversaw the building of a large addition to his church, which won a best-building award in his area of West Bloomfield, Michigan. He also designed his own house and houses for friends. Late in life Danny developed a muscle-wasting disease, Inclusion Body Myositis, which left him wheel-chair bound his last ten years. Like my father, he bore it graciously and until his death in December, 2010 was almost always productive and in good spirits. His children and nine grandchildren are absolutely wonderful human beings.

For a long time I looked upon the deep depression I went through at nineteen as part of the religious upheaval my first year at Wayne University. I wondered if for me this "dark night of the soul" was something I needed to go through before I could understand God's grace, and have an encounter with Jesus Christ on that snowy February night. In writing this memoir, however, it has become increasingly clear to me that my depression was mainly fueled by the heavy load of guilt I carried for wanting to have my own life in a family where I felt sorely needed.

It was easy to confuse the psychological struggles with the spiritual in that the psychological conflict expressed itself in religious symbols such as heaven and hell, guilt and redemption. I needed both Dr. Sellars, the psychiatrist, and Leith Samuel, the Anglican priest, in order to sort through these areas of confusion. Mrs. Murphy and the J. L. Hudson Company were also essential in providing the intensive psychotherapy that I credit with saving my life. If only every young person struggling with depression and suicidal thoughts could have access to the therapy he or she needs. It is hard to imagine a department store providing that kind of care today—I did live in a gentler time, and even then I imagine Hudson's was unique. What we need is a really good health care system.

As I come to the end of this memoir I shudder to realize how much would have been lost to me if I had ended my life at nineteen. All the special people to whom I dedicate this book, I would never have known—and would those two fine sons and five wonderful grandchildren have even existed? It is something to ponder. I was indeed fortunate to have such a valiant mother, a loving father, and a brother who was my friend, a Mrs. Murphy, a J. L. Hudson Company, a Dr. Sellars, a Rev. Leith Samuel, a Dr. Harvey Dain, friends like Mony, Pat Forbes, Bob Alexander, Ann Tittl, Dale Brown, Dr. Covensky, Dr. E. Lowell Kelly—all of whom I believe were conduits of God's grace.

www.ingramcontent.com/pod-product-compliance
Lightning Source LLC
Chambersburg PA
CBHW030828270326
41928CB00007B/941